Contents

Between Health and Illness

BETWEEN HEALTH AND ILLNESS

*New Notions on
Stress and the Nature
of Well Being*

BARBARA B. BROWN

Houghton Mifflin Company
Boston
1984

Library of Congress Cataloging in Publication Data

Brown, Barbara B.
    Between health and illness.

    Includes bibliographical references and index.
    1. Stress (Psychology) 2. Stress (Physiology)
3. Mind and body. 4. Health. I. Title.
BF575.S75B75 1984   616'.001'9   83-18632
ISBN 0-395-34634-7

Printed in the United States of America

S 10 9 8 7 6 5 4 3 2 1

Between Health
and Illness

Prologue

Between health and illness there are obscure, ambiguous states of unwellness, times when mind and body are taxed by the demands made on us by the different worlds of people we live with and by the demands we make of ourselves to be and do what we and our society expect us to be and do. These are the states of unwellness we are expected to cope with, live with, sometimes ignore or occasionally succumb to, and do it all with a minimum of complaining, surrender, hostility, or failure.

These states are not "official" medical or psychological ailments. They are, instead, afflictions abandoned by the healing arts when they decided that you cannot officially feel not-well unless you are certified sick. These are new *kinds* of unwellness, mental, physical, and psychical kinds of un-ease formed by the pressure of a jet-propelled society in which achieving, competing, winning, coping, and being loved and well regarded are new goals of a society whose hazards are all forged by human behavior itself. These are the myriad unwellnesses that come from living with stress. (For present purposes, think of stress as living with and trying to cope with some undesirable or unfortunate or worrisome circumstance of life.)

We call the intangible, cerebral, psychical pressures in our social lives "stress." The ills and distress they cause are not any of the familiar ways of being sick, nor are they the stress ills of hypertension, ulcers, phobias or other "official" ills. Instead, we "cope" with our social pressures and live with them and carry on — not really sick, but just sort-of-sick. Struggling with the stresses of life costs us dearly both in the psychic energy we use in coping with them and in the erosion of our emotional and physical well being.

Contrary to much promotion about health issues, reactions to the stress of life are not firstly nor even secondly a simple matter of body tensions that relaxation can dissolve.* Nor, despite pre-

*Relaxation procedures only very slowly take away tensions that have accumulated from past stress. Their chief effect is "teaching" the muscles how *not* to react to future occasions for stress.

vailing impression, are they the "official" ills of hypertension, ulcers, neuroses, or other recognized stress pathologies. What we call the stress illnesses are not, as a matter of fact, caused by stress itself but are, as we shall see, caused by the breakdown of mind and body systems *worn down by living with stress.* It may seem like a fine distinction between stress as the cause of our miseries and *not* the cause of the "official" stress ills, but as the story of stress unfolds, the differences will be seen to be critically important to human well beingness.

Both the marginal miseries of living with stress and the official stress ills are products of a long and complex sequence of events that come from living with stress, beginning with some set of social circumstances one feels is unsatisfactory or worrisome. This perception of stress then (1) initiates defensive mind and body tensions that are the sensations of stress, (2) creates concern about coping with the situation thus causing distress and diminished well being (the marginal miseries), (3) accumulates mind and body tensions when occasions for stress are prolonged, repeated, or come in clusters and (4) leads to the failure of one's coping abilities, that (5) in turn weaken the physiological systems until one or another system (6) becomes functionally disabled and is recognized as an "official" stress ill. The so-called stress ills are caused by the breakdown of physiological systems (as their names such as hypertension, colitis, etc., indicate). It is failed or frustrated coping with stress that causes the mind and body systems to be first distressed then damaged. It is not the stress itself.

Identifying signs of the covert psychobiological erosion caused by stress is not an easy task. The signs and symptoms of actually living with stress seem, in fact, so harmless and such ordinary kinds of complaints they are rarely considered to be signs of a "real" illness. (Headaches must be common if the headache remedy industry is a billion-dollar-a-year business and fully half of the headache complaints can be traced to stress). The lack of a definitive diagnosis of stress states *before* they break down mind and body systems is largely because stress is a rather new cause of disease that has its first effects on mood and mind rather than on the body, effects that cannot easily be detected. Living with any kind of stress, nonetheless, diminishes well being and saps the energy of both the psyche and the physical body.

Human reactions to the circumstances of stress are firstly, secondly, and always, the mental (intelligent) appreciation of an infelicitous impression of some social interaction — a mental concern about the possible consequences of the undesired event and a mental search for remedies for the difficulty. People — all people — react to stress *first* by rational, reasonable concern about their difficulties, and it is that concern that can generate either reasonably effective ways to deal with the difficulties or the mental distress of not coping. It is only after long periods of failed coping and mental anguish that the muscles or heart or gut may become involved. Stress wears down the body systems (including the brain substrate of feelings and emotions) and is felt as "stress," but stress *ills* are caused by disturbed physiological functions, not by the stress (but more about this later).

Both the flawed states of being and the more acutely dangerous stress ills are products of exactly the same mental task of striving to deal with the stresses of life. Coping, or more precisely coping and failed coping, undermines health in two very different and devitalizing ways. In its first phase, the frustrating struggle to cope erodes well being furtively and drains its energy, causes feelings of underachieving, frustrated fulfillment, and predisposes to other ills. In its second phase, the growing anxieties and body tensions that follow the failure to cope with too much stress or having lived with stress for too long or having too great a sensitivity to the stress of life ultimately disable the physical functions of mind and body and create the "official" stress ills.

The unique way stress saps the vitality of the psyche and erodes the physical apparatus of the body leads to signs and symptoms of unwellness that are very different from the signs and symptoms of recognized medical and psychological ills. Since the stress disease process operates covertly and can incubate for years before the disabling stress ills surface, it becomes an important health issue to examine the dis-ease process of stress in considerable detail.

The dis-ease process. The way stress affects mind and body

involves a series of social, psychical, and psychological events*
(and in that order), beginning with some set of circumstances in
which one person interacts with other people or things that represent people (like the automobile repair shop) and the impressions
that are formed about the interactions (I think they cheated me).
This step is followed by mentally evaluating the impressions (yes,
the car still isn't acting right) and the possible consequences on
one's well being (I can't afford a transmission job now). It is at this
point when troubling images begin to form and nag at the way one
is trying to cope (I'll have to borrow money; hell, I'll never get out
of debt). As the circumstances drag on with no resolution of the
difficulty, images ebb and flow between hope and despair. The
mental anguish over a dim future of debt can easily swing to the
elation of relief when the motor purrs and the shift is smooth.
Anguish, a particularly vicious judgment of one's plight, takes a
heavy toll of well being, but it can be relieved and reversed by
nourishing the coping process no matter how semi-sick one feels.

If, however, circumstances continue to be difficult (car breaks
down, needs new transmission, you can't pay the bills, have to
borrow money) and coping begins to run out, the fears and worries
of the mind signal the body to brace itself for the disasters to come
(images of no money, no friends, no food, no shelter). And as the
stress continues and new stresses come along and coping fails
more and more, the tensions of mind and body continue to inch
upward and the psyche's defenses become more and more de-
pleted until finally one or another vital function breaks down.

"Official" stress ills (the hypertension, ulcers, neuroses, phobias, delinquency, etc.) appear only after the stress process has
damaged some important function of mind or body seriously
enough to interfere with a vital function. Once the damage is done,

*As the causes and cures of "the stress of life" are described, the need to distinguish
psychical and psychological effects will become clear. Although "psychological" implies
that something pertains to, influences, or is derived from the mind or emotions, psychology
itself studies mainly the emotional and behavioral characteristics of individuals that can
be documented by some kind of measurement. It is my belief, however, that (a) the stress
process begins with an intelligent consideration of one's circumstances, and this phase is
rarely accompanied by any discernable emotional or behavioral change, and (b) "the stress
of life" attacks the psyche *first* (stress is a psychic hurt), and the effect of stress on mind
and body (distress) is more accurately described and understandable when the effect of the
effect of stress on the psyche — and *before* the emotions are aroused — is considered
separately.

the stress ill is diagnosed, documented, and treated according to the body function that is disordered, and *not* according to the stress that actually caused the function to become disabled. The "cause" of the stress ailment goes into the medical records as, for example, "perforating ulcer" or into the psychiatric documents as "acute depression" or some similar diagnostic term. Only occasionally is there a postscript that the condition was "probably brought on by stress."

Who was tending the health store all the time the ulcer or the depression was developing? It's a fair bet the patient knew something was going on all those months, perhaps years, before his ailment disabled him enough to cry for help. Virtually every person alive possesses some sense of knowing when the integrity of the self has been breached, not only the awareness that something inside is troubled but that it is ailing because of something "out there" somewhere. One of the wonders of psychotherapy, for example, is the accuracy with which the distressed sufferer can intellectually pinpoint the source of his emotional turmoil. But for the stress of life, the dilemma is that no matter how heavily our miseries or heartaches or frustrations of not coping may weigh upon our mental shoulders, there are no good ways to express those feelings verbally or to attach clinical numbers to mental worry or to the wearied body or depressed spirit we feel. We have been programmed to believe we are not "officially" sick as long as we can still struggle to cope. We have developed new kinds of unwellness but we have not yet found ways to report the complex nuances of inner distress. Inner misery does not officially qualify for the curing magic of the healing arts. Yet we are not well at all.

The distress of stress is the diminishing of potential it causes long before stress ills emerge, if indeed they ever do. States of diminished well being arise out of the struggle with everyday stress. They come from the wear and tear on the psyche and on mind and body as they strive to cope with the inconveniences and unsatisfactoriness of life. Stress ills — hypertension and all — occur only as coping falters and fails. Diminished well being and dis-ease come from living with stress; stress ills come from succumbing to stress.

Stress is a phenomenon generated almost exclusively by society's mad pace of the twentieth century. Diminished well being is the social Pac-Man that devours coping and psychic energy and inner strength. Before it wins the game of our lives, it needs some serious, sober attention. That's what this book is all about.

Chapter 1
Setting the stage

Clarifying the contents . . . The curing magic . . . When stress became STRESS . . . Dukha . . . Killer stress . . . Commercial stress . . . Two poles of unwellness . . . The challenge of underhealth and underachieving

Clarifying the contents

This book deals with new thoughts on new phenomena that are becoming critically important to personal health and well being and important to the general psychological and social climate as well. Mostly the thoughts concern what many physicians, psychologists, and natural scientists are newly feeling and intuiting about the origins of mental and physical unwellness and unfulfillment, but thoughts that have not been formalized into what, for many of us, looks to be a new channel for achieving healing and states of well being.

Because nowadays there is so much energy being devoted to learning about states of human beingness, I decided to take a different approach to this extraordinary new flood of information about health and healing. I selected the task of trying to put some order into the assorted volumes of evidence to see whether states of health, wellness, and illness, including states of achieving and the human potential, all share enough common elements to suggest new ideas about the nature of health and illness and why people don't feel well and why so many often feel denied their fulfillment.

Then, because insights bring so many old notions into question, I began to fear misinterpretation of these thoughts and this book. This prompted me to note a few caveats at the very beginning, as follows:

- This book describes a new way of thinking about wellness and unwellness that focuses on detecting and dealing with stress long before it causes the more serious damage of stress ills. It describes particularly those states between health and illness of the "I-don't-feel-so-good-but-I'm-not-really-sick,-either" syndrome that keeps people functioning below par. It deals with the dilemma of wearing down under stress, of not being sick enough for professional help but not feeling good enough to play the game of life very well.

- Stress is not a phenomenon of man's physical nature, but rather, his states of diminished well being evolve from interactions with people, people-things, and people-surrogates,* creating circumstances that are the unfortunate, undesirable events in life that can happen to anyone.

- The direct, most treacherous, and least recognized effects of stress are the tensions that build up in mind and body without our awareness of them. These effects are very different from those of recognized stress ills. This book does not deal with hypertension, ulcers, neuroses, or the other "official" stress ills. It *does* deal with the cerebral-biological processes that

---

*One of the great problems facing psychotherapists, counsellors and family practice physicians is the lack of words to describe the very ordinary events of life that cause us pain. The chief reason for this dilemma is because psychotherapy, counselling and medicine are traditionally structured around the signs and symptoms of *really sick* people (and the causes of ills are easy to identify). In sharp contrast, the miseries of people under stress (and still functioning) are not the miseries of true illness. They are, instead, the miseries and un-ease and distress that come from dealing with people and all the social interacting people do with each other.

As I describe in Chapter 5, almost any discomfort you can feel that is not organic is caused by something having to do with people. Mostly we implicate people by referring to them specifically, such as mother, my child, the boss, and we refer to the events involving our relationships with people as "your affair" or "your loss" or "a real problem," etc. All such round-about ways of trying to describe the causes of mental unrest or emotional distress haven't helped one iota in tracking down stress problems and relieving them.

So, I invented some terms. When I speak of such things as "people-things" or "people-surrogates," I am using a shorthand way of saying "things made by people" and "things or institutions that act like people or are run by people, such as the phone company or the IRS." And when I say "people-problems," I mean any kind of problem created by people. These terms are not simply the whims of a writer; they are useful in distinguishing the causes of hurts to the psyche from the causes of true mental or physical illness.

cause such ills because *all* stress ills and distress come from living with happenings that make life unsatisfactory.

- Stress is a *psychical* assault, an intangible blow to the psyche, the Center that functions to preserve the wholeness and harmony of the being.

- Because mental distress is caused by disturbing thoughts about the unfairness of life, the primary effects of stress involve the mental faculties subserving the intellect (the information-processing systems of the mind-brain).

- The principal mental faculties involved in the creation of distress are those that reside mainly in the unconscious, much as described by Freud.

The curing magic

There have been astonishing changes in our attitudes about health and healing. Ten years ago my dentist wore a starched white coat and his entire vocabulary consisted of "umm" and "here's a new cavity." Nowadays he wears a sports shirt, has model airplanes decorating his office, and he attacks my mouth in new ways that let me answer his running briefings, dental lecture, or just friendly chatter. And I am no longer apprehensive as together we discuss the causes and cures of various dental problems that haunt me.

The Healing Professions are smack dab in the middle of a revolution of thought about ways to relieve and heal human distress. I nearly fainted the other day when I heard an old medical curmudgeon from UCLA being interviewed on TV about pain. This medical fossil, whose security blanket has always been drugs and chemicals and lab tests, stunned me by describing the latest research on the endomorphins (the "brain opiates") as demonstrating how the mind could control the chemistry of the brain. How times have changed! Certainly yesterday's sanitized ritual with the healer in the role of the omnipotent, omniscient, canonized god and the patient in the role of the helpless, ignorant, contaminated petitioner has been replaced in many places by a spirit of cooperation between healer and healee and a sharing of healing resources and responsibility. Nearly everyone has come to recognize that some kind of curing magic exists, whether we call it luck or faith, positive thinking or mind power. What hundreds of physicians, thousands of psychotherapists, and millions of the unwell, their families and friends confirm every day is the profound realization that wellness is achieved by something more than drugs or surgery or psychological counselling. For some the extra drive to wellness comes from within, from the spirit or from the psyche, for others the extra ingredient is the spirit of the universe or God, while for still others the extra healing dimension comes from the world beyond. For me it comes from a natural intelligence possessed by every human being. Whatever the unseen healer is, it is a new dimension of healing.

And this brings up an interesting point. Most of the new helping and healing techniques and most of the new therapeutic approaches either depend upon using the mind to help or heal itself or they depend upon becoming aware of the fine tuning of the body and the feelings and insights these awarenesses create. Under ordinary circumstances scientists would conclude from this that since the mind is so important in the cure, then the mind must play a role in the cause of human ailments. And while this conclusion does float informally around professional psychological and medical circles, and there is a fair consensus that the mind does influence the course of emotional and physical difficulties, most orthodox practitioners and theorists tend to cling to the axiom that every aspect of health and illness is chemically ordained.

Nonetheless, the changing consciousness of professionals about healing, along with the growing evidence for the effectiveness of *non* invasive, *non* physical, *non* medical healing techniques has conspired to gain at least informal recognition of a nonphysical factor in health and illness. The emergence of the concept of "stress" as a potent influence on the health of human beings is a heartening sign of improved understanding of health and illness.

When stress became STRESS

The current interest in stress all began with Hans Selye's brilliant biochemical research on the phenomenon he named stress and, later, when he published a book on his equally brilliant observations about "the stress of life." Academicians and professional healers alike simply took it for granted that Selye's research on stress explained how "the stress of life" affected human beings and caused all the distress of stress.

What Selye's research actually revealed was that when living organisms (especially rats) are *physically* stressed (i.e., physically assaulted, injured, or infected), they react reflexly and biochemically in a stereotyped way that causes most of the body changes we associate with looking sick and feeling sick, regardless of precise cause.

BUT — and here's the rub — "the stress of life" is *not* physical stress. Stress, as we talk about it today, is the special pressure people feel as they face difficulties in life and as they interact with the inventions of people, such as business, politics, sports, or love. "Stress" grows from social situations and the pyschological reactions they create. It is psychic trauma, never physical trauma. If Selye's contention is correct that the stress of life initiates profound endocrine and biochemical changes in the body, then the question to be answered is: How can the intangible content of social situations and psychological encounters be converted into the body chemicals and endocrines that cause psychic distress and bodily ills?

Some theorists answer this question by referring to a widely held notion that "stress" evokes the "arousal" response. Stress, they say, is something that threatens our well being and survival, and so we react reflexly in some programmed way to protect ourselves from harm. That is, when a threat to the self is perceived, that causes anxiety and we react reflexly to rev up the body's defenses (physical) to be ready to take some action (physical) should the worst befall us. The anxiety about the threat reflexly excites (arouses) the muscles, the cardiovascular and respiratory systems and affects other body functions in appropriate ways so that the body is physically ready to defend against or escape the coming assault. Such physical reflexes, these experts say, are the way stress causes stress ills.

Such a theory, unfortunately, contradicts the universal principle of the survival of the fittest, the principle that holds that species survive when environments become unsuitable or hostile by developing specialized mechanisms to cope with and survive those specific environmental hazards. If this is true, then reacting *physically* to threats to *psychological* well being would not only be incongruous, but certainly would not help a species to survive. On the other hand, human beings for the most part have, indeed, learned how to cope and deal with most problems in their social environment. The evolution of *thoughtfully* developed ways to adapt to *nonphysical* (social) environmental hazards is not only congruent with the nature of modern human environmental hazards, but also provides the sole reliably effective strategy for survival and the maintainence of well being.

Dukha

Contrary to the popular "arousal" theory that stress presses body systems into a physical defense posture, all people experiencing or suffering stress, not surprisingly, show the familiar signs of symptoms of being under stress — feeling concerned, worried, having feelings of despair or frustration, feeling distracted or mentally upset. These are all signs of *intelligent* concern — warranted, legitimate, reasonable concern. If stress is, as we generally understand it to be, pressures related to problems with the job or family, love of school, then it *is* reasonable to worry. People who worry just don't wring their hands in anxiety and self-pity; they search their memories for clues about why they have a problem and they probe their mental resources for reasonable answers. People under stress do not become rigid with tension and have a pounding heart and sweating hands. They alert their *cerebral* mechanisms.

The problem is that it is so hard to express feelings of concern and to describe the faint body signals of distress. If our mental concerns and feelings and vague body distresses are difficult to describe, it is no wonder the health sciences hesitate to speculate on ways to overcome them. People complain, for example, "I don't feel so good but I'm not sick enough to go to the doctor," or "I wish I had more pep today," or "That has me so upset," or "Why did I have to get a headache?" or "I wonder what I'm worrying about — I couldn't sleep a wink last night," or "Oh God, are these chest pains?" or "I think I'm catching something," or "I must have a virus."

These are complaints of people under stress. Unfortunately, they are also the kind of complaints that helpers and healers respond to with, "I can't help you unless we find out exactly what's bothering you." And you want to scream because you feel awful yet there aren't any right words to describe your feelings.

The lack of systematic attention to psychical distresses has caused an enormous unhealthy breach between the orthodox healing community, on the one side, which requires a diagnosis to be confirmed by physical evidence of an illness, and by the people suffering stress (mental anguish), on the other side, who could use help and healing. People actually under stress (*before* the blood pressure skies or anxieties gum up living) rarely get help because they don't qualify as being sick. They are only semi-sick. You have to fit the textbook models of unwellness to get help, and semi-sick isn't in the books. Yet.

Nevertheless, it is exactly the affliction of being neither sick nor well that is the most widespread and insidiously damaging ailment in modern society. The stress ills such as hypertension or coronaries or phobias or alcoholism that most people talk about these days are not half so frequent as are states of diminished well being. The "official" stress ills do not reflect living under stress, but rather, *having lived* under stress for a long time. The effects of active, ongoing stress go undetected until they begin to interfere with mind or body functions. The asthma, ulcers, anxiety neuroses, or behavior problems are the end products of months or years of stress.

Does anyone believe that these devastating stress ills burst suddenly into consciousness or biological awareness without warning, without any clue or signs that a disease process has been incubating for an obviously hazardous period of time? Of course not. The doctor, the psychotherapist, and the patient all know *something* has been affecting the mind and body, but no one seems to know how to come up with neat little figures or descriptions to prove it.

The problem is that by the time someone under stress can identify enough body or mind distresses to convince a professional healer or helper that expert care is really needed, the effects of the stress have already gone too far. The stressee by now has developed hypertension, a coronary, some other physical disturbance, or has had his emotional equilibrium battered into alcoholism, an anxiety neurosis, insomnia, or any of the many disturbances of psychological or social behavior we attribute to stress.

What I began to become most concerned about as I analyzed the stress phenomenon is exactly those states of unwellness, of feeling neither sick nor well, that are the states between health and illness. There is, in the Zen literature of Japan, a word that perfectly yet paradoxically embodies both the feelings and the cause of our twentieth-century misery. It is called Dukha, meaning the suffering we feel because of the unsatisfactoriness of life.

My concern about these states is twofold: first, because they are rarely recognized or acknowledged, in far too many instances these nether states become the incubation periods for the serious stress ills. Equally as important and also because the states are rarely detected, in *all* cases such "minor" unwellness undermines the human potential for achieving and fulfillment. You simply can't perform up to ability when you are semi-sick.

Killer stress

There is good reason to believe that just living with the stresses of this modern world is more hazardous to the health than smoking cigarettes, being exposed to nuclear radiation, too much cholesterol, or any other much publicized threat to the safety of our society. We can start with a statistic that should be shocking and frightening but for some reason never seems to have impressed anyone.

Conservative opinion generally agrees that stress is the main cause or major contributing cause of 75 percent of *all* human illness although many experts now quote 90 percent. I am always surprised by how casually everyone takes this statistic. It may be that the implications of how widespread the stress sickness really is nearly exceed our ability to apppreciate its full extent.

If we really believed that 75 percent of all human illness is caused by the stress of life, I suspect we would be tackling stress with all the vigor and funding with which we support cancer research. One serious complicating problem is that the phenomenon of stress involves so many different subspecialties of medicine and psychology that no comprehensive, unifying concept of its nature has yet been presented, and so the seriousness of the consequences cannot be fully appreciated. It is almost beyond our ability to comprehend the idea that stress, as the familiar, common stresses of life, can be the cause of the great majority of human ills. We will see, however, that stress causes a host of human distresses — nearly all, in fact — as well as the serious "official" stress ills.

Some examples —

A wave of suicides among children in Austria in 1981 stirred up a hail of angry accusations that blamed the suicides on the excessive stress and frustration created by the school system. After centuries when university education in Austria had been limited to students passing rigorous examinations, the reforms of the Socialistic government had abolished both exams and fees and opened the universities to everyone. The experts now suggest that both the prospect and the reality of higher education exert undue stress on students, driving many of them to suicide in a desperate attempt to escape failure or disgrace.

In the United States, a 1981 report funded by the Department of Labor Occupational Safety and Health Administration concluded that coronary heart disease and other stress-related ills were now occurring as frequently in women office workers as in their male bosses. The study correlated the rising incidence of stress ailments in women office workers with stressful working conditions, particularly lack of promotions, low pay, monotonous work, heavy work loads, overtime, and frustrations over their inability to influence decision making in the workplace.

In the 1980s stress also invaded small towns. In Wyoming, activating the huge natural gas and oil deposits attracted thousands of workers. People crammed into trailer parks, women were left alone all day, isolated in their campers, and no one could find release for their interests or relaxation. The upshot of the intense stress of living was a tripling of police calls for help in family fights, and serious crimes soared — rapes, child neglect, shooting sprees, and bad checks as well as family abandonment.

In the 1980s, too, drugs moved from the street to the workplace. From marijuana and Valium to heroin and cocaine, drugs are increasingly being used at work to relieve office pressures.

At the Wadsworth VA Hospital in Los Angeles, Vietnam veteran Hopkins crashed his jeep into the lobby of the hospital. His wife spoke of his brewing anger and frustration and the stress of trying to cope with the VA red tape. A few months later Hopkins killed himself.

Surveys of alcoholism among congressmen in 1981 underscored the constant social-business rituals of drinking while working and the abuse of alcohol among congressmen who routinely explained their drinking behavior as caused by the stress of the job.

It's all there — coronary heart disease, drug abuse, crime, suicide — a veritable sea of iceberg tips menacing the health of society. Stress has come a long way since the times fifty years ago when ulcers were the diseases of executives and the first to be acknowledged as a real illness caused by stress. At that time clinicians feebly proposed such ulcers to be produced by the combination of some genetic weakness and excessive tensions peculiar to executive jobs. Today stress is one of the first things we think of when we have an off day or suspect we are developing some physical ailment.

Commercial stress

For months during the spring and summer of 1981, a disagreeable radio commercial repeatedly interrupted the early morning news. Every time it played I clenched my teeth, slapped fist into palm, and strained to choke off my frustration. The commercial started with a dramatic recitation:

Here lies Charlie Moore
His blood pressure went to two-o-four
No less, no Moore.

And, after a weighty pause,

Here lies what's left of Margaret Bent,
Her blood pressure got her and away she went.

The sponsor (Lincoln Savings and Loan) then urged the listener
to stop by the bank for a free blood pressure reading.

My ire over the commercials was never directed particularly
toward the sponsor. I assumed that some junior executive, all
wrapped up in new health programs or Pritikin-like regimes, had
overzealously sold the advertising department on what his stress
experts assured him was the hottest health scenario of the day. It
is the consensus among the health-stress stewards, especially those
who are holistically oriented, that hypertension (high blood pressure of unknown origin) is: (a) potentially fatal, (b) produces no
signs or symptoms until late in the disease, (c) is caused by stress,
and (d) this special kind of reaction to stress can be relieved by
changing to a more relaxed lifestyle. Thus the bank could legiti-
mately claim they were doing you a favor because, according to
the experts, learning you have the disease early enough in its
course may well help to prevent or delay its bleak consequences.

Well, so far, so good. The commercial was no doubt well inten-
tioned, and a good advertising gimmick to boot. Certainly it
echoed the consensus of the new medicine however much it ex-
ulted over a human physical frailty. After the rhyme and the offer
of free blood pressure readings, there were children's voices testi-
fying to the miracle of the readings. Saved my daddy's life, it did,
chirped one high-pitched voice, mommy said so.

Well perhaps.

If I can allow that the commercial was 90-percent kosher, why
did I become so irate? Why, morning after morning, did my blood
boil? Why be so concerned?

For three serious, important reasons.

My cry, first, is that long before blood pressure readings can be
reliably established and high enough to be taken seriously, *the
harmful effects of stress have already taken their toll.* Is this the
time to warn people?

The bottom line for hypertension (and for all stress ailments for
that matter) is that the ailment is detected only after the damage

of stress is done. Hypertension and other stress ills are the *consequences of long, long periods of stress.* What we identify as stress
ills are not the stress process in its active phase, but are ailments
and distress that are the end products of the active phase.

My second annoyance is because these blaring, insistent warnings of possible impending death (yes, Virginia, that's the message) have a hidden agenda of three frightening messages: one, you
have a good chance to be a victim (and a dead one, too, because
hypertension is the number one killer); two, chances are, too, you
are also a victim of too much stress (and they don't give you an
answer for that); and three, if you don't at least get your blood
pressure read so you will go to the doctor and so you can warn
your family you may die, you are blatantly guilty of a moral crime
against yourself, your family, and your doctor. Even the bank
could say, "I told you so." These interlocking messages literally
hurl stress after stress right into the vital milieu of your mind.

If the bank device does show I have high blood pressure, what
do I do then? What doctor do I go to? How much will the medicine cost? How long do I have to live? Will they cancel my
insurance? How will my family manage if I can't work? Oh God,
I'm scared.

It is, I believe, shamelessly irresponsible to foretell gloom and
doom and fear for life itself just to sell a product. And it is just
as irresponsible for the so-called experts to be so uninformed.

Which accounts for my third concern. This stems from the
shallow, flawed concepts about stress that so many professionals
recite enthusiastically, unaware that the principles they quote
about stress and stress ills and stress control are terribly old school
and not at all relevant to the stress problems of the twentieth
century . . .

The raunchy ad of Lincoln Savings illustrates the unfortunate
predicament of health and illness expertise. On the one side, concern for the afflicted takes a bizarre twist in advertising that, in
fact, dehumanizes suffering, while on the other side, the raucous
huckstering punches home the message that millions of Americans are suffering the agonies of a hundred kinds of ailments. I
become particularly saddened by the dozens of radio and TV
commercials that claim to warn the public about the hazards of

high blood pressure and its high risk state for coronary attacks or cerebral strokes. If it is true, as claimed, that millions of Americans are suffering high blood pressure and it is the number one killer, why must the commercials reinforce the doomsday despair of the sufferers?*

Two poles of unwellness

One of the first insights about disease we human beings absorb while growing up is the realization that most "real" illnesses give signals before they burst through the body's resistance. We learn that most ailments have an incubation period, some time period that can be either the time it takes for an infection to overcome the body's natural resistance or, more pragmatically, the time it takes before some physical or emotional distress becomes disturbing enough to be recognized. Usually infections have incubation periods of hours or days, occasionally a month, but rarely more than two. Some diseases, such as wear and tear problems, endocrine changes, and cancer can "incubate" (erode resistance with only vague and ambiguous signs) for months. *Stress ills can incubate for years.*

Most known human ailments are identified by the changes they cause in body functions while the disease process is active. Measles (rubeola), for example, causes fever, Koplik's spots, cough, malaise, and a rash, and when these signs are no longer present, the illness is over. A simple goiter is detected by extra growth of the thyroid (iodine deficiency and growth to compensate), and the presence of the ailment is judged by the physical size of the thyroid. *Stress dis-ease has no signs and symptoms we recognize as evidence of meaningful distress.*

*The figure of 60 million Americans suffering high blood pressure cited so frequently has long puzzled me. In terms of percentages, this would mean that nearly 30 percent of the general population suffers hypertension, and if we exclude children, who rarely have the disease, then the figure rises to nearly two persons out of every three. Common experience suggests this just isn't so — no one's poll, no matter how unscientific, can turn up 65 percent hypertensives in the population.

What is especially interesting is that recently a number of "medical opinions" have ventured that perhaps blood pressure readings are often inaccurate or that sometimes, perhaps often, momentary apprehension causes abnormally high readings, or that the body state just prior to eating, or excessive fatigue, etc., etc., may cause errors in readings. One can only wonder what the real statistics are.

During their incubation, physical and serious emotional ills often, perhaps invariably, cause changes in the body's physiology and biochemistry, or changes in behavior that can be detected and documented by standard medical or psychological tests. We call these prodromal (pro = forward, dromos = running, so, running ahead of . . .) signs, signals that foreshadow a disease in process. Awareness of a couple of wet sneezes or a scratchy throat is fairly convincing evidence that a cold is starting. Measles, *herpes zoster,* arteriosclerosis, syphilis, and nearly all other ailments give signals of their festering incubations. The same is true of mental ills. Signs of anxiety, depression, altered perceptions, phobias, psychoses, and other personality and behavioral disorders can be observed long before the ailment becomes irreversibly serious and damaging.

Not so for essential hypertension. Or for ulcers, angina, alcohol abuse, or any of the other ills and distresses modern medicine and psychology are now describing as caused by or triggered by or aggravated by stress. There are no obvious signs or symptoms, no clues about the hidden disease process that relentlessly erodes well being and can wear through the body's most rugged physical structures.

Stress ills are detected only after the stress disease process has been active long enough to produce erosion of a physiological or mental function serious enough to interfere with life's pursuits. The worrier who develops an ulcer or anxiety neurosis because of job stress becomes aware that he/she is really ill only when the fears and anxieties significantly interfere with doing the job. Nine times out of ten behind the apparent coping, the worrier is absolutely miserable (which to me means real distress) and chances are that the anxiety has already caused one or more secondary effects, such as insomnia, irritable stomach, etc. Depending upon the particular constitution, psychological heritage and emotional experiences, the eager, young worker may manufacture a physical disturbance such as an ulcer, colitis, high blood pressure, or varieties of psychological difficulties such as mini-neuroses or drug dependence. It is the appearance of these *secondary* effects that identifies stress as the cause of the ailment.

A few years ago I was surprised to read about the widow of a well-known county official suing for increased benefits in her pension because, she claimed, her husband's recent death had been caused by the stress of his job. What's more, a few months later, she won her case. Since then, stress has occasionally been officially recognized as a cause of disabling illnesses and death, and while stress is commonly accused of causing disabilities, for very obvious reasons pension funds, insurance companies, and employment compensation officials are careful to avoid even the mention of stress in disability or death claims. The media can call it Killer Stress all it wants, but the health insurance business will never, I suspect, admit that stress qualifies as a disease-producing agent. But it is. We simply have to learn how to identify and define it more precisely.

Let's examine the instance of the county official and his wife. Judging from the media's coverage of his many political problems over the years, his was certainly a stressful job. Occasionally the media mentioned his high blood pressure, and they covered his heart attack. Two coronaries later, he died.

The problem for the insurance company and for the pension fund was that the high blood pressure and the narrowing coronary arteries had been developing for a long time, and there was also the question of whether the medical or psychology experts could say whether the politician's cardiovascular system was inherently weak or just which of the job problems he faced might have caused the last failure of his heart. His widow was more fortunate than others whose spouses succumb to the effects of stress. She won her case, but I suspect she did only because the media had so completely covered her husband's job stress.

Most victims' cases are not so well documented. Usually stress problems or illnesses start and fester in the obscure, inaccessible networks that comprise the mind, and in the most subtle nerve activity of the brain that responds to the products of mental activity.

If, for example, your company transfers you to a different city and you have to find housing fast, the unexpected pressure to accomplish this in addition to performing on the job is one stress. But then you find the cost of housing is unbelievably more than you expected, and this unexpected undesirable is more stress.

Then you discover utility costs have gone up, and there are unexpected expenses in getting settled, and the new job has more risks in it than the old one, and so the stress builds. It is not one assault in one place at one time the way other illnesses strike. There is the thread of concern for the future and for the well being of the self that ties together clues from different happenings at different times. Your reactions may be mild annoyance at first, some worry, apprehension, making a great effort to adjust to many new changes, but always in the back of the mind is the worry about diminishing security.

Since life goes on, the worry settles down into the unconscious mind while conscious activity is devoted to solving the problems of each day. But this does not mean that the stress has decreased. Signals of its constant pressure disturb the ease of mind and body. Every time money or costs or job security comes to mind you feel a twinge of anxiety. Stress has established a beachhead within the mind, and because it incubates within the mind and the brain that serves the mind, it also reaches the neural networks that regulate the body's functions. The result is an inching upward of body tensions, a slow but inexorable shift in the body's physiological activities, keeping them from their usual balanced state. Depending upon the body's systems or organs involved in the stress, or because of some innate weakness or some association from experiences or images, one or another part of the body begins to suffer true physical damage.

The surreptitious nature of the stress process means, unfortunately, that remedies prescribed to relieve the damage need to overcome *two* serious disease processes, not just one. There is the first process of living with stress and struggling mentally and emotionally to cope that damages vital body systems.

The second process occurs *after* the stress damage has reached the point where it impairs necessary biological functioning or the ability to perform in life and it is this effect that causes the additional, and life-threatening, problems. High blood pressure, for example, causes headache, annoying pounding sensations, effects on the kidney, brain, and heart that can end in uremia, a stroke, or heart attack. These secondary effects are not due to the original stress but by the inability of a body system to function properly.

What we have, in fact, are *two very different disease processes during the development of stress ills.* The first is the mental stress that causes the breakdown of a body function, while the second is the effect of that breakdown on the operation of body functions.

There is another and profoundly important consequence of the silently eroding process by which stress damages the human organism that is seldom considered in discussions of stress therapeutics. This concerns the exhaustion of the body's defenses against harm to itself. Obviously, as the body's tensions continue to impair normal physiological functions, the body systems use their reserves to maintain their operations, and it is only when these defense reserves are exhausted that the damage becomes obvious enough for detection and diagnosis. This silent, surreptitious drain on the body's resistance (why we get more colds under stress, etc.) is added evidence that stress affects human beings very differently from the way other ailments produce their effects.

The challenge of underhealth and underachieving

What I want to do in this book is to make a statement about transactions within the mind and body that diminish biological integrity and erode the psychological potential of human beings. I want to describe as completely as possible why it is that so many human beings function below par, often for whole lifetimes, being neither sick nor truly well, and why it is that so many people endure states of diminished well being, underwellness, and underachieving their potential. These gray areas of emotional and physical beingness, when life limps along between health and illness in the states I call diminished well being, are created when the adversities and unsatisfactoriness of life begin to tax one's abilities to cope with the never-ending demands of life.

"Stress" is generally taken to mean the whole scenario when some change in a person's circumstances puts pressure on the person to react in some socially approved way, and that socially approved way is finding some way to adjust to the circumstances, i.e., "to cope." Misfortunes of any kind, from personal rejection to great disasters, are the pressures to perform despite the misfortunes, and although some allowances are made, for the most part society *expects* us to perform. The most concise and accurate description of "stress" is that stress causes emotional distress and mental or physical ills when people won't, don't, or can't cope.

One of the most scientifically puzzling observations about "the stress of life" is how such things as company policy, a disagreeable boss, difficult family relationships, love affairs gone sour, or the fear of failure can damage the mental and physical health of so many so much as to support a two billion dollar a year stress industry.

There are, in fact, a staggering number of unanswered questions about stress. What is stress, *really?* How can stress cause such an amazing array of very different kinds of ailments? Why are more and more people living under constant stress? Why are some people more susceptible to stress than others? How can the same kind of stress cause hypertension in one person, ulcers in another, drug addiction in another, and depression in still another person?

And, of course, do stress reduction techniques really work? How can stress management using relaxation methods help high blood pressure that has been developing for twenty-five years?

Every stress a person experiences leaves its mark on the mind and body, a numbing, sickening wound when loss or failure is sudden and unexpected, a small bruise of the psyche and body tissues when stress is the common, everyday kind. Even the most ordinary stress leaves scars that never truly heal (such as negative life scripts). When one stress follows another before the psyche and body can heal the breach, the stress wounds deepen and healing is slower and less sure. For the most part, stress builds up over time and can take years before it explodes into the damage of high blood pressure or neurosis or drug abuse. It is the gray areas of unwellness-but-not-"real"-sickness that incubate the erosions of mind and body's wellness that needs to be understood.

Chapter 2

Introducing
the "stress of life"
phenomenon
A synopsis of its causes and cures

Selye's revelations . . . Profiles of the stress that assaults the psyche . . .
Some problems in the understanding of stress . . . Living is hazardous to
your health . . . The strange dynamics of stress . . . THE stress ills.

Selye's revelations

Every now and then someone comes along with an observation
about life that is so on the mark and such a compact summary of
what we all know but can never say in words that the expression
is immediately adopted as the perfect way to express the feelings
we all share about one or another circumstance of life (stay cool:
it's the pits).

It was this way when Selye first used the expression "the stress
of life." Everyone knew immediately what he meant, and although
people have been talking about stress for hundreds of years, the
misery of life has never been captured so succinctly nor so well.
Before Selye, stress was usually related to especially unfortunate
circumstances or especially heavy pressures of business. When
Selye's expression revealed the ordinariness of stress, so common
it could be felt everywhere in life, people suddenly realized that
life was, indeed, stressful.

Selye's insight, like all sudden revelations, was disarmingly simple. And deceptively profound. What he was saying was that the
difficulties people face as they adjust to the ebb and flow of their
life situations create changes within human beings that disrupt

their psychological equilibrium. It is a simple observation and one that immediately suggests at least three more observations about the endless successions of ups and downs that punctuate even the most ordinary life. We know, for example, that sometimes the stress of adversity can galvanize our energies in such a way that we conquer the adversity. We know, too, that at other times we fail, and when adversity exhausts our capacity for the struggle, we become distressed. And most of us know that at still other times the stress can become more than our minds and bodies can endure, and we fall victim to true illness.

Out of this one simple observation — that life is stressful — has come a hodgepodge of new notions about health and illness. In a way, the health sciences were caught short by Selye's observation. The stress Selye was talking about were the nebulous, ill-defined difficulties people have when they are interacting with each other and with people-things, but difficulties that nonetheless cause real distress and illness. Until "stress" came along, the healing arts lived by the idea of one specific cause for one specific kind of distress, such as pneumococci causing pneumonia, or crowding causing violence or lack of insulin causing diabetes. Now suddenly the health sciences were faced with a very different concept about the cause of human afflictions, the notion that the intangible events of just trying to live can cause physical ailments. Almost from out of nowhere came research, clinics, authorities, and yes, TV commercials, proclaiming stress to be the number one enemy of health. Still, the new revelations focused on the drama of the grim consequences of stress and how to treat them rather than stimulating professionals to discover exactly *how* stress causes so much trouble for human beings.

As a matter of fact, Selye had uncovered some tantalizing clues in his work on a different kind of stress. Another of his profound observations was when, as a medical student, he observed that all illness, regardless of cause, shared the common feature of what we recognize as the look of sickness. That is, no matter whether the illness is caused by injury, infection, or chemical assaults to the body, each cause also produced a *second* kind of reaction that makes all sick people have a similar "look." Selye called it "just being sick." And in an arduous, prolonged research effort, Selye discovered the biochemical and endocrine mechanisms that were common to all kinds of physical ills regardless of the nature of the cause.

I have long suspected that a similar, parallel reaction occurs whenever the psyche is abused. Any impact on the mind or body or spirit not only damages the specific part of being affected, it also diminishes the whole organism. The parallel to Selye's "just being sick" is "just being stressed." That is, the effects of the stress of life are twofold: one is the specific stress such as job stress that very specifically disturbs the particular feelings about one's work and one's relationships with the work environment, while the second effect is the nonspecific effect on the psyche that diminishes participation in life in general and saps the energy of mind and body and spirit. If the psyche contains the drive toward fulfillment, then the main effects of all stress must be on the psyche. All other effects on mind, body, and spirit are secondary.*

Profiles of the stress that assaults the psyche

Stress has become endemic so quickly, it has literally stepped on its own toes. Dozens of stress reduction or stress management techniques have been newly devised, yet no one really knows the best ways to use them nor why they do what they do. There has been, in fact, little if any general constructive agreement about what causes the stress of life. Experts who treat stress problems list endless examples of things that are stressful, but there are no satisfactory explanations of what it is about those things that makes them stressful. Yet many people, including the experts, have little doubt about what stress is for them personally, and they can empathize well with other people about their stress. Everyone has felt the pressure of stress and everyone knows that more than likely there is more stress to come. They are, however, hard put to put their fingers on how it happens or why.

*Although it is widely accepted that moods, beliefs, and various states of mind affect health and healing, the hard sciences do not distinguish the intangible ingredients that ensure the existence and growth of human beings. In my discussions I use mind, body, and spirit as they are used conventionally and use the term *psyche* as Jung defined it: "the innate, inner organizing center and guiding force of the Self and the growth of Self during life," i.e., the inner mechanism that puts experience together for the well being and growth of the individual.

Ask a thousand people and you'll get a thousand answers about what is stressful in life. They will say, "Oh, it's the pressures I feel at work," or "It's the tensions in the family now that Dad is living with us," or "It's worrying about not being able to make ends meet," or "It's not knowing how to carry on now that poor Harry is gone," or "It's being lonely and not being able to make friends."

Almost by consensus we tacitly agree that the stress of life is the encounters we have in life that make living more difficult than we think it should be, encounters with people or people-things or people-surrogates (like the IRS) that challenge our abilities and our hopes and dreams.

Stress is Mom going to work at 42, starting over in the work-place that is no longer yesterday's familiar shop or office, while chores at home haunt her with demands on her time and energy.

Stress is a spouse's wandering eye and body, irregular hours, obvious excuses, changing moods, or being unbearably preoccupied.

Stress is not feeling well and not knowing why, waiting hours in the doctor's office, not knowing where to get the right kind of medical help.

Stress is worrying about getting through school, about finishing assignments on time, unfair tests, misleading courses, about how much school is enough.

Stress is changing jobs, buying new houses, hunting apartments, getting divorced, parenting.

Stress is suppressing anger, resentment, fear, and worry.

Stress is caring for a handicapped child, a child being bussed or not bussed, stumbling on drugs in an offspring's room.

Stress is paying high bills on a low budget, using less energy and paying more for it, the unexplained cancellation of car insurance, watching food prices leap forward, being audited by the IRS.

Stress is the grey pall of winter skies, allergies borne on the wind, hot weather, high humidity.

Stress is an unfriendly boss, scheming colleagues, being overlooked at promotion time, playing the work game and losing.

Stress is not being able to communicate well, fearing failure, feeling guilty, making goofs, gaffes, and faux pas.

Stress is the death of a loved one, being the victim of a crime, having a major accident, losing one's job.

Stress is coping.

The stress of life is, in short, nothing more — and nothing less — than the jostling back and forth of human beings seeking fulfillment within the very human surroundings they seek it in. The stress of life originates in the kinds of things that can and often do happen to most people in the course of a lifetime.

Some problems in the understanding of stress

Stress is, then, any obstacle in the way of finding satisfactions in life. The puzzle of stress is why, if it is just living, has it become the most insidious, harmful affliction man has ever faced? The stress of life can wound the psyche, wrench the emotions, derange the mind, impair the body, and extinguish life.

The most bothersome question about stress is one that is quite generally ignored. This is the peculiar (and frightening) way stress affects the human organism. Stress produces its effects on mind and body surreptitiously, accumulating silently, wounding the inner substance until finally the mind and body functions can no longer keep up any pretense of normal activity. Not until we understand the way stress abuses the body's functions (including the brain's) so quietly and malignantly can stress be managed effectively. For stress is a wholly new and different kind of ailment from the kinds of illnesses familiar to medicine and psychology. *What causes stress does not cause illness.* Stress, as "the stress of life," *first* disturbs the equanimity of the mind. As the mind absorbs a difficulty in life, it becomes disturbed, and it is the mental disturbance that causes the hundreds of emotional and physical illnesses.

The unique feature of stress that makes it so wholly new as a source of impaired mind and body function is that the entire process by which it produces its effects is carried out by the very ordinary (and normally functioning) activities of the mind. Most people of the Western world have been conditioned by every authority they know — parents, teachers, counselors, and doctors

— to believe that the only time thinking can cause emotional or physical problems is when thinking itself is sick (or lazy or too egocentric, etc.). The upshot of this cultural injunction is that we are thoroughly brainwashed to believe that if we are normal, then we should know how to cope with life's common difficulties. The result of this is that we become saddled with two worries instead of the one problem we first started worrying about. The first worry is the difficult situation we are facing while the second is worrying that we may not be able to cope!

The crucial role of the mind's activities in stress is underscored by the very personal way its effects are expressed. Everyone's stress is different, everyone's problems are different from everyone else's, and everyone handles problems differently. Each person has a personal, special way of handling the obstacles in the way of living a tolerable and reasonable, satisfying life. In these modern days of changing values, changing family relationships, confrontations, economic hardships, constant demands for performance in the marketplace, and confusing media messages about human strengths and weaknesses, only hermits can escape the stress of life. And because the circumstances for stress are everywhere yet each life is lived differently and moves in different spheres, the circumstances of stress are, too, very personal.

Living is hazardous to your health

So, living today is hazardous to the health. Why? If the physical hazards to life are no longer so punishing, why should just living in relative comfort and safety have such a great potential for causing illness? How indeed does this new, *nonphysical stress* disturb mind and body?

The answers to both questions lie within the nature of the human mind. The new stress of life is the endless stream of intangible obstacles along the way to self-realization and fulfillment, obstacles detected by the mind senses that alert the *inner* being to threats to the psychological well being of the self.

People generally believe the feelings they have about some stressful situation are caused by the situation itself. When Jane complains about unfair treatment at work and blows up in anger and resentment, the connection between the work situation and the emotional reaction is so strong it is seen as a straightforward cause-effect stress-distress relationship. A bad situation "out there" makes for emotions "in here." Jane knows things have not been going well for some time at work and she identifies her feelings with the disagreeable situation so completely she believes the situation is the cause of her stress.

It isn't. The situation is the cause *for* stress but not necessarily the cause of the *feelings* of stress. The feelings of stress are reactions to the *perception* that a situation is threatening to one's psychological well being whether the situation may or may not be. The situation itself simply *is* — it has no meaning at all until it is interpreted, and different people usually interpret the same situation very differently. Gutsy little Harry may be in exactly the same situation at work as Jane but he looks at it as an exciting challenge to prove himself. The difficult situation "out there" is an occasion that *can* trigger disturbing thoughts and feelings, but just as often it doesn't.

Situations involving people usually develop over time, in different places, and they depend upon the way each individual perceives the circumstances and how the people and their behaviors converge around some especially meaningful goal in life. It takes time to weave the story. In the workplace, for example, every exchange between worker and worker, between worker and boss, or between worker and other management personnel contains a hundred clues about the quality of the relationship between worker and the job situation, and it can often take a hundred clues before one knows whether things are going well or badly. Only when the last part of the puzzle falls into place do the feelings of satisfaction or frustration, anger or despair, or contentment emerge.

The confusing feature of the process is that much of it occurs with little, and sometimes without any, conscious awareness. If the boss, for example, selects a co-worker over me for a promotion I think I deserve, after my disappointment and resentment have cooled, I may recall a number of times when the boss subtly showed favor to the other person and I didn't attach any real importance to it then. But now I will search back for reasons and will reinterpret these and other episodes. The fact that I can later reconstruct a long story of subtle bias against me means I *did* know, I *did* take in the information, and the fact that I didn't react, consciously, until much later also means that I didn't draw a firm conclusion until my subconscious mind had become convinced the situation really did bode ill for me (after the fact, in this case). My desire to succeed may also have interfered with the ability of my subconscious to make an accurate appraisal of the situation.

Unlike job stress or family stress, awareness of a disaster needs no time to understand the problem; sudden loss or failure descends upon the mind like an avalanche. It is *adjusting* to the stress situation and to all its ramifications for the future that is a long process.

The strange dynamics of stress

Understanding stress rests entirely on putting some order into the chaotic mass of things we already know about it. We know, for example, that the stress of life is always concerned with people or people-things, that it is always concerned with coping with the adversities in life, and that the adversities are what we perceive to be difficulties in the way of achieving one or another goal in life. Nothing about stress is physical. Tracking stress within the mind and body and discovering how the mind can warp itself and the body as well is mainly an exercise in drawing conclusions from common experiences and from the experiential and scientific consensus.

The starting point is cataloguing the outstanding characteristics of stress. There are, as I see it, three special features of stress: it is unique to the individual, it depends upon interactions with other human beings, and it incubates within the mind.

While many people encounter similar kinds of stressful situations, the circumstances are always unique for each individual. Not only is every human relationship special in some way, but the meaning of events, circumstances, and relationships depend upon how each person perceives them, and that in turn depends upon each person's way of using experience, teaching, culture, and personality characteristics to shape individual attitudes and beliefs and expectations.

The dependence of stress and stress reactions on the circumstances and dynamics of human interactions means that stress cannot be separated from life itself. Everything people believe in, everything they value, love, respect, desire, admire, or long for, is rooted in what other people think, have thought, and will think. Human beings are not merely born of other human beings — what they are in life is how other human beings shape them during their lifetimes and generations of lifetimes before them. Stress is the pressure to be the way other people feel we should be and the struggle to reconcile a unique inner life with the pressures to be what the other people believe we should be.*

All reactions to stress begin as concerns about relationships with people or things created by people. When life becomes even slightly difficult, human beings instinctively try to remedy their troublesome predicaments, and they are successful more often than not. Most people learn during the course of life how to handle different kinds of life's stresses. But because stress comes from human interactions and always involves other people, even good solutions don't always work to quash the stress. Life's circumstances can sometimes be so involved no solution to its problems can be truly effective. As stress continues, mind and body brace for the next episode. Concerns about the stress builds, frustration sets in, worry begins, and feelings intensify and the reactions involve more and more of the mind's and brain's and body's energy. The energies are no longer devoted to trying to achieve goals or satisfying living; the energies become misdirected into two very difficult tasks: trying to cope *and* continuing to try to achieve and live a reasonably satisfying life.

The committed wife who becomes emotionally unsettled after months of domestic quarreling begins to understand that it is not just the quarrels that are distressing. She becomes aware that the

*Every human being thus lives by a double standard. At this stage in our social evolution, we have scarcely begun to discriminate the two realities of self and society, the self as a member of society whose survival and well being depend upon functioning for the common good (i.e., for the well being of human society as a whole or as some socially significant part of the whole) and the self as an individual for whom the standards and expectations and survival mechanisms of our social groups can often be inimical to *individual* well being.

emotions she has before, during, and after the quarrels interfere with all of her other activities in life. She begins to realize that *all* her functioning is disturbed. If she works, her work does not go well; if she has children to care for, she feels she is not doing a good job as a mother. In moments of reflection she can trace these changes and her diminished functioning back to the quarrels, and rightly so. But what she may not be aware of then is that she is incubating a stress illness, and that if the stress continues, or more stress comes along, she is a good candidate for therapy or will need treatment for ulcers or some other psychosomatic or psychological ailment.

The concerns about the self excite disturbing images, and with every ill-omened, unhappy, discouraging image, the body involved in the image actually responds. When images are not favorable for the welfare of the self, such as images of being rejected, the body responds with an unfelt, but nonetheless real, physical echo of a posture of rejection. The little known but profound effects of images on the body's functioning are discussed in detail in Chapter 10.

There are other, insidious, slow-growing psychotoxic effects of stress on mind and body. When the images of the past or possible future hurt involve the body and the body reacts to the images, the body tensions of the reactions also send messages to the brain where they become recognized as sensations of tensions, the feelings we call anxiety. The tensions are then "felt," and because the body tensions and changes are worrisome or frightening, conscious attention focuses on the sensations and not on the reasons for them, which would enable the person to solve the problem and relieve the stress.

As a matter of fact, there is usually such a long time and such a tenuous connection between the events causing the feelings of stress and finally becoming aware that the unsettled feelings are indeed caused by those particular events that people rarely connect the two until the body's reactions either begin to malfunction or cause some kind of distress (headache, insomnia). Within the brain, the messages about the body's tensions combine with the mind's concern about well being, and the mind is suddenly confronted with two unknowns instead of only one: why the body is disturbed and why the mind is disturbed. Relationships gone sour are worrisome — the first effect is worry. The second effect is the body's reaction to the images of worry, and the third reaction is the awareness of the sensations that come from the body's *reactions to worry* (to the images).

It only gradually seeps into conscious awareness that there is probably some relationship between what we are worrying about and the way we feel, emotionally or physically. Some people make a general association, such as, "I really feel lousy, but that's probably because I've had so much pressure on the job." Other people may make a little more accurate assessment, such as, "Being on this training program sure has my gut all tied up in knots," or "I'm so nervous about whether my husband may lose his job I can't breathe." Notice that we usually tie worries or anxieties to some physical symptom. The main reason, as I noted earlier, is because we never feel the physiological changes going on in the body until they reach a point where the disturbance of a function becomes uncomfortable enough to attract attention. Those physical changes, however, have been developing for some time.

With continued stress, or our continued reactions to a particular stress, comes an even more disastrous change in the body. The body adapts. That is, it accepts the higher levels of tension in the muscles or gut or blood pressure as a new "normal" state and pushes its functioning to compensate for the new strain on the systems. It is a peculiarity of human physiological systems, such as muscles and viscera, that they literally stop sending messages to the brain about their states of tension if earlier messages have not been noticed. Take the common tension headache, for example. The muscle tensions have been developing all day, but the mind has been forced to pay attention to more pressing problems, and so the muscle tensions around the head are not felt until they become strong enough to demand attention.

The most extraordinary feature of the stress of life is that *it is the only disease process in which events in the mind affect the actual physical functions of the brain.* Until recently such a statement would have been viewed as heretical to health science dogma; however, it is now being accepted, albeit somewhat vaguely that, as Dr. Sperry wrote, "Mental events determine brain events and brain events determine mind events."* This mutual effect between mind and brain during the development of stress is described in Chapter 10.

There are still more fascinating special features about the stress of life. The first is that the damage it does to mind and body is never "cured" in the traditional sense. We do not take away stress germs, nor can we surgically remove the stress of life. What we can do, and what is the basis of all stress management, is literally to teach the mind and body not to react to stressful circumstances in a harmful way.

For simplicity's sake, let's reduce all stress reactions, from insomnia to hypertension or unusually frequent epileptic seizures, to the single entity of tensions of the mind and body (which it actually is). The tensions are present because, over time, and without conscious awareness of them, mind and body have developed states of uptightness, and the physiological mechanisms of the organism have "learned" to operate in this state of tension. The tense state becomes the operational mode of the organism.

The psychological approach to relief from these tension states, whether therapy or counseling, is to help the person understand the sources of stress and enable him/her to develop mental and behavioral ways to deal with the sources of the stress. The result of this kind of therapy is that the more the person understands about his stress and how to handle it, the less he tends to react to future stress situations. With fewer reactions of mind and body, the innate regulating mechanisms of the body gradually allow a return to normal or near-normal states of functioning.

In a somewhat similar way, the body awareness techniques used in stress management help the individual to become aware enough of his body tension reactions that he comes to recognize that he is under stress sooner and so begins to deal with the stress sooner. That is, learning to be aware when body tensions *are developing* alerts the individual to begin coping with the tension-producing situations while they are happening. As learning proceeds, the individual learns to begin body relaxation more and more promptly. As the individual becomes more proficient in *not* react-

*R. W. Sperry, "An objective approach to subjective experiences: Further explanation of a hypothesis," *Psychol. Rev.* 77 (1970): 585–900.

ing to stress, here, too, as with psychological alertness, the body's normal physiological regulating systems are allowed to return to normal functioning and the effects of previous stress gradually diminish and may disappear.

The stress ills

The parts of the stress story that interest professional helpers and healers are the "officially" recognized disturbances that living with stress can cause. In Table 1 I have listed the major examples of human emotional and physical distresses that are caused by, triggered by, or aggravated by "the stress of life." The consensus of the medical and psychotherapeutic communities is that each ailment, disorder, distress, and emotional or behavioral problem is either caused by or remarkably worsened by stress.

The implications of the list in Table 1 for the health of our society is staggering. Taken together with the nameless mini-miseries of everyday stress that attack nearly everyone (and sometimes are the incubation periods of the ills in Table 1), these ills and difficulties can no doubt account for all but a relatively small part of all the discomforts and ills of the world.

In contrast, the causes of all other human ills are remarkably few in number. Infections, physical injury, and biochemical or tissue abnormalities, along with genetic and birth defects, are the sole causes of illness except for stress. And some experts believe that stress predisposes to the occurrence of nearly all of these other kinds of human ills.

The question so critical to human well beingness is — what signs and symptoms did the people show while they were developing all these ills? None? Oh come now, certainly some psychological change preceded the sexual impotency; certainly some behavior gave away the approaching delinquency; certainly some altered moods signalled imminent neurosis.

Certainly there are antecedents, some warning signals that the psyche has been bruised, or that some biological function is weakening. There are, of course, but the problem is how to capture all those fleeting, variable, indistinct, hard-to-describe feelings and forebodings that all is not really well, and then put them into some

Table 1
Examples of disturbances caused by, triggered by, or aggravated by "the stress of life"

1. Bona fide emotional disturbances ("official" signs, symptoms, or ailments)
   anxiety, insomnia, tension headaches, neuroses, phobias, hysterias, hypochondriasis, and a major factor in: aging, sexual impotency, alcoholism, drug abuse, sleep disorders, learning problems

2. Abnormal behavior
   delinquency, hostility, underachieving, compulsive behaviors (kleptomania), cult addiction, obesity, vandalism, aggression, withdrawal, chronic unemployment, crime, battered child/spouse/parent syndrome, sexual deviation, suicide

3. Psychosomatic illness
   essential hypertension, auricular arrhythmias, ulcers, colitis, asthma, chronic pain, acne, peripheral vascular disease, angina, bruxism, cardiac arrest

4. Worsening of genuine organic illnesses
   epilepsy, migraine, herpes zoster, coronary thrombosis, rheumatic arthritis

kind of sensible arrangement that can foretell the more serious ills.

There was a time when we knew nothing of the unseen forces of the universe. Then, bit by bit the forces, still unseen, were captured by the shadows they cast on time and space, and now we are in bold control of outer space. So too, I think, we can learn to capture the operations of the unseen inner forces that determine our control over inner space.

If we start an excursion into the nature of stress with what we know about stress, it is precious little. We have Table 1 and little else, except that stress is, well, uh, the stress of life.

Chapter 3

States between health and illness

Marginal miseries (varieties of nameless ailments) . . . Physical "maybe" ailments . . . Psychical unease (mini-neuroses) . . . The stress of coping . . . The stress of being ill or handicapped . . . The treatment void . . . Why name nameless ailments?

Marginal miseries (varieties of nameless ailments)

Unlike those who suffer "official" stress ills that can be diagnosed and treated (as in Table 1), there are countless human beings who hover in life's wasteland between true health and true illness. Medicine and clinical psychology put limits on health and illness, limits that define the extent to which their skills can be used for helping and healing and what has to be wrong with you before you can receive their help. The kinds of ailments and indispositions accepted for treatment are very specific. Not-feeling-good is *not* an ailment that qualifies for expert help.

By far the most prevalent kind of unwellness in the world is the kind that is never diagnosed: the states *between* health and illness. They are not recognized by practically anyone as genuine unwellness.

There is, too, an exasperating lack of words to describe not-feeling-good states. People who are neither really well nor really sick have a difficult time explaining what ails them, or often they are reluctant to discuss their inner distress either because they themselves are unsure why they are unwell or because they don't want to admit being afflicted by some nameless state, especially these days when antacids or tranquilizers or counselors are so handy. And anyway, it would seem bizarre to confide to someone, "Oh God, I think I'm semi-sick!"

It doesn't take a whole lot of serious thinking to catalogue a variety of not-well-not-sick states. We can all tick off times when we haven't felt too good physically but were not *really* sick, other times when we have been emotionally unsettled but not *sick,* times when we have felt sort-of-ill and scared about it or suffering the distress of actually being sick, and still other times when we are just plain sick of coping. These amount to five quite different kinds of states between health and illness (Table 2).

Why identify the gray areas of health? Because, in one way or another they all signal the stress of life. Each nameless ailment is either caused by or significantly worsened by stress. The predicament for both the people who are semi-sick and for the helpers and healers is that few of these nameless ailments are recognized as related to stress illnesses. The vague, ambiguous sensations of being semi-sick are — as we shall see — the signs and symptoms of living with stress.

Physical "maybe" ailments." Everyone has experienced times of feeling not quite right physically, aware something different is going on in the body but with nothing disturbing enough to suggest any specific kind of illness. Later we say something like, "I thought I was getting something," or "I thought for a time it might be something really serious, like a tumor." This nonspecific

Table 2
Varieties of nameless ailments
(Kinds of not-well–not-sick states and ways of feeling stress)

1. Physical unease (physical "maybe" ailments)

2. Psychical unease (emotionally unsettled; mini-neuroses)

3. The stress of coping (marginally coping with stress and losing the coping battle)

4. The stress of being ill or handicapped

5. Semi-sick and not knowing what to do about it (the treatment void)

physical unease is a common condition that, curiously, has not been studied for the remarkable implications it contains. The "maybe" kind of physical unwellness breeds stress at every turn. People worry about what may be wrong in the body, they have forebodings about how serious the illness may become, how much it may harm, and then, when the unwellness fades with no damage done, there is the curiosity about what it was and whether it might happen again.

"Maybe" ailments are those vague but quite real yet not fully crystalized physical signs and symptoms that hover between insignificant, minor physical distress and portents of serious illness. The discomforts can be caused by the 24-hour viruses, transient gastrointestinal upsets, funny little bumps suddenly appearing on the skin, low back pain, wandering chest pains, peculiar headaches, unusual fatigue or waves of lethargy, or awarenesses of any of a hundred other ill-defined, inexplicable strange changes in one's inner biological functioning.

From experience you know that chances are these nebulous, usually fleeting disturbances do not signal serious or imminent onset of any other serious illness, but on the other hand, you are not completely sure they don't. At the same time experience tells you that a visit to the doctor may not be very productive. The physical signs and symptoms are not specific or well defined enough to diagnose a definite ailment, and the inevitable counsel is, "wait and see," along with, "take two aspirin and call me in the morning."

But while you wait for further physical developments, uncertainty about the outcome grows. Everyone worries about these indeterminate states. Many people fantasize their consequences. A headache grows into a brain tumor, fatigue into a cardiovascular problem, muscle chest pains into an impending coronary. It is the uncertainty and not knowing that magnify the feelings and concerns and anxieties.

Psychical unease (mini-neuroses) is the stress state between health and illness when one feels emotionally unsettled but can find no reason for it. People often feel mildly, or even moderately, apprehensive, sad, depressed or irritated seemingly for no reason at all. Often the emotional distress simply fades away. Some of the time the feelings stay at modest levels and eventually become focused as worry about a specific problem.

I am still amazed by the artfulness with which the conscious mind ignores the signals of the subliminal mind. Ever since I began analyzing observations and other data about stress and the mind-body reactions to stress, I have become increasingly sensitive to subtle changes in my own feeling states. Whenever my emotions and feelings seem to change and I don't know why, I try to ferret out the cause. Yet many a time I will be stumped by an annoying depression or psychic hurt and may need many days to realize that I am subliminally grieving the anniversary of a loved one's death, or that other times I am indulging in self-pity because a friend has just had great success while I've been pummeled by bad luck.

These fitful plays of feelings and emotions, roused most often by the silent, uninhibited grinding away of the unconscious thinking machine could, I suspect, be called mini-neuroses, or perhaps micro-neuroses. With the roots of the emotional upsets unknown to conscious awareness, these small and transient disturbances of emotions can validly be termed irrational and hence neurotic.

The essential point of designating one kind of not-feeling-well state as psychical unease is simply to acknowledge that such states do exist. Modest swings of emotions are not half so disturbing as physical unease, but neither should they be dismissed lightly. Their cause may be some temporary stressful circumstance and so they disappear in a few days; or when the unease continues, it is a signal that a stress problem does exist.

The stress of coping. Even in the gray area between health and illness there are gray areas. The most damaging and the most diminishing of these is living with anxiety. Although psychologists tend to consider anxiety as either irrational fears or the next state to it, in the practical world of working people, anxiety ranges from mild concern about something to skillfully hidden terror.

The gray area within the gray area comes from the vagueness with which states such as mental distress, anxiety, and neuroses are defined. I prefer to label the anxiety that accompanies stress and coping as psychical distress caused by psychic assaults. These terms emphasize that the theatre of operations is the mind fabricating ideas and attitudes and beliefs and thoughts rather than a neurotic anxiety that suggests an instinctively reacting body as the source of the sensation of anxiety. I have distinguished two categories of psychical distress, the one being the psychical unease of unknown origin as a state in which "anxiety" is actually intelligent concern about something that nags at the margin between consciousness and the unconscious mind, and the other, the stress of coping as a state in which the emotions of uncertainty and anxiety can range from begrudging the energy spent on coping to a terror that is contained only by an enormous effort of will and mental discipline.

Many people live with marginal and near-incapacitating neuroses. During my career in industrial medical research, many of my colleagues were executives, and over the years I was confidante to many who suffered the worst of anxiety neuroses, men who felt their anxiety symptoms were signs of weakness of character. They could barely confide their problems to a special friend and certainly not to a psychologist or psychiatrist. Yet they carried on and muddled through and sometimes became models of the successful human being. Once at dinner I asked one of these friends why he wasn't having soup, and he confided that his anxiety was so bad he couldn't get a spoon to his mouth without spilling the soup, the hand would be shaking so. Then he wistfully added that this uncontrolled shaking when he felt anxiety was also why he refused coffee in public. He was so embarrassed by what he felt was a character weakness that he would never order anything that required high degree of hand-to-mouth coordination.

To the best of my knowledge, psychologists have not catalogued the length of time people who "cope" and live with intense anxieties or depressions, often for entire lifetimes. Not long ago a local TV station presented a collection of cases of people with common phobias such as the fear of flying, fear of leaving the house, the fear of cats, etc. The programs emphasized the panic episodes and the constant fears the victims had, and they also described some new psychotherapeutic kinds of treatment for phobias. But what impressed me the most was the incredibly long times these phobic people had suffered and endured and how many had not sought treatment, and for those who did, how often treatment had failed.

The average time the people suffered their phobias was over twenty years!

The stress of being ill or handicapped. The most tragic oversight of the professional healing sciences has always been, in my mind, failing to recognize the very special stress of being ill or having a handicap. Both healing specialities of medicine and psychology have skirted responsibility for helping to assuage the mental agonies of illness and unhealth.

The stress of illness or being handicapped is a terrible burden. And it is sadly aggravated by the suffer-in-silence martyr code that has somehow managed to brainwash generations of human beings into believing that it is virtuous and morally rewarding to bear pain without complaining. We are taught, "Nobody likes a crybaby," "keep your chin up," and to bear up under adversity as in the old camp song we children used to sing, "Mrs. Fox Terrier said to her pups, 'In all life's adversities keep your tails up, keep your tails up'." Old adages about keeping a stiff upper lip may be historically interesting, but they can seriously interfere with facing adversity and just make matters worse. It is another stress to cope with on top of all the coping the ill or handicapped must do anyway. Somehow the healing professions ignore the enormous stress of coping with being ill, and they seem oblivious to the fact that the coping cover-up of great stress and distress drains energy and shackles the human potential of enormous segments of society.

Every ill person perceives his wholeness diminished and his deprivation of the fullness of social activities, and the mind reacts as it does to any difficulty with the self. Recognizing the inability to perform up to expectations engenders emotional reactions. The anxiety about diminished ability to perform is increased by the frustration of not being able to perform. The effects of the anxiety, the intellectual concerns and frustrations are the stress that aggravates the primary illness or handicap. Without proper relief, the added stress delays recovery from the primary illness.

The treatment void. The worst stress is not feeling good and not knowing what to do about it. Strictly speaking, all stress is feeling upset and not knowing what to do about it. Despite the spread of the new psychologies that teach how to cope with wives, husbands, children, jobs, careers, insecurity, and other troubling circumstances and despite the availability of the new body awareness techniques to relieve the tensions of stress, truly effective relief is hard to come by. While some personal stress problems do yield to one or another stress reduction procedure, most stress problems are so personal, so unique to the one person, and depend so much upon how each individual can incorporate the helping resources into the real life situation that relief is partial at best. So many of the new ways of helping people under stress are specific to one special kind of circumstance that adapting them to other circumstances proves difficult (if not stressful), and much too often new helping techniques are available only in distant centers.

People with physical ills have the same difficulties in finding relief as do people with emotional distress. An interesting thing happened to the healing professions on their way to conquering disease and improving the quality of the physical life. Their research laboratories spew out therapeutic products to heal the sick of this world so magnificently one would think their silver bullets of eternal health can be bought in the bargain basement. You have to be sick enough to be obviously troubled or in pain or in serious jeopardy before you merit a parcel from the healing storehouse.

Why name nameless ailments?

Why is it important to pay so much attention to such seemingly minor, unimportant states of not-feeling-so-good? Because, quite to the contrary, distresses such as the marginal miseries and nameless ailments *are* important. They are important for three very serious reasons.

First, most people, including the professionals, don't recognize these "I-don't-feel-so-good-but-I'm-not-really-sick-either" states as warning signs that they are living under stress, and second, that semi-sick states not only signal the presence of stress, but can point to a covert struggle to cope with a stress problem that, if not relieved, can incubate the stress-making process until vital mind and body operations become eroded.

But most important is the value of this new information to the healing processes of the subliminal mind. Because stress originates from poorly nourished information-processing systems, having information about the ways and nature of stress is of paramount importance in relieving, healing, and preventing the harmful effects of stress.

Chapter 4
Searching for symptoms

In all life's adversities, keep your tails up . . . Thief of health . . . Thought tensions — signs of psychic distress . . . Tension build-up . . . Muscle tension — an inventory of how and where to find it

In all life's adversities, keep your tails up

For the most part, the healing arts do not distinguish the stages of the stress dis-ease process the way they identify the stages of most illnesses such as cause, incubation period, recovery signs, recommended treatment and rehabilitation. Only the end result is identified for the official stress ills.

It is not terribly difficult to identify stress as the "cause" of a heart attack when a sixty year old man trying to rescue a child trapped in a burning house suddenly stumbles and dies. Or when the young executive develops ulcers or a high-strung child develops asthma. The challenge of stress is to catch it *before* it maims or kills.

Some clinicians have developed "stress profiles" that describe special personality and biological patterns that indicate a susceptibility to stress, particularly the Type A personalities who are subject to heart attacks. The kinds of stress profiles used to predict susceptibility to coronary attacks are valuable in designing treatment programs for stress-related high blood pressure victims, but by the time people develop Type A personality characteristics that can be scored reliably *and* who have some degree of high blood pressure, the probabilities for a coronary attack are already high.

Stress profiles are predictive, unfortunately, only when personality characteristics are fairly obvious and just naturally seem to bode trouble (how many times have you heard someone say, "he's so hyper, he's bound to have a coronary"?). The white-collar worker who seems driven, hyperactive, and restless to be working or doing something is a classic candidate for a stress problem, profile or not. Hostages are another classical example. Anyone held prisoner, isolated from his world and unable to participate in any normal activity of life, suffers stress. We can all empathize because we all know what stress feels like. What we fail to recognize are the signs of the distress of stress *while stress is developing*. The really thorny problem of stress is identifying and treating effects on mind and body *before* they culminate in damage.

The dilemma is caused by the completely unique way stress affects human beings. There are no infectious organisms invading the body, no injury, no biological defect, no pathology growing inside. There are, instead, difficult circumstances in life to be coped with. Stress is an ever swelling and receding super-physical, psychical atmosphere made up of a number of difficult circumstances, each with different degrees of difficulty in coping. The impact is on the mind senses, not the body senses. The signs and symptoms of stress are submerged beneath the belief that this is just the way life is, and the striving to cope with life's problems. The reactions to stress are simply changes in thoughts, moods and feelings that most people accept as normal reactions to adverse circumstances, changes that have not yet been recognized as caused by stress (except casually) with its hidden potential harm. The reactions are, for the most part, private and not worn as badges of suffering or heroically surviving the difficulties of life.

During its incubation period and before serious consequences erupt, the signs and symptoms of stress are difficult to describe — often difficult to relate to stress. We are, in fact, so conditioned to the idea that any half-way intelligent person can cope with the problems of life that most people refuse to admit when they feel a despair or frustration or hurt because of the unfairness of life. As I noted, we are taught, "Nobody likes a crybaby," "keep your chin up" and "in all life's adversities, keep your tails up" and these insensitive moralizings often seriously interfere with facing adversity realistically and healthfully. Burying the feelings of stress behind customs dictated long ago by a bunch of masochists is a mean disservice to the health of individual minds and bodies. Conforming to some unreasonable command that bottles up emotions does nothing to relieve the stress causing the distressed emotions.

Most people do not recognize the potential harm of stress because most of us are used to the ups and downs of emotions in life, and except for the acutely occurring stress of failure or loss, the modern kinds of stress tend to be intermittent. A dying love relationship does not keep dying forever. At times partners cope, the next moment they don't. Stress waxes and wanes as people adjust to one or another part of a troublesome situation and fail to adjust to another part. Stress may ebb and flow but — and here is its harm — its memories linger almost forever. The girl who wants desperately to play in the high school band and is rejected because of a lack of talent never forgets; rifts between friends are rarely mended completely. The mind remembers the failures and hurts. The misfortunes of stress are that its effects linger in the body, too, the tensions of one stress building on the tensions of an earlier stress in both the mind and in the physical body that serves the mind, the brain.

The stereotype of the "loser" is a perfect example. Three losses, like three strikes, means you are out of the game of life unless some miracle comes along. The loser not only feels rejected by society, his body also feels the rejection. You can often spot a loser by his body language — tense, bracing, the sadness of defeat written in his face because the mind warns that more failures may lie ahead. It is the subtle changes in the integrity of the wholeness of the body that betrays the effects of stress.

The thief of health

Stress is the thief of health, elusive, stealthy, capricious, pernicious, and devilishly deceptive and dangerous. It is everywhere, unsettling, nettling, chafing on-again-off-again with the rhythm of life. Coping with kids and dogs, budgets and jobs, gardens and cars, marketing and shopping, schools and clubs, vacations and visitors, bills and repairs are the everyday sources of stress. The days everything goes wrong, all the mini-stresses add up. The pressures of everyday modern living are often expressed by, "What a day! The things I've had to cope with!"

Coping yes. Stress over? No. Every mini-stress causes mini-tensions of the mind and body. If the mini-tensions pile up one upon the other, mind and body cannot recover and the tensions simply add. Too much or too frequent stresses add up to a psychic toxicity that spills over the mind coping barrier to damage the body.

Although it is recognized that stress can be the unseen culprit causing disabling disease or dangerous emotional problems or disruptive social behaviors, and although the experts tell us these fearsome consequences result from "tension build-up," that emotional tensions can build into violence or suicide, and that the body tensions of our daily stress can break down vital body functioning, what we are *not* told is how to recognize stress during its long incubation periods when it silently erodes the vital substances of life. If stress were a linear disease, say like herpes, with one effect for one cause, then half the healing community would feel obliged to track its transmission, document its incubation period, and find a cure. Stress, however, is a *non-linear* disease whose signs and symptoms have not yet been explicitly separated from the common complaints about the rudeness of life or its traumas.

Over the years I have collected the considerable diversity of signs and symptoms people talk about when they are living under stress. Some representative examples are listed in Table 3. Any stressed person can feel any combination of the various subjective feelings and body tensions. At first glance, the kinds of complaints in Table 3 seem unconvincing and trivial because they are such familiar complaints in everyday life. They happen so frequently we pay no attention to the probability that they are the signs and symptoms of very real disease . . . stress. Yet the presence of any one of these signs and symptoms is diagnostic of the distress of stress.

Thought tensions — signs of psychic distress

It is not customary in the healing professions to consider thoughts and vague subjective feelings as signs of unwellness. *WE* know what we mean when we say we have the blahs or feel awful or icky, but these states do not qualify as "official" complaints. In

Table 3

Examples of the signs and symptoms of the distress of stress

(and during the incubation of stress ills)*

Disturbances of the psyche
  Altered moods, worry, unhappiness, misgivings, apprehensions, irritation, emotional tension, annoyance, heartache, crying on the
  inside, lump in my throat, dead weight in my stomach, feel drained,
  nerves on edge, sad, blue, can't concentrate, feel dissatisfied, feel
  distracted or disorganized, feel insecure, defensive, frustrated, troubled, guilty, have waves of anger or hurt, waves of anxiety or
  depression, feel lonely, miserable, notice change in work habits or
  habits of wearing clothes or of ways of using time and space,
  becoming accident prone, feeling "burn out" . . .†

Disturbances of the soma
  Muscle tensions, visceral tensions (gut uptight), shaky, tired, physically drained, catch more colds or sniffles, have more headaches (or
  physically down days), worse backaches, disturbed sleep patterns,
  troubled dreams, minor sex problems, fleeting hints of nausea, general malaise, changes in exercise habits

*The kinds of mind and body distress people feel while *living* with stress and *before* one
or another mind or body system becomes disabled and succumbs to an "official" stress ill
when one lives with stress for too long or with too much stress or is too susceptible or
sensitive to the stresses of life.

†For more descriptor words, see Appendix 4.

stress, though, it *is* the kind of thoughts that is important. When
someone is under job stress, say, or the stress of a difficult family
situation, thoughts change from the usual semi-neutral thoughts
busy with planning daily life to the nagging stress concerns and
speculations about what may happen because of the problem.

A quick survey of the jargon used by experts to describe stress
states reveals a number of problems standing in the way of developing systematic descriptions of the changes in mind and feeling
while stress is incubating. Professionals in the new holistic or

integral approaches to healing do talk about mind and body tensions, and for the most part everyone understands what they mean. Unraveling the exact nature of the tensions, however, is left to (or claimed by) theoreticians who are oriented toward diagnosing the disabling, pathological kinds of illness, not toward the simple stress tensions of everyday life.

Psychology tradition has it that emotions are strong feelings, generally of rather primitive nature, such as anger or fear that cause fairly obvious changes in behavior and indicate some loss of control over reason and behavior. In stress, quite to the contrary, *people tend to contain their emotions,* often even from themselves. If they are irritated by some adverse event, their anger is temporary, fading quickly to a controlled irritation because they know from experience that it is impossible to deal with their problem during anger. The person summarily fired from a job may be deeply hurt and despondent, but he is not pathologically depressed because he knows he must and undoubtedly will carry on. It has not yet been recognized that the kind of mind and body sensations that people have while living with stress (and before the "official" stress ills develop) are *covert, private* thoughts and feelings rarely displayed to the public. So, the signs and symptoms of stress are very different from those signaling the kinds of mind and body pathology that the healing professions generally deal with. The changes during stress are *sub*clinical and are usually contained within the inner being.

To get an idea how mental tensions develop in response to the impact of stress and how they can be described, we can look at examples of the two principal kinds of psychical stress — (1) stress caused by *ordinary* obstacles to achieving and finding fulfillment, and (2) stress caused by sudden, unexpected *calamities.*

The stress of most college students is a typical example of the commonplace stresses of life. Most students' goals are tied up with doing well enough in school to get a good job after graduation and at the same time enjoying college days as a once-in-a-lifetime experience. Their stress can be anything from a counselor's careless recommendation of courses later found useless to the stress of not being accepted in school's activities or the financial burden of tuition, housing, and books. There are hundreds of stressful circumstances during college days and any of them can cause episodes of anxiety, depression, insomnia, worry, heartache, despair, or any assortment of uncomfortable feelings and body malaise. The special characteristic of all stress is that it comes entirely from the world of ideas. For the students it is ideas about what is expected out of college, about how to perform, ideas about how well one is performing and achieving and preparing for the future. The pressures are mental pressures, pressures recognized by the mind and reacted to by the mind, with the mind reacting by searching for answers and ways to overcome difficulties and reach the goals. When the answers are *perceived* to be unsatisfactory, the feelings of stress are aroused.

The other major kind of stress circumstance is sudden, personal tragedy. Although the trauma of the stress appears to be dramatically different from the subjective tensions generated by daily stress, sudden disasters involve the same sequence of perception, mental reaction, altered feelings and body states, but the mental events occur so quickly they can scarcely be identified. When a treasured child dies suddenly, the parents are immediately numbed with grief and sorrow. There is the awful realization that a great part of life has suddenly ended, that a great part of the hopes and dreams for the future has been destroyed, that the object of so much love and care is gone. Most of the structure of life has collapsed. The first reaction is not the reaction of raw emotion; the first reaction is the *awareness* of the *meaning* of the loss. This cognitive, mental processing of information occurs largely within the unconscious or at best the quasi-conscious mind.

The next reaction blends with the first — images, images of life without the loved one, how life can go on, how to carry on and handle all the intimate details and affairs that must be handled at and after a death. The images of the loss are so vivid they overshadow the efforts the mind is making to recompose life. Yet the mind does attempt to understand and plan for carrying on. It is the process of adjusting to the aftermath of the tragedy that creates and maintains stress. It is often said, for example, that for most people mourning the death of a loved one may last for seven years. The loss of any part of life takes a period of adjustment and reconciliation to life almost as long and as intense as the attachment existed.

Stress is *always* the way people interpret life's experiences in their thoughts and in the attitudes and feelings they invent about the things that happen to them. Certain circumstances or events in life can be perceived as unfortunate, unlucky, disappointing, troubling, or calamitous — any judgment that the eventual outcome of the situation will interfere with achieving one's goals or hopes or dreams. The very moment the judgment is made, the mind instinctively reacts to try to eliminate the obstacle or to overcome it or deal with it in some way that will allow life to move along a satisfying path. Stress is the process of adjusting and adapting to circumstances, the process of healing psychic bruises and working out ways to deal with the difficulties that threaten one's psychological well being. It is the process of trying to think through ways to cope that is stressful.

Tension build-up

Tension build-up sounds more like a commercial than the name of a biological fact, but it is, however, the most insidious and potentially damaging of all the effects of stress on the body.

Persistent or accumulating stress also causes muscle and visceral tensions. Tension is a general term describing the state of the muscles or viscera, especially the arteries, heart, and gastrointestinal tract, when they are tending toward a contracted state. Anyone who has ever suffered an insult knows exactly how uptight the insides can feel, yet this kind of visceral response is almost impossible to measure precisely. Some examples of signs of body distress are listed in Table 3.

There are no easy techniques available yet to detect the visceral tensions that can forewarn of impending serious ailments, but unfelt muscle tension nowadays can be measured, usually with biofeedback instruments. Under most stress conditions muscle tensions are not felt until they become strong enough to interfere with some muscle activity or cause pain. The muscle tensions tend to accumulate slowly, particularly in chronic stress, and because the tensions occur in small increments but are sustained, the body tends to adapt to the tensions. The mounting tensions are not appreciated in conscious awareness because the attention is always elsewhere. Superior athletes, for example, often feel marked muscle tensions after performing, but they are unaware of them during performance when their attention is focused on the act of performing.

Tension build-up is something everyone has experienced. Sometimes we are acutely aware that inner tensions are building as, during economic recessions, when income can no longer cover emergency expenses and the hot water heater bursts and the car's brakes give out and Christmas is coming. The groundwork of stress is the lack of money and every unplanned for expenditure strains coping to its limits. The reaction is one of tension, waiting and bracing for the worst to happen with the tensions of anger and frustration and holding back the psychic hurt and pain rising as difficulties continue.

At other times the tension build-up is ignored or suppressed until finally the last psychic assault suddenly crosses the threshold of resistance and a stress ill erupts and begins to disable some vital function of mind or body.

The most insidious tension build-up happens when we must cope with many *different* kinds of life's problems, because then there is no connectedness among events that brings the presence of stress into conscious awareness. The white-collar worker, for example, may face daily stress as she/he struggles for job and economic security through the years but must also face added problems such as intense competition from co-workers, a mother-in-law who becomes ill and in need, a brilliant child needing special, expensive care, another child with dental problems and a complaining spouse. Stress is most often scores of stressing circumstances from scores of different sources.

The stress victim is perfectly capable of coping with one stress at a time, perhaps two or three, but there is a limit to human coping resources. Every "cope" calls on our fund of experiences and knowledges about how to solve problems, but every "cope" also means an expenditure of mental and physical energy. The defenses of the psyche run dry and the tensions that have been accumulating over the years can no longer be held at bay. As the mind's and body's defenses weaken, tensions increase until they burst the tenuous bonds of coping and emerge as almost uncontrollable bouts of anxiety or depression, or physically as high blood pressure, angina, colitis or asthma. Perhaps the most disastrous effect is the weakening of inner resistance to true organic problems or to the more remote psychical effects such as proneness to accidents.

Usually we do not feel tensions building because our attention is occupied with the business of living. After a long day of chauffeuring children, running errands, cleaning house, preparing meals, amending the budget, the housewife can feel an almost overwhelming depression or develop a tension headache. She has not been aware that each challenge to her energy resources has created tension and there has been no time for the psyche to rest and regenerate its energy. As each new hassle occurs, more tension is produced until finally the accumulation is high enough to break through the coping efforts that have blocked recognizing the tensions.

Equally as potentially destructive as the piling up of subliminal tensions are two other subtle, furtive reactions of the mind and body. One is a quasi-conscious, psychological "adaptation" that lets our emotions and behavior keep on going through rough times. We know we have to live on through difficulties and we keep our attention on trying to cope with the daily needs of life rather than on any stress sneaking into our lives. The second reaction is a *phys*iological adaptation in which the body and hence the mind come to accept the increased tensions as more or less normal for the situation at hand. The tensions thus remain (the new normal) and so when any new tension-producing situation comes along, the tension produced adds to what was left from the previous reaction to stress.

Muscle tension — an inventory of how and where to find it

The classical symptom of stress is muscle tension. I suppose nearly everyone knows by now that all the relaxation procedures so popular today were designed to relieve muscle tension, and that in some way relaxation also seems to ease concern, apprehension, and other tensions in the mind. What is not generally appreciated, however, is the incredibly intimate relationship between mind and muscles and that muscle tensions control our body language and can reveal the most inner secrets of the mind.

The union between mind and muscles is so profound and yet so delicate its effects in the stress process are almost unknown. Study of muscle tension has always been overshadowed in medical research by the need to explore more obviously disabling muscle disorders. The effects of the mind-muscle union in stress dis-ease have been lost somewhere in the therapeutic loophole between medicine and psychology. Only the most obvious features of tension and relaxation have been explored, yet it may be that tension and relaxation will ultimately be found — surprisingly — to be the least important elements in the role of muscles in stress.

If you can conjure up a mental image of how your muscles behave in different kinds of social activities and in different ways of communicating, you can begin to get some feeling of the extraordinarily intimate relationship between mind and muscles. Try to feel your muscles working as you drive, work, shop, and play. If you focus your attention on various muscles as you work and socialize and communicate with other people, you can begin to become aware of the way the mind controls not merely muscle movements but controls the expression of every thought and feeling we have.

As we explore the stress process and the ways stress can be relieved and coped with, it will become clear that learning to become aware of normally unfelt muscle tension is the key to relieving stress. Becoming sensitive to muscle tensions as they are developing creates an early warning system that stress is beginning to attack the health of both mind and body.

I am inserting a discussion of the role of muscles in thought and feelings at this point in the book because muscle tension is so widely believed to be THE symptom of stress and distress. This is generally true for the more disturbing stress ills, but for states between health and illness, the role of muscles is better viewed from the larger perspective of the role of muscles in activities of everyday life. For each individual to be able to recognize his or her own, personal, idiosyncratic ways for expressing the signs and symptoms of stress, nothing can be more helpful than becoming acquainted with the many ways muscles can reflect the mind's control of the physical body.

Little known facts about muscles. For the most part, health professionals are shockingly ignorant about the role of muscles in general health and illness. To be sure, there is expertise about neuromuscular disorders, growing skills in sports medicine, and a smattering of pop knowledge about the benefits of muscle relaxation, but there is little or no concern about muscles as a significant factor in general health and unhealth. There are a surprising number of properties of muscles that play a critical role in the new psychical, psychosomatic and stress ailments of human beings.

Muscles, for example, possess by far the greatest mass of the body, and thus they also contain by far the greatest amount of body biochemicals. They are subject to voluntary control; that is, they respond to mental commands to achieve a goal the mind sets, and they respond to imagery by subliminal activity. Muscles also possess the unique ability to learn special activities (to specialize, such as the hands in magic tricks, the arm in tennis, the feet in soccer), and their activities are so automatic and their mass so great that they can develop appreciable amounts of tension that are not perceived by the mind. And muscles provide the main signals to the mind-brain of fatigue; they store and expend enormous amounts of energy. But the strangest feature of muscles is that 99 percent of what muscles can do is contract, nothing else, and they can contract and move the body only by courtesy of the nerves that carry impulses between muscles and brain.

This apparent simplicity of muscles is an illusion; nerves make muscles what they are, and in addition to providing the movement for living things, the nerve connection endows muscles with remarkable properties that operate subliminally to realize the intellectual capacities of human beings.

The nerve networks that control muscles are so widespread and so complex that they interconnect with almost every area of the brain and spinal cord. As animal species became more complex and more dependent upon body agility and strength, the neural networks that regulate muscle activity also became more complex and forged more connections with the brain areas that are associated with the most evolved behaviors, such as protecting territories and caring for families. In time, as evolution continued, the nerves controlling muscles also connected with the parts of the brain that retrieve memories and with the integrative, interpretive cortex that constructs images of every kind, especially images involving the behavior of the body. Dr. Edmund Jacobson, the father of Progressive Relaxation (the tense-relax exercises), conducted many experiments demonstrating the relationship of muscle tensions to feelings of anxiety and showed that images involving the body actually do cause the physical muscles to become measurably tense (see Chapter 12).

While contraction is the principal action of muscles, there is, in fact, a second "activity" we call muscle tension and generally consider to be a part of the muscle contraction process. I suspect muscle tension will one day be discovered to be a process that functions separately from muscle contraction although it is, of course, a necessary part of contraction. Here are some of the reasons why I believe this:

The tensing of muscles is a fascinating phenomenon. Although little is known about the tensing of muscles and muscle tension is usually *not felt,* it can be proved by nearly everyone that muscles tense as an accompaniment of some of the most interesting activities of the mind. I can think of the following: 1) muscles tense in preparation to move parts of the body whether the movement occurs or not, 2) muscles tense when people "brace" to fend off the threat of either physical blows or *psychical* blows; 3) muscles tense when people are imagining or fantasizing something that involves their bodies or when they are mentally rehearsing a performance or "identifying" with a physical activity (such as watching a boxing match or an emotionally intense movie), 4) muscles tense when we are interacting with other human beings, and this kind of tensing is responsible for our body language, 5) muscles tense (and may move) as a memory device (when trying to recall something, the eyes roll up and outwardly, usually to the right), and finally, 6) muscles tense in anxiety states.

There is, I am convinced, no more effective therapy for stress than information. Understanding the role of muscles in health and

illness can be marvelously therapeutic. Simply knowing and learning to discriminate the many different reasons for the muscle
tensions of our not-feeling-good states relieves a great deal of
uncertainty and anxiety about vague body and mind distresses.
And when relaxation procedures are used, awareness of the behavior of muscle tension makes the relaxation exercises much more
efficient and effective. The following descriptions of the varied
kinds of muscle tension are given to provide a basis for discriminating the different appearances of tension and for developing the awareness of body states needed for true relief from stress.

Preparing to move. We all know that we actually prepare the
muscles for all the actions they take whether we carry through the
action or not. If you haven't had an awareness of this kind of
tensing, try the following: sit down and focus on the state of your
muscles, especially from the waist down. Now decide you are
going to stand up, but don't move yet. Can you feel what happens
first? The back muscles of the thighs and lower buttocks tighten,
then the muscles of the lower legs and feet tense, and all this
happens before you actually contract the muscles to stand up.

Or say you are in a foot race. When the starter says, "Get set,
get ready," you tense all the appropriate muscles needed for running and prepare them so that when you hear the "GO," the
muscles can contract immediately and you are off and running.

Bracing. Bracing is often thought of by researchers as a rem-
nant of our animal ancestors' main survival technique, the
fight-or-flight reflex (see Chapter 10), in which tensing the muscles
is preparing them to fight or flee the danger. Bracing is *not* a reflex
action. It is a much more sophisticated kind of defense maneuver
that involves *anticipating* some event.

The anticipation of something involves forming images about
what *might* happen and anticipation is an integral event in the
creation of stress. It seems much more like a first line defense
"holding" action that commits to no definite action but does buy
time to evaluate more information that may indicate the degree of
potential harm more clearly. To me this is a much more plausible
explanation of the tensions of stress than is the inference of the

arousal theory that muscle tension is part of the primitive fight-or-flight reflex. Bracing, in fact, is much more a component of reactions to either real or imaginary *social* difficulties than it is of reactions to imminent physical difficulties.

My own explanation for bracing (see Chapter 10) is that when the subliminal (or unconscious) intellect senses a potential psychical harm, the uncertainty about what it may be or even whether it may occur evokes a state of readiness to deal with an imminent assault to the psyche. It is not a muscle response evoked to defend against a possible *physical* attack. What the bracing muscle tension does is to focus attention on the situation and thus increase alertness to any clues or information that can be used to better define the possible psychic hazard and help to resolve the uncertainty. The increased alertness in turn stimulates mental activity.

Imagery and fantasy. One of the most exciting new discoveries in healing and psychology is that of the therapeutic value of imagery and fantasy. Although, as I noted, Dr. Jacobson clearly demonstrated these effects as long ago as the 1930s, it has taken a long time to liberate the inner world and admit that the inner life of images and fantasy is by far more meaningful and richer and exciting than the real world. It just isn't very practical to live there. But *that world is always with us in images,* directing every move, making every decision and every judgment. Images of home, school, church, work, play and people are abstractions we make of experience and all learning and all decisions. (Images are *not* always visual; in fact, most imagery is a hazy mixture of memory information from every sense and mind channel.) Images are really thoughts, memories, ideas, and feelings all tied up in neat little symbolic packages that open into every memory storehouse and capacity of the mind.

Mostly, images have *us* in them somewhere, we as people participating in some activity, most often in some relationship with people. When the images are strong enough (whether in conscious awareness or within the subliminal mind), those muscles represented in the image develop tensions just as if they were about to move (see also Chapter 7). An example of Dr. Jacobson's research shows how precisely images evoke muscle activity. Using patients who had learned Progressive Relaxation well enough to silence nearly all muscle activity, Dr. Jacobson asked them to lie down and assume a totally relaxed state. After he had prepared them for recording the activity of a number of muscles, he asked them to perform a task without moving any muscles, in fact while trying to maintain relaxation. The task was to imagine they were trying to lift a 200-pound weight from the floor. In every case, exactly those muscles that would be used to lift the weight developed muscle tension. From this and other research, it has been concluded that images can cause tension in those muscles involved in images.

I always feel a sense of awe when I think of the extraordinary implications of Dr. Jacobson's research for the more subtle aspects of muscle activity. The experiments on imagery during a completely relaxed state are of special importance to understanding how the mind and body behave during stress. If, as in the experiments described above, you imagine lifting a heavy weight and do not move any muscles yet muscle activity (tension) can be measured, then you are expending real physical energy. And moreover, you are usually not aware of the tension in the muscles.

Images of one's experiences readily activate one's physiology (not only the muscles), and often much more intensely than does the actual experience. Take the common example of imagining you are sucking on a very sour lemon. The image can cause more saliva flow and grimacing than the real event. Or sometimes when you remember that snake that suddenly slid across your path last summer, and you shiver and the body startle can be much more vigorous than the original reaction. The images, whether visual, auditory, tactile, feeling, or symbolic, can activate the body parts and body systems important in the image.

The imagery of fantasy can be a powerful stimulant of activity not only of muscles but of all body systems. Suppose you are watching the mile run at the Olympics, and your favorite athlete is ahead and within 50 meters of the finish when a pursuer starts to gain on him. Your favorite is in trouble and you can see both runners pushing hard, the other fellow gaining fast. You become tense, arms and legs ready to run, and you stop your breathing on inhalation. Your favorite wins by a hair's breadth and you heave a big sigh and relax.

Why do you have such an intense physical reaction? Because the visual nerve impulses construct an image of what you are watching on the visual cortex and is now a part of the interpretive cortex that also responds to the influence of memories and hopes as well as to reality. Watching the runner stirs up old memories of running, wanting to win, cheering on favorites, feelings of competition, the rewards of winning, calling on your muscles for more effort. But because all your running is in your head, all you do is tense your muscles and gasp.

The extraordinary effect of images on the physical body probably accounts for why it can aid healing. One of the most interesting features of the effect of images on the body is how extremely specific the body's responses are to the images. It is high-fidelity imagery — the body faithfully executes what the images have shaped in the mind. In the lemon example, the reactions are localized exactly for reproducing the original reactions. This special effect of imagery no doubt also accounts for why Autogenic Training relaxation exercises are so successful as well as why guided imagery can sometimes heal. These new healing procedures (see Chapter 12 for details) use self-suggestion phrases, such as "My hands feel warm," that are repeated with the image focused on the hands, and with practice, the hands do become warm.

The imagery of dreams is different but dreams also give us evidence of the remarkable relationship between muscles and the higher mental activities. I have never heard of relaxing dreams, but many people have experienced dreams of hard physical effort and have awakened greatly fatigued. Or often the dream can be of some hurt to the arm only to awaken to an arm numbed by "falling asleep." Possibly the most curious and challenging feature of this kind of dream is that "hurt" is a concept in a dream and *not* a real sensation (i.e., the sensation belongs to the awake body and is not appreciated physically as a hurt in the dream).

Social interactions. One can only wonder just how much images of the past, images of the future, or images of desire or of fear affect our everyday behavior. It is nearly impossible to measure people's muscle tensions while they are engaged in their social activities of work, home, school or play. But from what is known about human behavior, we can make a fairly good guess that during social interactions our muscles are performing and reacting with every nuance of thought or impression. For one thing, we move muscles in communicating and in all of our social behaviors. The way muscles move is also highly individual and depends upon how we are built physically, upon how much movement we have been taught to suppress for good social behavior, on how good or tired we feel, and on two very important psychological (mental) influences: how pleased we are by the way the interaction is going (and expressed by bracing or being relaxed) and by what kind of impression we want to make. All these influences flow through the mind as images. The net effect is body language.

Memory aid. One very surprising role of muscles is that they are often used as memory aids. There is no scientific data to explain this role, so we can only guess that certain nerve-muscle patterns associated with certain behaviors or experiences (or some abstract representation of them) are stored whole or in easily recovered chains in special areas and can be activated by certain movements. A universal muscle movement pattern used to jog the memory is the almost reflex rolling of the eyes upward and (usually) to the right. In some people, trying to recall something specific is also jogged by squinting the eyes and furrowing the forehead, while some (like President Reagan) give a sigh and say, "Well," and still others tap their fingers on a table or pace around.

One striking example of "muscle memory" is illustrated by some people who use touch telephones. It is my own experience that I have no trouble "touching" the telephone number of a friend from memory, but if I have to use a dial telephone, I get stuck and can't remember the number. The number is locked into memory somewhere as a pattern of muscle activity, and is activated by tapping out the number on the touch-tone telephone. Sometimes when I use a dial telephone and can't remember a number, I will pretend to use a touch-tone phone, and presto — there comes the number out of memory. A friend told me he always knew when he touched a wrong number because the tones were wrong. In his case, the number was locked into memory as a tone pattern and was activated by tones.

Performance rehearsal. Anyone whose performance depends upon perfect muscle performance, such as concert musicians, athletes or actors long ago discovered that imagining the performance is a good and often excellent way of rehearsing. Many modern day athletes, especially in golf, tennis, basketball, and track and field events, use imagery to rehearse the muscles to a perfect performance.

The rehearsal of specific body actions is a feat absolutely unique among all human activities. When the muscles of the body are mentally rehearsed to perform a specific act, it is an effort that recruits both the psychical (desire, motive) and (potential) physical energy into a single, unified effort. It is always a very special experience either to accomplish or to watch someone accomplish a perfect performance. We sense perfect performances as manifestations of inner unity.

Judging from athletic performance, performance rehearsal also would seem to *prepare* the muscles in some way, so that when the actual performance occurs, the muscles behave in a very special, synchronized way.

Anxiety. Most, but not all, anxiety states are characterized by professionals as states having muscle tension. The tensions of anxiety are typically attributed to a reflex action to fear for personal well being and survival. As I have traced the mental and physical events of stress, there appear to be many other, probably more important causes for the muscle tensions of anxiety than fear, such as any or all of the muscle effects described above, particularly bracing and images.

Let's take an example of how the tensions of anxiety can begin. Suppose you are competing for a job along with fifty other candidates. It is important for you to get the new job, but there are endless forms to fill out, endless tests to take, and personal interviews with personnel management, supervisors, etc. You start out with some confidence that your qualifications are great for the job, but as you go through the hiring process, many questions arise in your mind. You begin to wonder if what you've got is what they want, whether you are making a good impression, what the other candidates are doing, and hundreds of other questions. This is uncertainty, and uncertainty becomes insecurity, and when uncertainty and insecurity about one's situation exist, there is immediate anxiety. The uncertainty, insecurity and anxiety all lead to defense reactions and the body braces against the possibility of failing and having to face an unknown future.

You are only marginally aware of the body tensions because the mind is so completely occupied by the mental effort demanded by this critical social situation. If the hiring procedure lasts for any length of time, you may develop insomnia or tension headache, or suddenly become superstitious, or you may feel awful or your back may begin to ache. You may be seized by any or all of the varieties of nameless ailments, but regardless of the other signs and symptoms of distress, the most pervasive and persistent change is usually increased muscle tension.

Jacobson's concept of muscle tension and anxiety was/is that the muscle tensions of anxiety were caused by the imagery accompanying the mental effort of trying to solve the problems causing the stress (see Chapter 10). When he found that deep relaxation relieved anxiety and its physical consequences, he concluded that anxiety and relaxation states are mutually exclusive.

Another marvelous bit of evidence for an intimate relationship between muscles (actually, between the brain's muscle control areas) and thinking, feeling, and emotion is the sudden release of muscle tensions that occurs occasionally during the process of relaxation. When the mind suddenly understands that there is no reason for fear or bracing or anxiety, there is a sudden release of the mind-brain's mechanism that has kept the muscles tense and bracing (see also Chapter 11). That is, nerve impulses mobilized by the concerned cortex sending messages to the muscles to stay on the ready have been stored up at the point where the brain activates the nerves to the muscles. Then, when the mind understands that there is no reason for fear and thus no reason to stay alert the mind took away its messages and suddenly the piled up "keep tense" messages spill over the mind-muscle dam and fly helter-skelter to the muscles. The result is the uncontrollable shaking that marks the "anxiety reaction." The healing power of this mind-muscle release is truly incredible. Within minutes anxiety disappears, and rather than being fatigued by the explosion of muscle energy, the muscles and the whole being feel fine and energetic and healed.

For now, the most important point to remember for the stress story is the extraordinary, intimate relationship between muscles and the thinking mind.

Chapter 5
Stressors and stressees

Him Dr. Holmes, me Watson . . . The circumstances that precipitate stress . . . Customary, anticipated life events . . . Unexpected life events . . . Progressive, accumulating, situational stress . . . Personality Glitches . . . Value Dependent events

Him Dr. Holmes, me Watson

Despite some amazing misinterpretations, the research studies most often cited as evidence of the serious consequences of "the stress of life" are those of Dr. Thomas Holmes and colleagues, beginning with the Holmes and Rahe report in 1967. In various studies the researchers surveyed people for the kinds of events in their lives that they felt were the most important to them and then these life events were correlated with how many and what kinds of illnesses these people suffered in later life. One series of studies showed that the number of such important life events was related to the time of onset of real, diagnosable illness. Other studies showed that people exposed to a critical accumulation (cluster) of rather ordinary "life events" were the frequent victims of physical illness requiring medical care.

Nearly everyone working in the field of stress has assumed that the many studies of Dr. Holmes and his colleagues actually dealt with the stress of life as most of us know it, yet nowhere in their reports did they actually write that they had studied stress. One scientific objection to their studies has been the lack of a standard interpretation for the phrase "degree of difficulty in adjusting to a life event." Yet, as the researchers noted, the scores they reported indicated the degree of difficulty of adjusting to certain life experiences but do *not* indicate the degree of stress as the stress of life is generally understood.

One of the things that I find very ho-hummy about scientific research is that it often merely gives numbers to things everyone already knows. But what the studies did bring out was the persistent failure of people to acknowledge that so much — perhaps all — *stress comes from the struggle to achieve socially desirable behavior.* Such life experiences as gaining new responsibilities at work, job promotion, marriage, having a child, graduation, buying a house, taking a vacation, or even celebrating Christmas are all considered by people as desirable events in their lives. The stress comes from feeling obliged to perform in these events in a socially desirable and traditional way.

It is important to understand that *life events themselves are not stressful,* but that *they are only the conditions or occasions for stress.* What is stressful is the process of adjusting to the occasions of stress, or, more accurately, what is stressful is either worrying about not adjusting or worrying about not performing well or failing to adjust (or, to be blunt, most of the worry is about what other people will think about you and what you will think about you, even though what you think of you is shaped by what other people have thought about you in the past!).

The circumstances that precipitate stress

One of the things that occurred to me early in the course of my analysis of the stress of life was that the sole scientific study of stressful things was the Holmes and Rahe list of life events. When I reviewed all the publications carefully, I became more and more puzzled by the many misinterpretations that had been made about the studies. As I noted, the researchers themselves made no claims that the life events they studied were universally stressful (difficult to adjust to), not that they had studied stress illness at all. There was no doubt that many of the events they studied could be stressful to some people, like a change in church activities or a change in kind of recreation, but no single event in their list could be said to be difficult for everyone to adjust to (stressful). I remember my mother getting upset (stressed) whenever a new president was elected for her church group, but our next door neighbor loved the changes. On the other hand, Mother loved the excitement of Christmas while our neighbor would get tied up in knots anticipating the preparations and ceremony. Sometimes one person's stress is another person's challenge.

When we think about it, the kinds of life events in the list actually comprise only a very, very small and highly selective portion of the stress of life. It occurred to me that all of the listed events were the kind of important things that might be *expected* to happen during the course of an ordinary lifetime. And if the events were all commonly occurring events in life, one might guess that most of them could be anticipated. Certainly the majority of people grow up expecting to be married, have children, buy a home, change jobs, add responsibilities, move to a new community, have a parent die, take vacations, have an occasional illness, buy major appliances, and retire. As I continued to muse over the list of life events, I realized that if most people expected them to happen, then most people are exposed to ways of handling them and are prepared. Whether it is having a baby, moving, or changing a job, we not only expect to do these things and have been preparing for them, we have also learned from the experiences of others. The question then became more urgent — why should anticipated, prepared-for, commonly occurring events of life be stressful? It became obvious that since the Holmes and Rahe list of life events covered only a small and special kind of stress that could be expected to happen sometimes or other to most people living the usual kind of life, then there must be many other kinds of stress *not* in the list.

It was on this basis I distinguished two different kinds of life events and labeled them *customary, anticipated life events* and *unexpected life events,* as in Table 4. From this perspective it became clear there are other quite different and *much more important kinds of stressful events* that are, *specifically,* circumstances that can lead to stress.

Anyone who has felt stress would know almost intuitively that even combined anticipated and unexpected life events comprise a very small part of all life's stress. For most people, in fact, most stress comes from still different kinds of situations. The most common occasions for stress are those that continue over time — family problems, school problems, financial problems, love and sex problems, work problems, problems of competition and performance — all problems involving relationships with other people on a continuing or recurring basis. Education these days, for example, has become a highly complex problem of finances, changing job values, requirements and fads, time for study while working, coping with inflexible yet irrelevant course requirements, crowded, expensive housing, crowded classrooms, computerized records, and the struggle for personal attention and to define the future. Each facet of the educational experience contains the seeds of stress, overlapping and mixing, adding bits of stress, repeating over and over. No matter what part of life it is today, any part that is a continuing part of life is stressful for most people. Few escape.

I have called these commonly occurring, repeating kinds of stresses *Progressive, accumulating, situational stress*, and they are by far the most frequent sources of modern stress. This kind of stress generally centers around one particular aspect of life, such as love, sex, family, job or school, etc., and because these aspects of life are ever present, the effects of stress accumulate. It is the kind of stress that increases over time, the kind that takes its toll in bouts of anxiety or depression, the kind that leads to heart attacks or asthma or colitis or high blood pressure. It is the kind of stress that builds up to a crescendo, that may disappear briefly only to reappear, the kind of stress that keeps the body tense, the kind that distresses the mind throughout all phases of life.

We have now described three quite different kinds of the stress of life — those life events we usually expect to encounter some time during our lives, other events we hope will never happen but sometimes do, and those events that are the chronic, accumulating stress we are all exposed to throughout life. To these we can add a fourth — the stress of being inadequate in one or more dimension of human beingness needed for fulfillment and self-realization, the stress of *Personality Glitches.*

People who lack self-esteem and blame themselves unduly for their circumstances and failures (usually imagined failures), people who are too passive, people who overly repress emotions and feelings, people who feel helpless against the odds of life, people who are insensitive to other people or who show volatile emotions or who find pleasure in hurting people are all the kinds of people who suffer what I call the stress of personality glitches.

Ordinarily these kinds of defects would be classified as personal trait or personality defects but I was afraid some overzealous psychologist would interpret them in the context of emotional pathology which is *not* a trigger for stress. It seemed to me that the notion of personality glitches could convey more accurately the fact that the personality faults causing some of the ordinary stresses of life are rather mild and are mainly temporarily distorted perceptions of the self. The unfortunate fellow, for example, who was not endowed with communicating skills is under constant stress. He cannot express his feelings, explain his behavior, verbalize his motives or hopes, or establish a foundation for loving, caring, and sharing. His personality glitch haunts every experience and every memory. It skews every life event toward denial or fulfillment. Such idiosyncrasies of personality infect every action, every happening, every activity of life of those afflicted. It is a constant, all pervasive stress of life.

The fifth kind of circumstances in life that precipitate stress is, perhaps, the most treacherous. I have called such circumstances *Value Dependent Events* because their effects depend exclusively upon beliefs in one or another code of human behavior. Whenever one's beliefs are denigrated, there is hurt; whenever one is the victim of a moral transgression, such as being duped, the psyche tears and weeps; whenever the object of one's trust or love or belief is revealed as deeply flawed, there is psychic pain.

Precisely because beliefs are the supports of the inner life and growth of the psyche, when beliefs are violated or when they fail us, there is little intelligent moral substance left to resolve the moral difficulties we face.

The psychological and physical effects of even the seemingly smallest assault on beliefs can have life-time effects. Take the very common example of a house theft. Let's say you walk into the house one afternoon and discover the TV set is gone. As a matter of fact, the set in the bedroom is gone, too, but nothing else is missing. Do you know what comment most people make when they describe the episode? It's, "but I felt so . . . so . . . violated!"

Violated by someone stealing your TV sets? No. The feeling

comes from the distress of having your privacy violated. And why is that so harmful to the psyche? Because Americans believe they have a fundamental right to privacy. It is the belief that is violated. And years later you will say, "I had the strangest feeling of . . . uh, uh . . . being violated!"

The stress of moral problems or of having one's thoughts or beliefs abused erodes the health of mind and body surreptitiously. No one seems to have worried much about the effects of moral conflicts on *health.* Yet the damage can always be detected; the psychic damage that moral injury causes never truly disappears from memory. And depending upon the intensity of belief, behavior and health can be forever changed. For some people the moral dilemma of deciding how to care for a severely handicapped infant is a lifelong, life-determining stress and far too often there is the added stress of wrong but irreversible decisions. By social custom, the stress of moral difficulties is consciously concealed and the effort to perform up to acceptable social standards despite the psychic suffering is simply added stress.

Tables 4a and 4b give some examples of the five kinds of circumstances that precipitate stress, along with short summaries of their distinctive characteristics. For people interested in a more extensive analysis, please refer to the full text.

In the following sections I will describe the special features of each of the five major kinds of stress.

One of the things we have to recognize is that *stress is not just stress,* that is, "stress" is not the usual kind of disease-producing agent. Unlike most other ailments human beings suffer, the distresses and ills of stress occur only when a cluster of influences (personality, predisposing circumstances, immediately preceding events, images of the future, social values, etc.) interact in some way that triggers the stress dis-ease process.

Once the dis-ease process is begun, the operations of the process are always the same. The results, however, can be any combination of the signs and symptoms of distress because they depend upon the psychobiological pattern of the individual and in some non-linear way relate to the clusters of influences that triggered the whole stress process in the first place. It's a bit like the common cold, where, depending upon the kind of virus, some people

Table 4a. The Five Kinds of Circumstances That Precipitate Stress

CATEGORY	EXAMPLES	MAJOR DISTINGUISHING FEATURES
1. Customary, anticipated life events	marriage, divorce, beginning or ending school, changing residence, children leaving home—any major change in life pattern or lifestyle	events anticipated by most people events determined in part by decision (capacity to influence consequences) usually single, spaced, unrelated events stress symptoms only when events accumulate
2. Unexpected life events	unexpected death of a loved one, sudden failure, sudden loss of job, major accidents, sudden loss of home, learning of terminal illness, being the victim of a crime—any major life event occurring suddenly and unexpectedly	stress symptoms usually sudden and severe events cannot be influenced by individual usually nonaccumulating single events stress usually not chronic
3. Progressive, accumulating, situational events	job stress, family problems, love and sex problems, school stress, competition—any continuously recurring problems in life's activities; also nuisance overload (daily hassles)	events centered on human relationships stress source from many dissimilar situations (depends upon many events in social time and space) events concern values, attitudes, beliefs, perceptions, and communications situation control depends upon interaction dynamics stress symptoms usually develop slowly

4. Personality glitches	moderate degrees of low self-esteem, insecurity, lack of confidence, poor decisionmaking, poor communi-cations, fear of failure, guilt feelings—any personal trait that creates social problems.	stress events related to personality traits events center on a single theme stress source pervades all time and space dimensions a perceived failure to influence situations chronic stress symptoms
5. Value dependent events		
social transitions	any circumstance generating thought-feeling conflicts	stress circumstances arise from *beliefs* about social or moral behavior
	aging, fractured families, displaced homemaker, being orphaned, revolution	stress circumstances concern conflicts between two sets of beliefs, either between the individual and others or solely within the individual (dilemmas)
moral transgressions	incest, person abuse, victim of toxic waste dumping	source of stress centers on one specific kind of social value
social thought abuse	being duped, disillusioned, victim of scripts and images, being devalued, being ill or handicapped, expected to cope	stress symptoms usually well concealed and evident only as changes in long-term behavior and changing attitudes and beliefs.
moral dilemmas	cheat or fail, betray trust for personal safety, the fallen away Catholic, peer pressure vs. personal conscience	

Table 4b. Distinguishing characteristics of the different kinds of "the stress of life".

Characteristics	Anticipated stress	Unexpected stress	Accumulating, situational stress	Personal trait stress	Value Dependent stress
time-space dimensions	unrelated, spaced single events	single events	recurring, related events	through all time and personal space	enduring through time and space
feelings/emotions	mild to moderate	marked	fluctuating, accumulating	continuous, low grade	mild to intense
reaction time course	gradual	sudden	gradual	continuous	gradual, then continuing or rejected
symptoms appear	late in process	immediately	late in process	continuously present	continuously
focus of attention	on coping	on loss	on uncertainty	on defects	on conflict
expectations*	predictable; reality-oriented	none or vague	modest; variable and intermittent; some fantasy	pessimistic	excessive hope
perceptions*	accurate; transient	focused on event	depend upon interpretational "set"	negatively skewed	skewed by beliefs
problem solving*	customary mode	"automatic", slow	depends upon situational information; directed toward situational control	poor, inhibited	approaches narrow
social adjustment required for relief	conventional; to situations	rebuilding life, compensating, psychological rehabilitation	adjusting to social interactions	personality development	examination of concepts, morals, values, and beliefs

*Described in Chapter 9

mainly sniffle and blow, while others suffer a sore throat and still others have congestion of the chest as their chief symptom. And rather similar to the common cold, while all colds are treated pretty much the same, the chief symptom of the particular kind of cold gets the main attention. Becoming acquainted with the special characteristics of the different kinds of stress means that treatments can be tailored to be the most effective for each kind.

There are a number of important reasons for identifying the five different kinds of the stress of life. The most important reason is that defining the kind of stress one has is the best way to determine the ways to relieve that stress and prevent the further effects of stress on mind and body. Another reason is because the different characteristics and qualities of the five different kinds of stress can be used as guides to tracing the sources and reasons for the stress one suffers, and this step is critical to determining the best way to deal with the stress.

Customary, anticipated life events

As the name indicates, this kind of stress arises out of the kind of events in life that can, and usually do, happen to everyone during a lifetime. Since they are expected, a good bit of experience and learning about how to handle the situations have already been gathered before the events occur. That is, most people have some idea about how to cope with situations such as changing jobs or some social rejection, but this only makes matters more difficult because they know people *expect* them to cope with the situation. The stress they experience is worrying about how social peers will judge their coping, worrying about whether they are coping and performing well, and later worrying about whether they did perform acceptably. Of course many ordinary life events contain other concomitant problems, such as the emptiness when a child leaves the nest or the apprehension about making new friends after moving, but these are problems that have also been foreseen, at least to some degree.

Since to be forewarned is to be forearmed, reactions to anticipated kinds of stress are generally mild. Rarely does anticipated stress cause anything more than moderate degrees of anxiety, worry, or sadness. There is, moreover, usually time to recover before the next anticipated stress comes along.

The only truly serious stress caused by anticipated, customary life events is when they occur in clusters. One event happening right after the other leaves no breathing room or time to recollect the coping resources. Too many such events too soon fragments the attention, blocks coping, adds feelings to feelings, and lets too many memories spill out, disturbing the emotions. Each life experience affects body and mind in ways that subtly weaken their resistance; too many too soon can be just as seriously disturbing as unexpected life events.

Suppose you get a better job. It fulfills your hopes and dreams, and you are excited about it. Where is the stress in this wonderful heart-fulfilling experience? Two places: psychologically and behaviorally there is a new challenge to perform, not simply up to your own expectations, but to your colleagues' and bosses expectations as well. Every challenge means mobilizing your interior resources for performing, being on your toes, being constantly alert. Being alert means biological changes, too, for the body is held expectant, ready to answer the challenges, ready to foresee problems, ready to perform. The body does not distinguish this kind of alertness from the kind of alertness it needs to be prepared to act against threats to its well being. So it is all one and the same stress to the body.

There is one characteristic of anticipated, customary stress that does not bode well for the future — or for the present for that matter. This is the fact that there are not only more *kinds* of everyday life events happening today, but potentially stressful events are becoming more and more *frequent.* Twenty years ago did you actually expect an offspring to become a drug abuser? Fifteen years ago would you expect your offspring or best friend to cohabit without marriage, expect an open marriage, to be jailed because you participated in a political demonstration, have Chrysler Motors fail, double digit inflation, letter bombs, teachers' strikes, police strikes, plane hijackings, muggings in a small town, terrorists in New York, have to plan meatless meals? The extraordinary changes in our living environments and in our beliefs and values and the incredible rapidity with which the structure and rules of life change are the circumstances of still a different form of stress. It is a stress of life made up of the clustering of the little things in life that go wrong.

Unexpected life events

These are the kinds of things in life that we know can and do happen to people but never seriously expect to happen to us. Rape is a common example these days, as is being robbed. Any sudden loss or violation of the self and psyche is not merely loss or violation, it is a psychological pillage of every investment in one's being. A major accident is not merely an event in life (as studies of stress would seem to indicate), it is a major rupture in the total process of living, and the stress it produces is far-ranging.

Any person suffering sudden and unexpected loss or violation or failure is faced with both immediate and long-range changes in the pattern of living. The physical and mental suffering is intense. The financial support may be taken away, an event of life that spews out a stream of lesser stresses like the time release cold capsules. Unpaid bills, less food on the table, unemployment lines, becoming a depersonalized job hunter or welfare client or yearning for clothes are the daggers of stress that cut so deeply into the psychic fiber of every victim. The sudden loss of a job long believed to be permanent or losing a home through a natural disaster is the loss of a substantial personal investment in life. The suddenness of the loss allows no time for preparation to cope with the loss, and because these kinds of events are not common within our circle of acquaintances, our experience in handling such disasters is very limited.

The stress of loss or failure comes from the difficulties encountered in *adjusting* to the loss or failure. A large part of life has been removed, and in addition to blows to love or pride or to an investment of love or the labor of life, there is the need to rebuild life in a major way. The stress is the struggle to rebuild life. It is generally a long process, taking time to heal the psychic wounds and time to compensate for losses or failures, and time to learn where and how to risk new investments of love and labor.

Unlike any other kind of stress, the occurrence of such events cannot be influenced or controlled. There is no anticipation, no preparation, and no fund of experience in ways to deal with the stress. No one experiencing disaster can fully explain the feelings or the pain nor how to ease the pain. Each experience is deeply personal, affecting only that life. For most people there is no time to think, only to feel. Every other event becomes focused around the disaster because every activity of life has been affected. Adjusting to dramatic change is, therefore, the difficult process of adjusting to a thousand bits of life turned upside down. In a way it never ends until the life is completely rebuilt.

Progressive, accumulating, situational stress

This is the common stress of everyday life. It is, for the most part, the kind of stress we are expected to cope with, and most of us do most of the time. But it is also the kind of stress that can wear out the coping resources from time to time because the stress never completely leaves us.

One special feature of ordinary stress is that its major focus is usually in one particular kind of situation. The most common situations are love, family, sex, school, jobs, and any kind of group participation. These are all activities dominated by the way people interact with other people. People interacting with people create all the situations that cause stress.

What complicates daily stress is how the frustrations of having to deal with a continuing problem drain the coping resources. Being occupied with saving a marriage or struggling with school leaves little time or disposition to deal with the other daily stresses. If Grandad's stress is his hurt and anger about his enforced retirement, every event of every day is a reminder of how he is being excluded from fulfilling his deep desire to participate in life. The smallest aggravation of the bottle that won't open is added stress. It is the little stresses on top of continuing stress that, I suppose, brought on the phrases, "that's all I needed," or "I didn't need that."

The distinctive feature of everyday, situational stress is that it isn't any one event but tends to emerge slowly over time and out of different places. Job stress illustrates this process and why this kind of stress has such profound implications for the health of mind and body. The average person has been schooled to expect some kind of recognition for a job well done. Let's say a man has a fairly responsible position and has a big investment in his job. Then he begins to feel uneasy. He becomes aware that company policies are changing yet the situation is not clear. An expected raise does not materialize and a layoff is rumored. He discovers a co-worker is doing extra work; another time he learns another worker is looking for a job; and at still another time he finds the boss clearly unfriendly. Each is a different event taking place at a different time and in a different place, but every event centers around the theme of a growing uncertainty about the job.

Situational stress is put together in the head. Clues about the situation are gathered from widely separated circumstances, with the mind interpreting the meaning of each as a link in a chain of circumstances. At first the process is observation, later the jelling information arouses vague feelings of impending problems until finally the evidence crystallizes a focus on an emerging difficulty. It is, essentially, a judgment that things are going wrong, and at the moment of the judgment the observations clash with expectations and held-back feelings spill out. The inner process has produced stress.

The special stress suffered by blacks illustrates progressive accumulating, situational stress almost too vividly. Stress has been identified as the probable reason for the great susceptibility of blacks to high blood pressure. The source of the stress is the frustrations of blacks trying to function in a white dominated, deeply prejudiced society, frustrations that cannot be expressed in behavior or language (if the black is to survive) and the suppressed anger causes the blood pressure to rise.

Personality Glitches

Even the best-adjusted, most successful person will admit to worrying about some personal defect. The pressures our peers lay on us to perform, or to be special (but not *too* special), and win at *something,* pervade every aspect of life. We have been trained, overtrained, and brainwashed from infancy to believe that everyone should be able to achieve happiness and success, have a pleasing personality, good looks, participate in social activities, be responsible, and in general live up to what most people feel are the proper qualities of human beings.

Personal traits that cause stress are those one feels prevent satisfying relationships and social approval. Feelings of shyness, insecurity, inadequacy, helplessness, or ineptness are all feelings generated by social and psychological influences. They represent an awareness of what society expects a successful personality to be and a perception that one's inner resources fall short in meeting those expectations. The perception of deficiencies of abilities needed to win social approval are mainly how one learns to perceive one's self, a feat that is achieved only through what we are taught. Aside from inherited tendencies, personalities are shaped almost entirely by traditional concepts of child-rearing attitudes and practices, the teachings that competing and striving for success are the conditions for survival and fulfilling the natural potential of human beings.

Low self-esteem, lack of confidence, fear of failure, and other personal traits that can cause stress are not the lack of self-esteem, lack of confidence, fear of failure that debilitate and immobilize the personality. The person still functions; he/she simply doesn't function up to potential.

These personality glitches nonetheless can be part of "the stress of life." They are, also, all aspects of the larger picture of how each person values himself, his attributes and his potential. In psychology this self-appraisal is known as self-esteem or self-concept, a phenomenon of man's nature made up of a "sophisticated" need or drive to feel as capable as most people to deal with the good and bad of life and to be successful to some degree. The partner of this need to feel capable is the need to feel of some personal value in the total scheme of life. There are many parts of the self-esteem picture. One can feel, for example, a lack of confidence without feeling worthless. Many people who feel they lack confidence are not lacking in confidence about *everything* — they may lack confidence about their ability to balance a checkbook or to give a speech or to be a parent, but this feeling of a special lack does not paralyze the mind. Some may feel they can't be good parents, but they may also feel they are good artists or business managers or engineers. The stress comes when the special deficiency (actually one's perception of one's self) meets the situation requiring that special talent.

Value Dependent Events

Beyond the inevitable mundane events of life that can cause us stress and distress, from time to time there are severely distressing circumstances that thrive solely on thought and in the cerebral environment. These kinds of circumstances concern our *beliefs* about human behavior. The distress these circumstances cause come from the private world of inner thought-feeling conflicts.

The stress of Value Dependent events ranges from the nibbling away of self-esteem by destructive life scripts or the sometimes trivial moral dilemmas of cheat-or-fail to the horrendously soul-searing stress of being a victim of moral transgressions by institutional power (when you are a victim of toxic waste dumping or an innocent victim of war).

Yet it is rare that mental conflicts about beliefs or moral dilemmas are acknowledged to contribute to unwellness. Nearly everyone has experienced the intense mental distress of a moral dilemma or the anguish of being the victim of a moral transgression or the disparaged ego of social mental abuse. These events in the intellectual environment tear at the foundations of morality and belief. The distress of "just thoughts" is very real. Their intense afflictions of the psyche can easily cause as much inner tension or insomnia or anxiety — and ultimately the serious stress ills — as any other kind of stress, but their elusive, intangible causes are not yet recognized as authentic causes or contributors to human stress and distress.

The anchor for nearly every human being's raison d'etre is belief in the rightness (and safety) of particular codes of human social behavior. In the 1980s beliefs in beliefs continue to be the most potent reason for war and violence. Beliefs cause war and terrorism between Muslims and Christians, between Marxists and Republicans, between English and Irish, between the Texmex gang and the Maxibandits — even between preteens on opposite sides of the my dad is smarter than your dad argument. Beliefs in what is justice and what is injustice create revolutions and human migrations; beliefs in what is proper etiquette and what is gross behavior creates leaders and outcasts. Every code of moral and social behavior, whether it is religious or some special cultural etiquette or the trivial behavior of the classroom, can produce profound effects on both mental and physical behavior. The assaulted reacts with a vigorous defense of the mind's intelligence and often with remarkably intense physical involvement.

The Value Dependent events that strike most shatteringly at the psychic core are the assaults on one's beliefs. Quite literally, *any* attack on one's beliefs is thought abuse and assaults on one's beliefs produce victims of social thought abuse. Think for a moment about your religious and political beliefs. Two of the hottest issues of the day are abortion and prayer in schools. No doubt you know dozens of people who argue vigorously for one side or the other and you've probably watched people debating the issues on TV become angry or flustered in the heat of discussion. "He sure got steamed up over that," people will say. They observe an intense *physical* reaction to an assault on a belief. Psychologists are wont to attribute the physical reactions to fears about one's safety or well being that can be implied in the fear of failure. While I prefer explanations implicating the more sophisticated mechanisms of the intellect, whatever the nature of the cause, it all starts with the thought processes.

When you feel strongly about an issue and someone impugns your *beliefs,* you almost immediately tense yourself, bracing to resist the attack on your beliefs. Anyone who has ever suffered an assault on a deeply held conviction knows the pain and stress of having those beliefs disparaged. Some people become flustered and confused, some react explosively, some hide a deep hurt with retreat and some mobilize arguments for a debate, but *everyone* reacts strongly. And note that while the assault is nonphysical, an attack on ideas and not on the self, the reaction almost always involves reactions and sensations over the *whole body.*

There can be actual physical bracing for even the subtlest censure for a minor social transgression (you confuse signals and start eating when your host starts saying grace); or the angry outbursts during debates; mental turmoil over being accepted or rejected by a social group (it only takes one blackball!); the total physical effort of acts of heroism; the whole being involvement in terrorism.

The physical reactions to assaults on one's beliefs are so intimately related as to be literally innate. There are dozens of studies showing how vigorously the body reacts to even the most remote and harmless questioning of one's beliefs. My favorite study used a questionnaire covering attitudes about the Church (yes, with a capital C) given to volunteer subjects while various of their physiological activities (heart rate, respiration, etc.) were being recorded. The results showed strong physiological reactions to even the most benign challenge of one's beliefs about one's religion.

It is, perhaps, even more extraordinary that *beliefs about one's own body state* can remarkably influence both mind and body activity. Laboratory studies have shown that when individuals were made to be nervous and anxious and their own (fast) heartbeats could be heard at the same time, when the experimenters substituted *false,* nice slow, calm heartbeats, the subjects not only became calm but their own heartbeats became slowed.*

The most obviously intense kind of Value Dependent events are those moral transgressions against the person — person abuse. The physical pain of incest or of child, parent, or spouse abuse can be relieved, but the psychical pain is stinging and deep and enduring. It casts dark shadows on nearly every part of living for despairingly long periods of time.

Becoming victim of an unfair exercise of power is another way one can become a victim of moral transgressions. The dumping of toxic wastes, for example, is an infinitely greater psychical hazard than it is a potential for physical harm. The hazard strikes at the roots of survival and concern for survival is the primal concern of all living things. In view of the statistics, it is truly incredible that such hazards are classified and treated almost exclusively as medical hazards, and in the distant future at that. There is definitive data about the physical risks but little about the potential psychical harm.

The following was gleaned from news reports about the String-

*Elsewhere I have accounted for why consciousness misreads the body's signals (Chapter 10).

fellow dump site in California (one cause of the EPA crisis). The calculated *possible* future number of cases of cancer, for example, is variously estimated from such contamination as 1 case per 100,-000 people to 10 cases in each 100,000 people exposed. But of course not all of the people in such statistics are equally exposed ... some live nearer the dump than others, but all are counted as potential victims. Nor do the statistics account for the influences of family history of cancer, susceptibility to illness (especially concerning the immune system), present state of health, age, etc.

On the other hand, the psychological impact affects virtually 100 percent of that same population, now, in present time. And the severity of the psychical damage is enormous. Not only are all varieties of emotions aroused, but they can never truly be relieved. Only time can resolve the uncertainty of who and when and how an illness may strike. In the meantime the worry and fear frequently cause stress ills and mental difficulties. And the anxiety of uncertainty and the fear and resentment can last a lifetime. From time to time a few of the more distraught are selected for psychological counseling, but there is not yet any formal or official or systematic approach for recognizing the psychic hazards of moral transgressions that can far outweigh the potential for psychological harm.

Psychical stress may indeed be the most critical factor determining the future of human well being. To underscore the significance of psychical stress and complete the comparison between the physical and psychical effects of toxic waste dumping, let me outline the surprisingly wide range of its effects on human emotions. When one is the victim of an immoral abuse of social power, there is:

- the hopelessness and despair and anger of being a victim;
- the fear and anxiety of the "medical uncertainty";
- the frustration, anger, hurt, and heartache of being ignored, neglected, and rejected by a government "of the people and for the people" that appears insensitive to the needs of the human psyche, and the hurts by a bureaucracy that prefers obeying inflexible, inhumane rules to searching for ways to help the victims of an abusive commerce;

- the anger when medicine and science weasel about what constitutes illness (endless colds in the family, frequent headaches or gastrointestinal upsets do not qualify even though you know your resistance is getting lower and lower; the standard is being sick enough for medical supervision. And that's what gets counted in the statistics, too).

Possibly in many, but not all, instances, the least intense and most easily remedied Value Dependent life events are those involving the more socially evolved (sophisticated) beliefs. Being duped, for example, arouses feelings of resentment, of being maligned or insulted or of diminished self-worth in varying combinations and intensity depending upon one's personality and maturity.

Being disillusioned is the stress of broken values as when you learn that the pastor or priest that you idolize is arrested for molesting small boys. The psychic hurt is a trust betrayed, a crack in the supporting fabric of your moral code. From then on, time after time the betrayal comes to mind and spurs a mental conflict between belief and wonder about human nature and human mores.

The psychic pain of arbitrary, misleading life's scripts (boys don't cry) and images (I'm going to be a rock star), the hurts of being sick or handicapped, the agony of being expected to cope are discussed elsewhere in this book. The message here is to emphasize the role of social thought patterns and beliefs and how these become exerted through peer pressures to spawn stress and distress.

Moral dilemmas are probably the greatest challenge to the human psyche. They are "no-win" circumstances in which there can be no truly satisfactory way to resolve conflicts of beliefs. The time-worn example is the priest hearing the penitent who confesses murder in the confessional. The priest's beliefs and feeling-beliefs collide. On the one hand is a crime against person and the commandments of God and a belief in the Christian concept of punishment. On the other hand is the Catholic doctrine of the sanctity of the confessional. The victim of the dilemma is confronted by a head-on conflict between two deep convictions, and no answer to the dilemma can truly resolve all aspects of the problem. The anguish can be extreme, flailing the emotions and sickening the body.

The intensity of the distress caused by moral dilemmas is universally and almost inhumanely underestimated. Take a tiny, seemingly inconsequential event that is, in fact, a frequently occurring moral dilemma — lying about something and getting caught at it. Let's suppose friends had invited you for dinner for Tuesday evening and you declined with a quick lie that your daughter was acting in the school play that night and she would be devastated if you weren't there. You just couldn't think of any other reasonable excuse quickly enough and at that particular moment you just didn't feel like seeing your friends for dinner but you just didn't know how to say you didn't want to go out then. Then, by Tuesday you've forgotten and on the spur of the moment the family decides to go out for dinner. Of course! That's when your friends decide to dine at the same place. It just had to happen, didn't it! And it's panic time. Because you had forgotten, you don't have a prepared excuse, and worse, you had never told your daughter about the call and heaven forbid what she will say! And naturally, your friends can detect in a moment that you had lied.

Is this really stress? The kind of stress that can lead to real difficulties and ailments? Indeed it is. Think for a moment how many ways and for how long a time you react to such incidents.

At the moment your deception is discovered, you react vigorously both mentally and physically. Your breath catches, your pulse starts to race, your hands get clammy, and you'd like to go through the floor. You search your mind for a reasonable excuse, and stutter and stammer, all the time both trying to hide your social blunder and trying to cope with the present embarrassment.

But that's only the beginning. The incident haunts you. It springs to mind at every unbusy moment and you tense and brace with the fear of getting caught all over again and you shiver with embarrassment. The moral slip is permanently embedded in memory. And so are its effects on the body. Years later you will say, "I'll never forget the night we ducked an invitation to the Joneses and they found us in that restaurant." And when you say that, you catch your breath all over again and feel a chill.

Moral dilemmas *are* stressful. Their impact can be felt for a lifetime. Being so aware of this kind of forever reaction no doubt strongly influenced me last week. I gave the gas station attendant a twenty dollar bill and he counted out change for a fifty. The thrilling prospect of a quick doubling of my money surged through me. At the same time there were a half dozen moral warnings wrestling in my semi-consciousness. Despite the attendant's arguing that I had given him a fifty (he'd thrown it in a box with a jumble of other bills), I won the argument but lost the profit. But the intensity of the inner conflict hung over me all week.

Now let's look at a Value Dependent stress where one becomes the victim of changes in one's own personal social environment — ordinary, inevitable changes like the stress of life. We've all identified with one or another of the kinds of psychic bruises and puzzlements described in such books as *Passages, Transformations, Games People Play,* and other new looks at the human psyche.

Take the events that occur when people suddenly become Senior Citizens. Social value has it that one day you are an ordinary human being and the next day you are a Senior Citizen. Now people perceive you very differently. You are urged to retire, get rid of accumulated belongings, give up the old house and move to someplace smaller, play games like shuffleboard or just sit and relax. Time is different, the spaces and places of living are different, the elements of the surroundings are different (even the chemicals are different). There are reminders of the differences and the rejection and the undesirableness of aging in every nook and corner of life. And the changes are stressful and painful because they are so different from the way one believed society was supposed to behave. The feelings are expressed as feelings of loss of dignity, respect, of rejection, and facing the approaching end of life.

Yes, aging is stressful. The attitudes of society — the social climate — see aging as falling victim to something undesirable. The aging one is besieged by the attitudes that aging is undesirable and a circumstance to be conquered or ignored or obedient to its myths, and the victim must cope with this, too, as stress.

Yet it is much the same for the displaced homemaker whose divorce forces a dramatic change in lifestyle, or for the newly orphaned, for the abused wife, child, husband or parent. And for the ill or handicapped, or for the immigrant fleeing oppression. Society taught that human beings have worth and intelligence and can take charge of their own lives. Any circumstance that denies exercising the innate drive for independent and individual feeling of being constitutes a stress.

The intensity and duration and harm of value dependent distress depend, of course, on a complex relationship between the circumstances of the abuse of beliefs and the depths of belief, upon the kinds and depths of beliefs, upon the security of the moral intrusion, and upon the moral and psychological support that is available.

As the world's population races toward its limits and people become increasingly well informed and the world becomes more a world of thoughts and ideas and changing beliefs, the occasions for value dependent stress seem likely to increase considerably.

There are, thus, five very different *kinds* of circumstances that create "trigger mediums," i.e., the special circumstances that can trigger the mind to interpret them as warnings of potential or real trouble in achieving one's goals.

As we piece the stress story together and identify the various influences that converge and intermix to cause our highly individual, personal perceptions of stress, we will be able to isolate each factor causing our particular stress with a fairly high degree of accuracy. It will be, strangely enough, a rather simple process of self-diagnosis. The various tables of this book that describe the several influences contributing to stress, the ways for accurately pinpointing stressful events and the ways people react to them provide an easy and convenient guide for identifying both the *exact* nature of one's stress and distress. The importance of accurate, reliable diagnosis is that it allows the development of treatment programs designed exactly to attack the causes of the distress.

We will find that the "cause" of stress is, in fact, the product of a reaction between external circumstances occurring in the social environments in which we live (the extrinsic factors) and the "internal" events that produce our impressions about those external circumstances and how we perceive them (the intrinsic factors). Both the outside and internal events are complex, the external circumstances being the many and variable ways human beings meet and interact and create various situations. The internal events are the complex processes of mind that interpret the external events and relate them to the way they can affect the life of the self. It is the product of the interaction of circumstances and the mind's understanding of their meaning that leads to stress.

Chapter 6

Where stress breeds

The *sources* of those circumstances that cause stress . . . Personal circumstances . . . Social changes . . . Social pressures . . . Covert environmental influences . . . Limiting factors of the physical environment . . . Unhealthy lifestyles . . . Being ill or handicapped . . . Scripts and images . . . Nuisance overload. The hazards of hassles

The sources of the circumstances that cause stress

There are circumstances and then there are circumstances that lead to stress. The biggest problem in relieving stress and distress is the lack of a systematic way to identify the critical influences causing the feelings of stress. If the major contributing factors could be easily identified, then measures could be designed to be more effective. This prompted me to search out and label all the kinds of things that cause stress.

If we consider all the sources of stress, we see there are some circumstances, such as those described in the preceding sections (the circumstances that precipitate stress), that tend mainly to trigger stress directly while other kinds of circumstances leading to stress tend mainly to be background settings that favor the development of stress. The latter can be more properly called the *sources* of the circumstances rather than the circumstances that directly trigger stress.

In Chapter 1, for example, I described the frightening rise in youthful suicides in Austria attributed to the stress of open admissions to the university. The circumstances of university life were the backdrop for stress and for some students implied such high levels of performance to be achieved that they could not face any hint of failure while other students found the circumstances of university "cope-able." Whether or not people react with stress to potentially stressful circumstances depends upon the interaction of their own special, personal constellations of stress influences that include personality, experiences, culture and all the rest.

Table 5 provides summary descriptions of the different sources of stress. Added detail is as follows:

1. Personal circumstances

Although they happen to most people, there are circumstances of stress that are unique to each person and have a special, personal bearing on hopes and expectations for achieving special objectives in life.

From whatever influence, people are obliged to perform up to some standard, either personal or social, to achieve either self-realization or meet some social standards of achieving. The result of performing and competing in any activity in life is either some degree of success or some degree of failure. For the stress susceptible, any touch of falling short sets off a comparison between the dreams of achieving with what wasn't achieved, usually ending in heightened awareness of one's shortcomings, real or imagined.

Success also can be stressful especially when it carries with it the images of living up to some hoped-for success. The stress of success is vividly illustrated in the recent experience of the man who was unexpectedly named head coach of a major university football team. Immediately after being notified, he held his first press conference. And promptly fainted.

Circumstances that contain the potential for stress, as listed in Table 5, underscore the many ways in which modern life has become tilted toward the hazards of psychic, rather than physical, hurts. Midlife crises, discrimination, or people problems can all function like a constant low level background of stress like Muzak playing in the background. Nebulous clusters of thoughts, impressions and feelings about one's personal circumstances prick away at consciousness with concerns about achieving and weaken the psyche's resistance. With the psychic defenses so eroded, when a new pressure appears, the whole ego protection system may collapse in stress.

Stress can simmer within any circumstance of one's personal life

Table 5
Sources of the stress that leads to states of unwellness

1. **Personal circumstances**
   Circumstances that individually influence one's expectations and desires to achieve personal goals:
   (a) ordinary circumstances (e.g., adjusting to family, job, school, life changes, etc.)
   (b) nonordinary circumstances (personal disasters, spouse/friend desperately ill, investments fail, custody battles, aging, retirement, midlife crises, etc.)

2. **Social change**
   Widespread changes in social policies and in social and moral values that affect significant segments of the population: (e.g. the economy, unemployment, discrimination, epidemics, wars, liberation movements, etc.)

3. **Social pressures**
   The standards imposed by society for behavior and the limits of toleration of behavior: (e.g., standards for levels of earnings, education, work performance; age behavior criteria; standards for caring and sharing; being expected to cope).

4. **"Covert" environmental influences**
   Weather, pollutants, allergens, radiation, artificial light, high noise levels

5. **Limiting factors of the physical environment**
   Time, distance, mass, heights, viruses, bacteria, gravity

6. **Unhealthy lifestyles**
   Lifestyles that put minds and bodies out of their natural balances (e.g., excesses, deficiencies, passivities, drug abuse, psychological addictions)

7. **Being ill or handicapped**
   Being mentally, psychically, or physically diminished in any way

8. **Scripts and images**
   Scripts about expectations and behavior inflicted on one by authority figures (e.g., "you'll never be the student your brother is"; "boys don't cry")
   Images as specific mental pictures that represent projections of achieving and the outcomes of achieving as either dreams fulfilled or as catastrophes (e.g., the macho image, the perfect performance, Murphy's Law)

that interferes with realizing goals. The boy who wants a new bike for Christmas when his parents can't afford it lives with the circumstances for stress. The grandmother neglected by her grandchildren feels the presence of stress; everyone concerned in a divorces swims in an environment of both real and potential stress; the victim of a crime may live for years with the ogre of stress hovering in the background. In each case the simmering background of stress drains the coping resources. Any new psychic bruise becomes the trigger for reacting cerebrally, behaviorally, emotionally, or physically. If the boy's skates are stolen or grandmother suffers a bad fall or the crime victim has his rent doubled — each is an assault to the psyche that can become the last straw of stress.

2. Social change

In contrast to the kinds of circumstances that affect only one person in special and personal ways, there are the kinds of circumstances that affect nearly everyone in a particular population in much the same way. The most common and widespread stress spawned by social change comes from failure of the national economy. And although financial pressures or unemployment or welfare do have deeply personal stress effects, they usually produce less intense effects on the psyche than do other stress circumstances for some interesting social and psychological reasons. The causes, effects, and solutions are actually *shared* problems and the concerns of large groups of people. This in turn generates new information about how to cope and more insights into causes and solutions to individual problems, and all this help in turn relieves feelings of guilt and self-recrimination or personal helplessness.

There are a fistful of unseen forces turning new screws on society virtually every day. This century has seen extraordinary personal social changes and the meaning of social has changed from meaning to be sociable to meaning to work, live, and deal with people. The great change in living is the extraordinary socialization of human beings until today how life is to be lived is determined more and more by groups of people than by natural circumstances or imperial command.

It is difficult to absorb just how much change the process of socializing has caused in individual human lives. We tend to discount the effect by saying we have always had to live with families, bosses, peers or unjust governments. The difference between now and even two decades ago is that a hundredfold more people are participating in virtually every facet of the social growth process of nearly every social group on earth. As more and more people participate in group affairs, the more fulfillment and achieving depend upon interacting with people. The groups reinforce feelings of individual worth, but at the same time realizing one's own worth depends upon one's success in human relationships and in meeting social criteria.

As people multiplied and massed and knowledge expanded, beliefs changed and the values people placed on beliefs and social behavior changed . . . and changed and changed, faster and faster. I call the phenomenon the "cult of transiency." Not too long ago we were able to count on the relative permanence of the things and attitudes and values we encountered in everyday life. For the majority of people there were home and school, church, social clubs, and the Sunday excursion to the park. The school process remained pretty much the same for decades — subjects taught were much the same, schedules were similar, the roles of the teachers were similar, and the extracurricular activities varied little throughout the years. Then suddenly there was the new math, then busing and integration, a growing dominance of social studies, open classrooms, school curricula that were more electives than required courses, pro-prep athletics, teacher strikes, and classroom violence.

Society changes but for most people the old values remain, hand-me-down reminders of the good old days but strangely incongruous in an environment where social behaviors shift with the winds of whim and whimsy and media hype. The result is inner conflict between the invading new values with their unknown effects and the familiar security of the old.

Our ways of coping with stress are mostly what is left over from past ways of coping, sprinkled with a spate of new, almost impromptu, techniques. Yet modern stress has little to do with the kinds of stress the last generation faced and is much different from the stress of the generation before that.

When Mom and Dad, moral to the core, discover their offspring "living in sin," they are convinced they have failed. Their stress is incalculable. A lifetime investment in training, love, and moral support has been snatched from the gates of heaven, their beliefs impugned, their expectations ridiculed, their parental performance embarrassed, and they feel they have lost love, child, and respectability. They "cope" by showing disappointment or anger, by arguing, rationalizing, putting up a front or insulating themselves from the perpetrators of the moral crime. Traditional ways of coping have been little more than maintaining an unswerving devotion to the conventions of behavior, faith, weeping, and carrying on in adversity. Problems are rarely solved.

Even today we retain a curious ethic about our behavior under stress. Few people acknowledge the deep, personal and emotional impact stress has upon them. One standard leftover from the past is the feeling that admitting to emotional pain is a sign of weakness. After all, nearly everyone faces difficulties in personal relationships or problems with jobs and finances, so any admission of the depth of emotional strain would be a sign of incompetency in the business of living. Culture has told us that we can persevere no matter what the odds, and Horatio Alger and Prince Charming stories still nestle in adult dreams about how life can be.

The kids, on the other hand, live in a completely new culture. They have had to understand the frailties of beliefs because their world has been a world of almost constantly changing beliefs and values. They went from segregation to integration, from war to peace, from restraint to liberation, from saving face to "letting it all hang out." It has not been the usual generation gap where a few notions here and there worked their way to change. The last quarter of the twentieth century is *an entirely new world* — a world in which values about people and life and ways of living are not just different, they are in constant flux, always changing with a speed that belies their impact on the psyche and forestalls recovery of the psyche before a new trauma comes along.

There are, today, always new challenges to our abilities to deal with life. The new fear-of-crime stress, the stress of being a newly liberated male or female, the stress of rearing kids overly wise at ten and adults at sixteen are only a sample of the new stresses of life. If we understand that each small stress bruises the psyche and that new psychic stresses are appearing at an alarming rate, it should be clear just how important it is to learn new ways to handle stress. It is the *accumulation* of stress that leads to all the emotional forerunners of diminished well being — frustration, irritation, anger, despair, feelings of helplessness, and the building tensions of the body.

For the first time, also, the sources of stress have become so global, so completely impersonal, so immune to appeal that no ordinary coping can relieve its effects. We must, apparently, develop new ways to protect against emotional runaway and the drain of mind and body resources.

3. Social pressures

The price the individual pays for the benefits of civilization is the need to conform to the rules the group makes to ensure the *group's* (not the individual's) well being and survival.

As society has more and more become a universe made up mainly of ideas, concepts and thoughts, the more evolved the rules of society have become until modern day civilization is regulated mainly through libraries of laws that govern human behavior, by dozens of religious philosophies that direct behavior via beliefs, and by stacks of social customs. There are also mechanical socializing influences such as urbanization, condominiums, satellite communications, and television — all of which operate to influence social behaviors and individual behavior by persuasion to beliefs.

The battle of beliefs rages over abortion, nuclear energy, prayer in schools, nude beaches, horror films, sexploitation, laid back attitudes, dress codes, or anything that offends beliefs. Individual human beings are caught between two conflicting pressures — the pressure of personal allegiance to family, school, and church and the pressure of wanting to know and learn and be one's own person.

The way society as a whole and each of our individual social groups expects us to behave and perform is probably the most potent hazard that predisposes to stress today. Social pressure on individual human performance has never been greater in man's history. TV and the print media see to that. Achieving — winning — being number one — are all powerful pressures to perform. The stress they generate is the crashing realization of some inability or failure to perform. Kids in organized sports are subject to incredible social pressures to perform. The whole kid world expects kids to compete and perform athletically to perfection and, of course, the adults expect them to win.

Some social standards of behavior are incredibly picayunish. I remember my mother being constantly put down for not being able to remember things the way other people could and for being so stupid she had to make lists of things she was to do and remember. It was great stress and psychic pain for her because it meant she wasn't performing as well as other people. When I grew up and found I suffered the same memory fault and that I, too, needed endless lists to remember things, the social environment had changed and the social pressure to remember without lists had disappeared.

A heavy, heavy fallout of the new social pressures to perform and achieve is the general assumption that nearly everyone can cope with the difficulties they encounter in life. One of the important new revelations of the new psychologies is that, on the contrary, most people have trouble coping. In the stress picture it is important to remember that coping itself is stressful simply because everyone expects us to cope. For many people, being expected to cope is as stressful as the circumstances they are trying to cope with.

4. "Covert" environmental influences

There are a peck of unrecognized or at best poorly recognized stresses percolating in the environment. Weather, for example, can cause many different kinds of stress. Hot weather makes some people irritable and interferes with their performance while for other people cold weather drains their energy and creates stress.

For still other people, because of special biological sensitivities a changing barometric pressure or changing humidity or change in ions in the atmosphere can physically stress the being and cause malaise. It takes a greater effort to perform and that sets off a creeping awareness of not being able to perform well.

It all becomes the stress of not feeling well and is exactly the same kind of stress that drains the body's resistance and can predispose to sinusitis, headaches, arthritis or any stress aggravated ailment. The stress is just as much the psychic sadness of being unable to function well as it is the physical weariness. Whenever the body must use its resources to defend against a breach of its integrity (physical or mental) in addition to performing the necessary work of living, it uses some of its biological defenses — the immune system. If the intact defenses of the body can hold off 5000 microorganisms before infection begins, under stress the immune defenses may be so weakened they can fend off only 100.

Much the same wearing down of the body's immune system occurs when weather brings smog or other airborne pollution or the materials of allergies — pollens and viruses. But perhaps the most profound weather stress is the constant eerie wind that is known as the mistral in Provence, the foehn in the European Alps, the sirocco of the Sahara and Britain's east wind of autumn. Today, as for centuries, these winds can become an unbearable stress and cause melancholy, depression, anxiety, erratic behavior, and suicide.

It may seem contradictory to include "soft" environmental influences as triggers of nonphysical stress, but most experts agree that stress does play a dual role in the way we react to environmental influences. There is no question that some people are very sensitive to one or another kind of environmental stress, but it is also true that people under stress are much more likely to suffer the effects of soft environmental influences.

5. Limiting factors of the physical environment

I often marvel at the patience of the settlers of the Old West who waited months on end for word from loved ones left behind, especially when I see the instant annoyance at a busy telephone signal or a TV set that takes more than a second to come full on. One of the interesting changes in reactions to the physical environment is that the more man has come to control the physical environment, the more stressed he becomes when he can't control it instantly.

Not long ago officials in some local drought areas couldn't wait for the spring rains and under the stress of the environmental intransigence, they ordered up expensive cloud seeding. The results coincided with the onset of the natural rains and the result was disastrous flooding. We are learning how to create stress out of inert physical nature! Impatience with distances, for example, has gotten us enormous highways, and when we become impatient with these, we fly in airplanes. How strange it is that we have become so "evolved" that the physical environment itself — inert and immovable — can be a source of nonphysical stress.

One effect of the limits of the physical environment that has impressed me the most is the overcrowding of human beings. From one of my first plunges into the frontiers of psychopharmacology came the discovery that animals reacted to drugs much more dramatically when they were in groups than when they were alone. Later other researchers demonstrated the chilling effect of overcrowding in rats, and while human beings don't react to crowding by either cannibalism or apathizing themselves to death, there is no question but that limiting people's space radically changes behavior.

Rather than science, it was the young people who developed the idea of psychological "space." I remember how delighted I was when I first heard the expression. A college student, talking about a friend's problems said, "We shouldn't get into his space." And while science only occasionally deigns to measure psychological space, most people know what it means, how we use it in living, and what being deprived of our personal space can mean. These days the time and space for solitary thought are hard to come by and perhaps the clear awareness of psychological space grew out of the scarcity of real physical personal space. How remarkable it is that we have come to identify psychological space. I suspect it is a necessary evolution of our crowded times and the stress it causes.

6. Unhealthy lifestyles

The media make a great deal out of Americans' love of junk food, their sedentary lifestyles, their excesses and peculiar psychological addictions such as credit card living or compulsive shopping, being the first to use new slang, needing to top other peoples' stories, being macho, excessively lib or anything else that can be labeled a fad.

People seem to get swept up in certain lifestyles that put their minds and bodies out of a natural balance. Any excessive swing away from a balanced nutrition and care of the body, or excesses of emotion or displaying excesses of prejudice or beliefs are all signs of habits frequently formed to avoid stress. Unbalanced lifestyles nearly always signal the presence of stress and the peculiar way a person shows and handles his stress.

7. Being ill or handicapped

One of the most unrecognized stresses of life is the stress of being ill. When a person is ill from any cause, whether the illness is mild or severe, short or long, mental, emotional or physical, the primary ailment is always accompanied by the stress of being ill.

The stress comes from the impact of feeling removed from the mainstream of life. Because living any kind of satisfying life requires participating in the general flow of life, any time a person cannot participate in one or another of even the most ordinary of life activities, the quality of all life is perceived as diminished. And although the expectations for self-fulfillment and for achievement in life are modified according to the constraints of the ailment, expectations for fulfillment and achieving still remain ("hope springs eternal . . .").

Strangely, the stress of being ill is much the same whether the illness is formidable or only an annoying discomfort. Contrast two very different kinds of physical problems: chronic sinusitis and the paralysis of a stroke. Attitudes of people about these two conditions are totally different. Yes, of course, sinus problems are admittedly annoying, but the paralysis of any body part is regarded as a *genuine* rupture of the essential physical nature needed to participate in life. The only friend the sinus sufferer has is the manufacturer of over-the-counter nose drops while the paralysis victim evokes awe and sympathy and concern from everyone.

Yet both physical problems are accompanied by very similar effects on the psyche. The person with sinusitis has few, if any, obvious signs of his problems, he *can* perform, he can participate in nearly all of life's experiences. His real problem is that he can't perform or participate very well, certainly not up to potential. And there is the nagging pain and diminished vitality. Worse, he gets few strokes — no sustained sympathy and precious little help in his efforts to keep functioning up to the capacity he knows he has. The psychic hurt can be more painful than the physical hurt because he is aware of his diminished ability to function well. This is the edge of weakness that frustrates every hope and dream for even the smallest accomplishment. It is difficult to enjoy life and difficult to contend with the small but constant annoyance most people view as a rather trivial physical problem.

The psyche of the stroke victim is hurt in a similar way. This mind is also tormented by fears and worries about the struggle to live a useful and some kind of productive life. The concerns are not too different from the sinusitis victim, and although the intensity of the concerns may seem to differ, often they do not because the stroke victim has already adjusted his understanding about what is expected of him. Both victims have obstacles to overcome in their pursuit of living a meaningful life. And both suffer the psychological pangs of not being able to live life as they hoped.

The same is true in mental and emotional illnesses. We have only recently learned of the stress the mentally retarded or the schizophrenic can feel. People with neuroses or phobias suffer the same kind of stress because their illness removes them from the mainstream of life and frustrates their hopes for personal fulfillment.

Undefinable "maybe" ailments are a special case of the stress of being ill. They lie at the crossroads between real or imagined sensations and real or imagined causes. "Maybe" ailments are those odd, worrisome states between health and illness when one feels that something about the body is not functioning quite right. It can be nonspecific aches and pains or a general feeling of malaise or a real physical distress. And it can be real or imagined — either way it is not-feeling-good. It can be, of course, the nondescript beginning of a real physical ailment such as a cold or hepatitis, or some slow-moving physical disturbance such as a tumor. But it can also be the effects of the accumulation of gradual and scarcely noticed (or chronically suppressed) stress when the mind blocks the cause from conscious awareness but finally can no longer prevent the stress from escaping its mental restraints to distress the body, almost as a way of drawing attention to it. Maybe ailments are stressful because people fear the unknown.

Fortunately they do not last long — only hypochonriacs stay undiagnosed or unhealed for long. If the cause of the un-ease is physical, symptoms usually either increase until they form a pattern that identifies the cause, or the unease disappears. On the other hand, if the cause of the distress is nonphysical, then that, too, usually either emerges as an emotional problem or it disappears. If the problem is physical, it gets physical attention. If the problem is psychological or social stress, it becomes recognized as a stress problem and gets psychological attention at least by a friend if not by a therapist.

8. Scripts and images

Not long ago I chanced on a TV special on child abuse called "Sticks and Stones." The title jerked me up sharply, recalling the sing-song childhood comeback to taunting insults. "Sticks and stones can break my bones, but words will never hurt me." Somewhere within me old memories stirred, shadowy recollections of chanting that saying, steadying my quivering jaw and running to my safe house where I could cry about the words that hurt so much more than any stick or stone ever could.

I didn't watch the TV special. Instead, the words collided in my head with all the thoughts stored there about the stress of life. And I realized that there are, in this childhood saying, the seeds of a macabre, hurtfully mistaken understanding of human feelings that has infected millions of Americans with conflicts between honest personal feelings and a perverted view of reality. It is an incredibly imbecilic saying, illogical and careless. It is bad enough that the saying is misleading, but worse, adults teach it to children as a prescription for psychic trauma, oblivious to the reality that words do wound and only experience and maturity can prevent their sting.

The saying is diagnostic of the age-old disregard for the most vital contribution to human health — the reasoning, thinking mind. Words do hurt, and far beyond their immediate wounds they can fester forever, a source of hurt that can unexpectedly and unwanted be triggered to rise from their hiding place in the unconscious and wound again and again. Words hurt because they have meaning and they are, as well, abbreviations for the way people think about each other.

The most difficult hurts in the world for most people to handle are the words that denigrate the psyche. Transactional analysis (T.A.) explains a great deal of human distress and emotional suffering by the harm words do. Although the psychiatrist Eric Berne used the word *scripts* as a symbol of influences on the course of life, it is often popularly interpreted as a simplified one-line description of some particular influence that shaped behavior. Scripts like "You're such a klutz" or "Your sister is so clever, why can't you be like her?" or the classical Japanese script "Don't show your feelings" are all nuclear thought weapons that wound the psyche irretrievably.

Another important implication of the "words can never hurt me" myth is its implication that some time during growing up you should have learned how to protect yourself against hurtful words, like using experience to create some kind of mental shield that wards off hurtful word arrows. Yet we give the "sticks and stones" saying (and hundreds of other equally inappropriate maxims) to children and neglect to help them make their mental shield. These scripts hurt so much and wound the psyche because they put down our potential and chances to achieve a satisfying (usually The Big Dream) life (you're too short for the basketball team; ugh, you should never wear blue and green together; don't you know how to do *that?*).

Images may be much more powerful stress inducers than life

scripts. Images easily become circumstances for stress because they are essentially compact symbols of thought-experience patterns that monitor problems and coping. Since images are cerebral constructions, they can activate all kinds of related memories — ideas, feelings, questions about life and people's behavior, and all manner of mental activity. Their global influence means that images can both perfect and destroy the human potential.

The most marvelously positive image is that of the concert pianist who can project a perfect performance in imagination and then identify with the feeling and totality of the image while performing (Horowitz does this and performs as perfectly as is humanly possible). The worst image is Murphy's Law. If the worst does happen, it becomes a script — as did Murphy's Law almost the minute it was formulated. Psychologists know such a script as the "catastrophic expectations" script or as the less noxious "wish fulfilling prophesy" script some people write for themselves. The images we have of success or failure, of winning or losing, of being O.K. or not-O.K. are the winds that blow the windmills of the mind.

Nuisance overload. The hazards of hassles

These are the common mini-stresses of daily life. Take, for example, the new stresses of the 1980s — waiting in line, being put on hold even on a call to the police, full parking lots, searching for clerks in department stores, trying to open the aspirin bottle, the transmission failing in a new car, a computer error in the utility bill. These are some of the little stresses of life, little stresses that can add up to big stresses.

It used to be that we could learn how to handle run-of-the-mill, garden variety problems in life because there were not so many of them and we had time to calm down and regroup our coping mechanisms before the next annoyance came along. Today's scene is very different. New stress appears every day, a new kind of stress that we have little experience with because it is constant barrage of little stresses.

If you would like a glimpse of just how serious the stress of daily nuisances has become, try living in Los Angeles. That is where the gas lines started, where people camp out for weeks to bid on new houses, where the utility companies responded by taped messages, where the line of cars waiting for service at automobile agencies every day can stretch for two blocks.

We have gotten used to built-in obsolescence, to the probability we will be ripped off by used car dealers, to missing bolts in build-it-yourself kits, to slow postal service, to shoddy workmanship, to the lies of politicians and sports people, and to the new wave of senseless crime. But we have not yet faced how psychologically abusive hassles really are and that they are, indeed, as stressful as any other stress when too many follow each other with no relief.

A few years ago, for example, slow, inefficient postal service annoyed millions of people who depend upon mail service for everything from personal needs to corporate decisions. Early in the failing service, friends were lost with lost letters, business deals were wrecked, and all kinds of important plans were mangled or lost in the mail. Gradually people learned to "cope" — that is, they reconciled themselves to putting out more energy not only to adapt to doing things differently to overcome the postal difficulties, but everyone also had to adapt to overcome the subliminal but very real psychic distress of losing a bit of social stability people had come to rely upon psychologically. Then, just as people were learning how to use alternative ways for important communications, the alternative ways themselves changed. The post office kept changing the ways they handled express, registered or certified mail, and the costs skyrocketed; private companies developed overnight postal services while others began to restrict the size and weight of packages that could be sent. At every turn, just as people learned how to use new ways of mail service, the services changed and they had to learn new ways all over again.

It is true that nearly everyone can cope with a few minor frustrations, even when they come in showers, but when hassles become a way of life, most everyone's coping wears thin. Hassles are, I'm sure you've noticed, becoming remarkably more frequent in everyday life, so much so we often say, "It's just one of those days when everything goes wrong."

Hassles pose an unsuspected but nonetheless serious problem to human health. They affect mind and body with unusual cunning. Every tiny stress saps the energy reserves because each mini-problem involves frustration and the effort of coping (problem solving), and there is the despair as well, because the security of know-how has been wrenched from one's repertoire of coping techniques.

As the mini-stresses add, so also do their effects accumulate. Every episode leaves an invisible mark on the substrates of the mind and body, tiny traumas of the psyche that take their own time to heal. The relentless wear and tear on the psyche easily exceeds its ability to cope or become reconciled to its frustrations. We lightly call this process one of adjusting to conditions, but that is an abstract term and does not reveal the potential of daily hassles for the inner tragedy that the build-up of daily stress can cause.

The treachery of nuisance overload is the constant weakening of the mind-body-psyche's resistance to more serious assaults. It is, of course, common experience that after a day when things do go wrong and coping is nearly exhausted, the ability to control emotions is weak and can burst out into temper or tears to release the emotions and inner tensions and let the psyche heal a bit.

At other times, in other people, marginal coping day after day can keep the emotional overflow in check, but the visceral erosion can, and usually does, weaken the body's physical defenses. The real message is: *stress gnaws inside* — and if it is not relieved, sooner or later mind or body controls rupture and stress ills burst forth to claim their toll of life.

Whenever the natural course of any activity is interfered with, the inner, delicate operations of the psyche are disturbed. The mind-body-spirit network reacts to all stress in *all* its parts, and when they are disturbed the psyche must mobilize its defenses from all its injured parts before it can restore itself and all this takes time. As the sensitive bond of the mind-body continuum the psyche always strives to return to a state of balance and harmony after any assault on its integrity.

A pinprick, for example, assaults only the tiniest bit of tissue yet it not only leaves a tiny red dot on the skin, it also causes a prickling sensation that can run through the entire body. And the psyche, too, reacts sharply. It immediately wants to know why there was a pin prick in the first place — why the integrity of the body has been breached.

It is exactly the same with tiny psychic hurts. The reaction is a sudden mini- (or micro-) convulsion of the body and the psyche's demand to understand why its balance has been shaken. Only then, after understanding, can the psyche begin to reorganize and restore itself.

Think back to some very small frustration, say buying a gift for a friend's birthday party that same night, and when you get there and the gift is opened, you find the store gave you the wrong box. Now recall how you felt. Was it feeling resigned to fate? Annoyance? Frustration, hurt, failure, despair, anger, embarrassment? Try to remember also what else went on inside you. You can probably remember a momentary feeling of tenseness or feeling upset inside, perhaps a bit shaky, like wanting to cry or scream or shout in anger. At the same time the mind's inner voice was saying things like, "Why did this have to happen to me?" or "Damn that clerk" or "I should have made sure before I came." Each mini-stress causes its share of mind-body-psyche reactions.

The most worrisome yet neglected effect of stress is the way it can incubate for so long before "real" illnesses appear. The accumulation of mini-stresses has exactly the same effect eventually as do the major crises of life, it just takes longer before the effects become obvious. Take the common experience of finding the morning newspaper in a flooded rain gutter. After the paper is dried out or you have gone out and bought another one, the annoyance fades away quickly. But now suppose this becomes an everyday event. We all know the reaction. Annoyance builds. In each succeeding day the reaction becomes more intense until finally there is an outburst of anger and you are goaded into some action to end the affair. On rare occasions someone shoots the newsboy. Such is the stress of life.

Nor do the occasions of stress need to be similar at all. It makes no difference what interferes with the pursuit of even the most mundane goals, the effects of any hassle are always the same. The endless hassles of daily life drain the resources we have for dealing with stress, dilute our healing reservoirs and leave our psyches vulnerable to assault. I suspect this accounts for the disturbing increase in all kinds of stress problems these days, including unpremeditated violence and suicides as well as coronary attacks.

I have used the word "hassle" for mini-stresses because it is so often used to describe the difficulties of modern daily life. Shopping at the supermarket can be a hassle, getting the car repaired can be a hassle, keeping track of work records for the government bureaucracies, the bus strikes, the cost of heating oil are all hassles. Incidentally, the word *hassle* apparently came from blending the words *haggle* and *tussle,* and originally it was used to describe how hoodlums bothered passersby. Now it means anything that gives you a hard time. The history of the word, growing out of descriptions for arguing and fighting or scuffling into its present popular use to describe undue fuss about getting something accomplished pretty much reflects what has happened in our society.

Chapter 7
Games theorists play

A question of territory... Stress research (chuckle, chuckle)... Psychological and psychiatric notions ... Ideas from the medical sciences. .... To summarize

A question of territory

The main obstacles to constructing a unifying description of stress such as I describe in Chapter 10 are the long traditions of treating psychology and medicine as completely separate sciences and an obsession to have physical data before venturing any serious speculations. In the following summaries of the most popular views offered by different schools of experts, the great informational gap between psychology and medicine is painfully clear. All the healing disciplines — medicine, psychosomatic medicine, psychology, and psychiatry — are concerned with stress and stress ills, yet these specialities have always remained peculiarly segregated. Physiologists rarely speak to psychologists and psychologists rarely speak (scientifically) to psychiatrists and psychiatrists rarely speak to psychologists. And to make things more complicated, even though the role of intelligent mental activities in the cause and cure of stress problems has become an inescapable conclusion, most scientists do not chance speculations about this very crucial aspect of stress because mental phenomena defy reliable measurement.

Theories about stress have sprung from psychiatry, psychology and a number of the basic medical sciences — a surprisingly diverse background (not surprising since the disciplines don't talk to each other). Most explanations of stress are actually "borrowed" theories because they were all originally developed to explain some other phenomenon, such as neurosis, certain aspects of physical ills, or the origin of emotions.

Research in each speciality, from psychiatry to physiology, has contributed important information to the stress story but no one speciality has developed enough information to make the story complete. The approaches of psychology, psychiatry and a part of psychosomatic medicine generally describe the unconscious and psychosocial factors of stress but don't account for how the emotions can cause physical ills. And on the medical side there are physiology, biochemistry, neurology and endocrinology that can explain how changes occur in the physical body *after* a stress state has already occurred but can't account for *how* the stress state causes the physical changes. The lack of a unifying, comprehensive theory in the face of a plethora of incomplete notions about "the stress of life" reflects quite accurately the great schism between the sciences dealing with the mind and the sciences dealing with the body.

Stress research (chuckle, chuckle)

Clinical correlation studies. The most suggestive evidence about the nature of stress comes from what are called clinical correlation studies. These kinds of studies simply estimate how much stress people experience along with how often they experience it, make various measurements of their current state of health, and then statistically analyze the data to determine the probability that the two items are related.

In one study, for example, bus drivers and conductors were studied over a five year period based on the assumption that daily conditions for both were the same but that the drivers had a greater job responsibility than the conductors since they had to make more decisions and thus were under more "stress" than were the conductors. And the study duly showed that there was a much higher incidence of heart disease among the drivers than among the conductors. In a similar kind of study tax accountants were found to show a marked rise in serum cholesterol levels (a stress indicator) in the weeks just before April 15, their period of high job stress.

These kinds of studies are more tantalizing than enlightening.*
They take situations in which reacting to some kind of social
pressure is almost impossible to measure and correlate them with
a hodgepodge of physical changes that can be measured. The
statistical analyses do show that some people in stress situations
do develop adverse physical reactions, but the studies give no
information or insights about which kinds of people react nor why
they do nor even whether they have more or less stress in areas
of their lives not under study. The time lapse between the stress
situations and the appearance of physical signs of stress also raises
extremely important questions about the mental events occurring
between the onset of stress situation and the much, much later
occurrence of the adverse physical effects. No studies to date
throw any light at all on this crucial aspect of the stress process.

Laboratory studies are designed to answer part of this problem.
Unfortunately, they have done a terrible job. I have argued vigorously with my psychophysiology colleagues that their laboratory
studies on stress are impossibly irrational, inappropriate, and
poorly conceived, but with only small success. I will describe the
nature of such studies and let the reader decide about their relevance to stress.

For a very long time, laboratory studies of stress have used
physical conditions to elicit strong reactions, i.e., to create a stress
situation that could be standardized. The two most common conditions were (a) thrusting the hand into a bucket of ice water and
(b) electric shock to the skin. If you think these conditions have
little relationship to "the stress of life," I agree. "The stress of life"
is mental pressure, not radical physical stimulation. How the body
reacts to physical trauma is completely different from the way it
responds to mental activities. Researchers who use physical
stimuli to simulate "the stress of life" do so because they are
convinced that human reactions to stress are an instinctive reaction to avoid or do battle with a threat to physical well being,

---

*There is an old saying in biological research that correlations between two features or
events can never prove a cause-effect relationship. We know, for example, that the Amtrack
train whistles by the crossing every morning at exactly the same time we are leaving for
work. The two events coincide but one does not cause the other.

having nothing to do with any kind of mental activity (see "arousal" theory, to follow). Of course, facing the stress of life involves mental reactions rather than primal physical reactions, but it is a lot easier to stick someone's hand in ice water than to explore the complicated sequence of mental events that changes how one perceives a situation into a reaction of physical distress.

More recently some researchers, answering the criticism about the nonrelevance of physical stimuli to the stress of life phenomenon, took to using a variety of "mental tests" and measuring such physiological changes accompanying the mental tasks as change in heart rate or skin electrical activity or respiration. The new test conditions are said to use emotional stimuli, at least the kinds of laboratory stimuli psychophysiologists traditionally use to study anxiety. But here, too, the laboratory conditions bear very little resemblance to the conditions that cause stress in life. Researchers use: mental arithmetic tests such as counting backwards by 7's, tests for manual dexterity, anticipating electrical shock (not knowing exactly when you'll get an electric shock to the skin), and sometimes asking their subjects to visualize stressful situations. The latter is, of course, the closest approximation to real life stressful situations although it really takes an actor of the Stanislavsky school to conjure up a surefire, deeply felt stress situation in the mind.

The point is, "research," as in academic research, that attempts to study the stress of life is actually many dimensions removed from simulating "the stress of life." Counting backwards by 7's has about as much resemblance to job stress or family stress or to the stress of loss or failure as a flea has to an elephant. Most research studies of stress have very little relevance to the causes and mechanisms of real life stress.

Drs. Friedman and Rosenman (the A and B personality researchers) have used some very imaginative devices to simulate stress situations. For example, they used a cassette tape of someone talking slowly, interminably, and quite vaguely about a particular topic, never seeming to get to the point. The A personality people reacted to the tape quickly, becoming exasperated with its slowness, and generally asked to have the darned thing turned off. The B personalities, on the other hand, tolerated the tape with no fidgeting. This kind of mini-stress certainly distinguishes people who react vigorously from those who tend not to react much to stress. Unfortunately, the test is used mainly with people who already have physical signs of stress illness.

A great deal of experimental psychology has also tried to track stress reactions as a learning phenomenon. This approach is based on the assumption that we learn certain ways of responding to stress situations, much as we learn to behave properly at the dinner table or at school. There is some rather impressive evidence that some kinds of learned behaviors do play a role in some reactions to stress. Such behaviors as learned helplessness, passivity, fear of failure or fear of success do indeed seem to be learned kinds of reactions to stress, but they are, at the same time, related to personality patterns and may or may not be important influences determining the way one reacts in real stress situations. So many times we hear about a Mr. Milktoast suddenly becoming a hero in times of stress. It seems more likely that learned reactions to stress are only one influence among many determining the reaction.

Psychological and psychiatric notions. Psychiatry, or rather, pure unadulterated Freudian and Jungian concepts, contributed the "psychodynamic" theory. According to this view, stress and stress reactions are attributed to "psychosocial circumstances" that create unconscious conflicts that in turn stimulate the unconscious to develop defenses to protect the ego from further psychic trauma. Such defenses are usually judged by psychiatrists to be inappropriate and unrealistic. The theory suggests that emotional distress bubbles up from the depths of the unconscious where emotional conflicts are kept submerged and hidden from conscious awareness. Since the unconscious (or conscious/unconscious barrier) screens the conflict from the practical reality, resolution of the conflict without benefit of the conscious mind is seen (by the experts) to be unrealistic and not relevant to the particular stress situation (a conclusion I view as highly arguable, see below).

There is, however, one difficulty: the question of whether mental illness (severe emotional/behavioral problems) — or psychoses — are caused at all by the same kind of circumstances that cause stress ills such as neuroses or psychosomatic disorders. The disabling mental illnesses, such as schizophrenia or mania, are identified largely by episodes of losing contact with reality. In sharp contrast, in emotional problems such as neuroses and other emotional or psychological difficulties, a sense of reality may be all too acute. The differences between emotional (mental) pathology and emotional distress ills suggests they are neither caused by similar agents nor circumstances nor are the intrapsychic activities that affect mental behavior similarly involved. It has not been proven that sick minds and normal minds stewing about an ordinary amount of trouble actually do function in the same way (as is generally assumed). On the other hand, the dynamics of the unconscious, as elaborated by Jung, do give clues about the way in which the intangible stress of interpersonal relationships can lead to emotional difficulties.

Two dynamic concepts elaborated by Freud and his physician colleague Breuer do appear to bear upon the stress process: the notion of resistance (that there is psychic opposition to expressing disagreeable memories) and the idea of repression (keeping unacceptable desires or impulses within the unconscious and not available to conscious awareness except as a disguised or unrecognizable symbol — as in dreams). There is a great deal of psychological evidence that consciousness tends to reject anything that is undesirable or unacceptable to one's self-image, tucking most undesirable impacts away in the unconscious to fester rather than troubling the conscious awareness that people need to have working on day-to-day survival.

As Freud created, with his colleague Breuer, the techniques of psychoanalysis and formulated psychodynamic theories, so, too, did he lay the foundations for psychosomatic medicine. The field of psychosomatic medicine has had an odd history, and for a speciality devoted to physical ills caused by problems of the psyche, it is even more curious that it has contributed so little in the way of understanding stress phenomena. As psychosomatic medicine limped along, it did do its research chores, at least the psychiatrists interested in the field did. From many studies a potpourri of rather unrelated findings emerged. It was found that certain personality patterns could be roughly correlated with certain kinds of illnesses; that types of unconscious conflicts (family, sex) correlated with certain kinds of psychosomatic ills; that certain individuals seem to inherit or acquire special kinds of organ susceptibilities or vulnerabilities to illness. The thesis of psychosomatic medicine was reduced to the formula: "personality plus emotional tensions plus precipitating circumstances can lead to physical distress of the body." What everyone began searching for was, what triggers stress ills? This is where psychosomatic medicine has been stuck for some time.

Thinking activity as the cause of stress. The other major notion from psychology about how stress might cause the effects it does on mind and body is the "cognitive" theory (role of intelligence and reasoning). It postulates processes operating between stressful events and the individual's reactions to stress and just sort of leave it at that. Just what these reasoning processes may be in the circumstances of ordinary, everyday stress has not yet been described, nor, as in the case of psychodynamic theory, does the theory suggest *how* cognitive activities can create emotions and cause physical changes within the body.

Ideas from the medical sciences. From physiological and psychophysiological research has come two theories that begin with the physical end products of stress and argue backwards to a nonspecified cause. One theory, called "arousal" theory, holds that psychological stress activates the autonomic nervous system and the endocrine system to become aroused (i.e., to tense, ready to take some action). It is seen as an instinctive reaction, identical to that of an animal reacting to defend itself against a threat of physical harm. The second theory comes from Selye's General Adaptation Syndrome concept, particularly the initial aspect of the biochemical, endocrine, and immune reactions to physical stress which he identified as the "alarm reaction."

Most experts working with stress ascribe to bits of all theories but particularly to the arousal theory. This is the major part of the fight-or-flight theory that states that when animal life is faced with an imminent threat to physical well being, animals and human beings alike react reflexly by either fighting (aggression), fleeing (escaping), or (and this is the usual but questionable interpretation) freezing in place (submission). In order to take any of these actions, the body must first be prepared to act. So the first part of the fight-or-flight reaction is "arousal" of the body's physiological systems (they are alerted and made ready for action).

Because it is the muscles that have to carry out the action, the first event in reacting to a threat to physical well being is tensing of the muscles — very much the way runners tense in a race when the starter says, "get ready, get set" before he says "GO!" Another part of the preparation of the muscles for action is to concentrate the body's energy in the muscles. The cardiovascular system shifts its activity to supply the muscles with more blood, and everything not necessary to the emergency activity stops. The motility of the gut, for example, stops and the secretions of the mouth dry up. This "arousal" prepares the body to take some lifesaving action.

The arousal theory has been buttressed by the work of Hans Selye who described a stereotypical response of biological systems to a variety of physical forces (trauma, injury, infections, chemicals, heat, etc.), and his research indicated the responses are caused by activation of the pituitary, the hypothalamus, and the autonomic nervous system. As Selye followed the physiological and biochemical reactions to physical stress, he identified three stages of what he called the General Adaptation Syndrome. For example, if an infectious organism invades the body, the reaction is first the *alarm* phase in which the body's defenses are mobilized. This is followed by a phase of *resistance,* which is the way the organism resists or adapts to the stress of the infection, and the third and final phase is that of *exhaustion* of the resistance, when the organism succumbs to the stress.

I want to make it perfectly clear that there is little question but that these biochemical and endocrine changes probably do *implement* the principal biological reactions of living things to physical stress and are, probably, the mechanisms responsible for the physical reactions to emotional stress once they are set in motion, and that if the stress is overwhelming, then adaptation may fail. The important question that has not been answered, however, is: how are these reactions set in motion (i.e., *initiated*) by intangible, nonphysical stimuli?*

How indeed does a bad day at the office cause a tension headache or executive stress cause ulcers or coronary attacks? Certainly there is nothing physical in these circumstances, nothing that can physically excite the nerves and endocrine glands. There must be something else, some other factor, some intermediary between outside circumstances and the physical elements that converts the social intangibles of life into actual physical events. My concepts of this psychical to physical transformation is described in Chapter 9.

The adaptation theory. Adaptation is another one of those mystery words science uses that tend to become so muddled and ambiguous that the term becomes much more important than what it is supposed to stand for. Originally, in medicine and psychology and anthropology, adaptation meant the process by which life forms respond to changes in their environmental circumstances by shifting and changing their biological structure and behavior so as to maintain a state of relative well being and favoring survival. As applied to the phenomenon of survival of the species, adaptation is used in a general sense to mean the process of functional and structural changes that foster survival. Or, more optimistically stated, adaptation is the process of changing the functions of life forms as the environment changes in such a way as to maintain a harmonious relationship with the environment.

As applied in physiology, the meaning of adaptation has been essentially the same. As applied to specific, separate physiological or biochemical systems such as the way the auditory system

*Here also, traditional terminology and certain scientific assumptions are strangely ambiguous. To biochemical physiologists, for example, the presence or absence of endomorphins (the "brain opiates") "causes" the presence or absence of pain. And it is true, that *when* the endomorphins are present or absent, their immediate and direct effects do relate to the sensation of pain. The *chemical* process that implements the effect does not, however, account for how the concentrations of endomorphins can be changed by psychological influences. When my attention is diverted I can easily "forget" my pain; even the worst physical ravaging can often be allayed by a comforting presence and love and understanding. Biochemicals carry out effects, they don't initiate them. This very important difference in interpreting the word "cause" is a critical factor in understanding health and illness. It is, unfortunately, a factor that is often ignored in the rush to scientific recognition.

"adapts" to a repeated noise by not responding (not "listening"), the usual interpretation is that responding to the noise stops or diminishes because the system has determined the noise has no harmful significance. Most physiologists and experimental psychologists are disinclined to attribute any "intelligence" to physiological systems and, insisting on greater objectivity, call this kind of adaptation simply "decreased sensitivity after prolonged stimulation." Such a conclusion of course avoids meaningful interpretation. I prefer to speculate that somewhere in the mass of interconnecting nerve networks that make living things whole and operating in harmonious, unified ways, there may well be the means to evaluate "intelligently" the meaning of elements in the environment.

When psychologists got hold of the term adaptation, they began to talk about "adaptive behavior," meaning that human beings and certain animals could modify their behavior in ways that allowed them to continue to satisfy their needs, reach their goals, and interact with their social environments in a way that could promote their own psychological well being.

And finally, when Selye designed his elaborate biological model of the complex ways living organisms react biochemically, endocrinologically, and neurohormonally to physical assaults such as injury, infections, or tissue abnormalities, he saw that his model of reactions to physical stress was a highly sophisticated form of biological adaptation. As viewed by Selye, when a living organism is physically assaulted, it reacts first by sounding an alarm. During the *alarm* phase of the General Adaptation Syndrome, signals are sent to the pituitary-adrenal system and, depending upon the intensity of the physical assault and how long it persists, a variety of biological chemicals can be released. Some of these biochemicals are capable of resisting or neutralizing or overcoming the effects of the physical assault, and Selye called this the *resistance* phase of the G.A.S. The final stage is the stage of *exhaustion,* when the primary resisting mechanisms become exhausted. The entire sequence of this kind of response to physical damage is, indeed, an adaptive phenomenon because it stimulates an outpouring of the body's defense processes, and if the resistance is successful, then the organism continues to survive in a state of relative well being.

As a result of Selye's remarkable research and theory development, "the adaptive syndrome" has come to mean the extensive
and profound changes in the endocrine, autonomic, and immune
systems caused by stress.

There can be, however, some damage to living organisms by
exactly these same adaptive processes that are involved in the
body's defenses. It has been assumed by Selye and advocates of his
model of stress that some neurohormones provoked during the
alarm reaction can become excessive and can, in themselves, cause
organ or tissue damage. It is also believed that when stress is
chronic (when the impact outlasts the body's defenses) if the stress
is not too severe, the body can adapt to the assaults and live with
them. This is one plausible explanation for why blood pressure
continues to rise under stress indicating that the musculature of
the blood vessels are adapting to more tension yet the cardiovascular system can still perform its function of contraction to keep the
blood circulating.

On a more popular psychological and social level, we often talk
of adapting but we use two quite different meanings of the phenomenon. For some people, adapting to difficult circumstances
means submission, while for others, it means overcoming, as in
"we shall overcome." Whichever way we use the word, we mean
it is a way of coping.

Notions gleaned from stress reduction effects

The final stimulus that exploded stress into the modern health
picture was a curious mixture of events Jung would call "syn-
chrony." Almost at the same time that some therapists discovered
or rediscovered relaxation techniques and yoga as beneficial in
stress ills (especially emotional and body tensions), biofeedback
and other body awareness techniques were found to relieve the
effects of stress, and society itself became more and more aware
that life was stressful.

Back in the 1930s, Dr. Edmond Jacobson conducted extensive
research on anxiety and muscle tension and concluded that images
of uncertainty caused the muscle tensions of anxiety, and that
because the muscles were under voluntary control, they could be

"trained" to stay relaxed. He demonstrated repeatedly that various psychosomatic illnesses (that we now call stress ailments) could be remarkably relieved through the assiduous practice of relaxation exercises. He proposed that "anxiety and relaxation are mutually exclusive" (also see Chapter 12). Jacobson's concepts were contrary to those of most professionals who, still today, tend to believe that stress tensions and anxiety are caused by some problem "out there."* Jacobson interpreted his research as indicating that *anxiety (stress) is caused by the effort to solve problems* and that the feelings of anxiety are really *patterns of muscle-tension images.* That is, when one thinks about a situation that seems to be related to one's anxiety, subconscious images related to the situation activate the muscles into particular patterns of tensions — such as bracing for another assault on one's psyche.

Then, since the tension-images get buried in the unconscious, Jacobson felt that imagery could be used to search for and recognize the special muscle-tension image patterns involved in the anxiety. Once these tension patterns are recognized, then with the practice of relaxation exercises, one could learn to maintain relaxation while learning to eliminate the disturbing images causing the tensions. No tension, no anxiety and vice versa — no anxiety, no tension.

A second repopularized relaxation technique, Autogenic Training, was developed by systematizing and ritualizing certain effective self-hypnotic techniques (see also Chapter 12). Using self-suggestion messages about relaxation, the idea is to allow relaxation by keeping the attention in a passive state. During anxiety (stress), the body is kept tense by messages from the brain that relay the information that the mind-brain believes danger is lurking, so the body should stay alert. And the body is also kept tense by messages *from* the muscles that tell the brain that the muscles are tense and in the ready-defense posture. The brain (at one level) interprets this to mean that there really *is* danger, so it increases *its* messages to the muscles, saying that since there really is danger "out there," then it is best to tense up and be ready to defend the self.

We will learn later that this confused nonsense is not quite the

---

*That is, it is the *nature* of the problems around one that is the chief influence determining distress from the stress of life.

way the brain-muscle connections work. Actually, the sustained tension is caused by a lack of information to the brain regulating centers that should tell the mind-brain that (a) the "danger" is *not* a physical danger, so tensing the body is of no help, and (b) that any tensions signals *from* the muscles are false signals and are to be ignored. When the attention shifts to feeling the relaxation, fewer and fewer messages are sent from muscles to brain and so relaxation can continue to deepen.

When the body begins to relax and there are fewer messages going to the brain about tensions in the muscles, the brain translates these fewer messagess into feelings of relaxation. The net result is a lessened cortical (brain) control. In some cases in which tensions have been pent up for some time, or extreme tensions have been held in, when the reduced number of tension messages passes a certain threshold of brain control, they are suddenly released in a flood of downward messages (like opening a clogged drain), and the leftover tension message race down the nerves helter-skelter instead of flowing down in their usual orderly, controlled way. The result can be all kinds of uncoordinated muscle activity such as twitching, jerking, and shaking and all these wild motor activities are accompanied by marvelous sensations of relief from tension (see also Chapter 11). Some neurotics, wise in relief techniques, often try to induce shaking in themselves as a way of releasing the feelings of tension. The mechanism is a safety valve for the body and emotions.

Biofeedback, especially muscle (EMG) biofeedback, produces its relaxation effects operationally much like Progressive Relaxation (tense-relax exercises) and Autogenic Training. That is, the biofeedback instrument measures mainly *unfelt* muscle tension and when the patient can see or hear the signal monitoring muscle tension he cannot feel, he nonetheless can learn to change the tension level.

Many experts believe that all three relaxation techniques effectively reduce the sensations of stress (especially apprehension and anxiety) because the learned relaxation neutralizes (decreases) the tension messages sent from the muscles to the brain, thereby lessening the *sensations* of anxiety which they equate with the arousal of fear of an imminent disaster.

To summarize: Briefly, psychodynamic theory from psychiatry (mainly Freud) has contributed the concept that the dynamics of the unconscious can cause emotional ills; psychosomatic medicine has confirmed that the stress of life does cause physical ills; cognitive theorists suggest that the barrier at the unconscious/conscious interface plays a primary role in the development of emotions; physiology contributed the "arousal" theory that uncertainty and anxiety and fear evoke instinctive, primitive, physiological responses (when stress is strong and terrifying); and Selye's alarm concept showed how the physiological mechanisms behave during stress and that the reaction is a process of adaptation.

And while experts, authorities, researchers, theorists, and clinicians each have more experiential, intuitive notions about stress than they have rock-solid data, most professionals do tend to agree that: "psychosocial" influences trigger stress and stress reactions, that when human beings perceive stress some respond by subjective and physical tensions and hormonal imbalances, and that reactions to stress involve both general and selective activation of the neurophysiological, autonomic. endocrine, and immune systems.

The most widely accepted theories about stress, thus, are based upon notions of emotional *reflexes* and reflex biochemical changes in the body. *None* of the theories explains anything about *how* "psychosocial" influences cause stress or *why* some people react to stress by subjective and physiological tensions or *how* the intangible psychosocial influences activate the neural, endocrine, and biochemical systems of the body.

My specific criticisms of the ideas about stress prevalent in academia are that stress ills with obvious measurable physical changes usually occur only after long periods of living under stress (hypertension, neuroses), and people living under stress do *not* show signs and symptoms of intense anxiety and fear but they have signs and symptoms like those listed in Table 3. Moreover, these kinds of symptoms are the products of cognitive (intelligent) concern.

Chapter 8
A need for new notions

New ailments need new concepts. . . . Feelings are creations of mind.
. . . Modern day feelings are sophisticated thinking emotions. . . . Stress
and the evolutionary ladder.

New ailments need new concepts

It cannot be emphasized too often that the kinds of unwellness
and states of diminished well being that nearly everyone endures
living with the stress of life are *very new kinds of ailments* with
very new kinds of complaints and very new kinds of remedies.

Accounting for the extraordinary prevalence of stress and how
it causes the distress of mind and body it does also requires new
ways of thinking about the nature of health and illness. For most
people stress is not an illness defined in pathology texts nor by
changes in any of the biochemical or physiological systems we can
relate to physical ills. The complaints of people living with stress
are the kinds listed in Table 3. Moreover, most of the symptoms
of stress come from concerns and worries about problems in life,
such as the kinds listed in Tables 4 and 5. These are *not* the
disturbed emotions that make people seek psychotherapy, rather
they are the kinds of mental concerns that make people want to
talk to friends, to seek out counselors, or to start self-help programs. The complaints are *feelings,* beginning as concerns and
always the result of thinking activity.

Most of what the healing professions know about emotions has
come from studies of intense emotions such as rage and fear, and
documenting their presence by recording various physiological
activities. But these are the emotions shared with animals because
of common biological roots and have little to do with the main
range of human emotions. Theorists generally explain feelings as

simply weaker versions of emotions. Under certain conditions feelings such as apprehension and irritation do progress to the stronger emotions of fear and anger. On the other hand, feeling disturbed, annoyed, unhappy, in love, peaceful, inadequate, depressed, or feeling a lack of self-esteem are feelings that *can* change to strong emotions but rarely do. What we generally call feelings are mental observations about the way one is interpreting one's circumstances, and the meaning of those circumstances to the self.

One problem in discussing feelings and emotions of states of unwellness that are not "official" ailments is the tendency of healers and theorists to assume that feelings are more indications of emotional pathology than they are merely mild exaggerations of common feelings. For example, therapists tend to interpret the fear of flying as the neurotic avoidance of flying while, actually, thousands of people have a fear of flying they can and do control and can scarcely be classified as neurotic. Such silent sufferers have every bit as much the symptoms of unwellness as does the neurotic with an uncontrolled fear, but their symptoms aren't "official." And the neurotic gets treatment while the not-well person must cope as best he can. The difference lies in the beliefs of helpers and healers as to what constitutes unwellness. What professional therapists believe about the origins of emotions is an extremely important factor in how they treat the underlying stress.

The arguments about whether feelings and emotions are products of our bio-evolutionary heritage, raw and primitive, that we work to keep under civil control or whether feelings and emotions are products of intelligent functions of the mind is important to resolve. If we recognize that the vague, often uncertain feelings of the "don't-feel-so-good" states are, in fact, signs and symptoms of being under stress, then not only can we begin to discriminate stress and its distresses from the signs of serious emotional ills, but we can select the most efficient treatment programs.

Feelings are creations of mind

A great deal of the new thought about the human potential and new ways of healing centers around feelings. The new techniques are aimed at changing feelings, feelings such as, "He makes me feel stupid," "I feel lonesome," or "I just don't have it." The feelings are changed by venting feelings, by becoming more involved with people, by self-acceptance, by rooting out childhood emotions, recognizing when people are playing games, becoming responsbile for one's own life, etc., etc. Note that most of the techniques aim mainly to relieve bad feelings and disturbing emotions; few focus on a role of the intellect in either the cause or the cure of stress.

But where, in fact, do feelings come from?

Let's first take a look at what we usually mean when we talk about feelings. Actually, we use the word to describe many different kinds of thoughts *and* sensations, such as "he hurt my feelings," "I had a feeling he would be here," "she made me feel very sympathetic to her cause," "I had a strong feeling of empathy with that girl," or "we had good feelings about the reunion." It certainly is not a very precise word whether we use it in the singular or plural. Feelings can mean anything from describing a mind state of awareness to a body state of strong emotion, or in between states of opinions such as "I had the feeling that was wrong," or states of sensitivity such as "those were people with feelings." So if we have to explain exactly what we mean by the word *feeling* or *feelings,* we have to say that sometimes it means an impression, sometimes an emotion, a sentiment at other times, and a sensitivity at still another time.

But now, let's look at what is meant by the word *emotion.* If I look in a standard dictionary, I see the word defined as "a strong feeling, arising subjectively rather than through conscious mental effort," and "agitation of the passions or sensibilities, often involving physiological changes." Emotions are explained in much the same way in the various psychological dictionaries, — that is, emotion is "variously defined but generally agreed to be a complex (behavioral) reaction involving a high level of activation and visceral changes" or defined as "behavior that is primarily influenced by conditioned visceral responses. . . Our viscera are always reacting; but in emotion, their reactions affect perception, learning, thinking, and virtually everything we do." Notice the emphasis on physiological changes here is somewhat greater than in the general dictionary. The definitions make it sound as if our emotions spring uncalled for, from overpowering animal instincts, with the body involved the way an animal's is when it is upset.

This popular theory implies that emotion is a behavior, — that is, the way one conducts one's self, acts and reacts in particular situations, that is mainly dependent upon how our gut, heart, blood pressure, and muscles are reacting. Reacting to what? What causes the gut and the cardiovascular system and muscles to "react" in the first place? Does some outside event reach into the body and twist the gut or heart? And conversely, how does the uptight gut or blood pressure or lungs or muscles "influence" learning, thinking, and "everything we do?" Does the gut or blood pressure (when reacting) interfere with thinking? I remember Hubert Humphrey, wasted by cancer, in pain, with every tissue and organ in his body reacting to the invader in his body, still not only thinking lucidly and effectively but creating new ideas.

Modern day feelings are sophisticated, thinking emotions

The prevailing academic notions about the origins of emotions raise some questions that seem very odd indeed, especially in the light of changing perceptions of the role of the mind in health and healing. For example, do "emotional problems" such as anxiety or depression or other neuroses mean that people with these problems act the way they do mainly because their inside organs are uptight? And further, does it mean that when people with these problems seek therapy that the psychotherapy deals first and foremost with uptight inner organs.

Of course not. People who have emotional problems usually behave quite well out in society, letting their emotions get in their way only in private moments, and while emotions can make their lives difficult, most of their behavior is not affected by the emotions they feel. When therapy is helpful, it is not directed toward changing the reactions of the gut or blood pressure. Not at all. Psychotherapy and counseling for disturbed emotions is directed at gaining insights into the causes of the disturbed emotions and working to change behavior through these insights.

Feelings the average person often calls emotions are really reactions to our judgments — judgments about the things of life that fall short of our expectations. That is, we judge how a certain part of life is going, compare it to how we would like it to go, and then react to how the events are different from what we expected or hoped for. Feelings are the reactions and they are the products of thought.

This kind of mental concept formation occurs in the development of nearly all feelings. Let's say you invite someone to your place for dinner, and at the last moment the guest calls and has to cancel. You are disappointed. You feel let down, especially after having made some special arrangements for your guest. Things won't go quite so well at dinner as you had hoped, although it certainly won't be a disaster either. The disappointment is your reaction, a feeling that is not at all dependent upon how your gut or heart is behaving physically.

I can't think of a single emotion that isn't preceded by intellectual activity. Theorists invariably cite sudden, intense fear as an innate, instinctual reaction of the body's physiology, a physical reaction of the body that comes first and is so intense it often seems to paralyze the mind. The argument is patently illogical. If, for example, you are home alone at night, ill, and you hear the back door opening into the darkened kitchen, most likely you *will* be seized by fear. The heart races, the muscles tense, breathing stops and gasps, the gut seems to bunch up, and you freeze for a moment.

The classical interpretation is that when a person's well being is seriously threatened, the person instinctively, reflexly mobilizes a "defensive set" of the body known as the "fight-or-flight" reaction. But what theorists don't explain is (a) why did you interpret an ordinary noise as a threat to your safety and well being? and (b) why did you decide the threat really was serious? Certainly, if a potentially dangerous intruder is coming in the back door, the mind has to put together a few facts and make an interpretation *first*. There are, as a matter of fact, *many* pieces of information that have to be put together sensibly and intelligently *before* any interpretation is made.

In this case, for instance, the intelligent processes of the mind first make a diagnosis about the particular noise and its source. This involves making a number of comparisons and interpretations. The noise is not the side door or the garage door — they make different noises. The interpretive mind almost instantly classifies the many characteristics of the noise and concludes it can only be the back door. The interpretive mind also reviews the possibilities about what is making the noise and concludes that no family member is coming home at this time; therefore, taking all things into consideration, the mind decides that the probabilities for danger are high. By comparing the *meaning* of many different signs and symbols the mind arrives at the most likely interpretation. Obviously, if the mind interprets its information as signaling an imminent danger, it is then most reasonable to recruit the body's physiological potential to its maximum alertness. (But it was the mind that was alert first.)

It is imperative to update our notions about emotions from the older ideas of emotions as originating from animal-like instincts to concepts that can account for the intelligent concerns and worries of people who lives with stress. As we explore the operations of mind as it creates stress and then as that stress the mind created undermines the vitality of mind and body, it will become clear that the greatest share of the stress process occurs via the thought mechanisms, and that relief from stress can be effected only via those same thought mechanisms.

Stress and the evolutionary ladder

Several hundred years ago, our English cousins conceived of stress as "some adversity over which the individual has no control." Later physics adopted the definition that stress is an external force or pressure that causes a change (response) within the system being stressed and most of us have grown up hearing about stresses and strains (the strain being the response to stress). Stress has been classically viewed as some external pressure that causes changes within the systems of things, and those systems of things the pressure is exerted on can be anything from steel or airplanes to gnats or human beings. Put simply, any external force affects the operation of the system it is acting upon. Force on steel causes internal strain on the molecules, weakening the bonds of the molecules holding the steel together; wind forces on airplanes affect their altitude and speed; air currents acting on gnats can blow them for miles. These are all physical forces and, of course, human beings can be severely affected by external physical forces such as heat, pressure, infectious organisms, and injuries to the body.

But human beings are also subject to other, very different pressures — the nonphysical forces of social pressure that is how society in general expects human beings to behave. These are forces that act on the mind and brain and change the way they function. For the human species it is the intangible forces and pressures human beings exert on each other by their words, ideas, attitudes, beliefs, and behavior have come to far outweigh the stress of physical forces.

A Table is a Table is a Table — usually. But tables like Table 6 can almost dance with exciting new information. This table compares the general phenomenon of stress in the different major systems of the universe. Note particularly that as life systems increase in complexity, the nature of stress as a force exerted directly and locally on the organism (stressors such as a blow, a bite, a sting) *become represented by bits of information* to indicate *impending* harm (the possibility of a direct, local assault — a nearby snake, a buzzing bee). Then, with further evolution the sensory information about things in the physical environment is integrated and interpreted to mean threats to the *whole* organism (a charging elephant), and finally the stress becomes nonphysical threats to social survival and well being (rumors of an impending layoff).

The evolutionary changes these changes in the nature of stress represent are truly staggering. Living beings shifted from primitive, insect-like systems with capabilities only for reacting to direct, immediate physical assaults to developing an ability to detect dangers not yet present and to react to them in a way that could ensure a prepared defense and continued well being.

These were truly quantum leaps in evolution. For any organism *to sense danger not yet present* means it has the capability to integrate information from many physical senses and create a very specific representation (image) of the danger within the mind-brain complex, and *then react to that image.* The implication that images may have played a fundamental role in the survival of

Table 6 Operational classification of stress systems

(where stress is an external force causing a change within the system it acts upon)

System	External force	Response	Response mechanisms	Resisting mechanisms
Inorganic	physical (pressure, heat, cold)	strain (change in shape, structure)	molecules/elements	opposite force
Primitive life forms	physical	change in shape, structure, location, direction	ion exchange reflexes	inclusion, secretions regeneration
Higher animals, primitive man	physical; threats to physical well being; threats to group	local and general arousal; fight or flight; aggregation	interacting neural networks; specialized organs fostering systems	coordinated neural and hormonal systems; primitive control of external force
Socialized man	predominantly nonphysical threats to social well being, intellectual pressure	primarily intellectual, emotional, perceptual; change of consciousness secondary—physical arousal	integrative brain functions; language; imagery; thought; logic	exploring resources and alternatives; securing relevant information; awareness; social coping; understanding

species strongly implies that the imagery tool of the mind-brain is important also in determining the well being of human beings and in coping with the stresses of their social environments. (The important role of images in all aspects of stress, the stress itself, the distress of stress, and relief from stress are described in Chapters 9 and 10.)

In Table 6 I identify today's human beings as *socialized* man to emphasize just how very different both man and his environment are from other species and their environments. The human species created a highly social environment, and as the social environment has become more and more complex and more and more an environment of thoughts and ideas and images, human survival has come to depend more and more on how well human beings can cope with the social conditions (the need to make a living, to perform in an environment of people, to behave according to the rules of the people, etc.). In the environment in which modern man lives, the physical stresses his evolutionary predecessors knew scarcely exist.

If it is true that only those survive who come to terms with their environment, then modern man can survive only by coping with the stress that comes from the interaction dynamics of the social environment. And for the most part people do cope and adapt. It is, as we will discover, only when people *lack* the information they need to cope and adapt that their well being becomes impaired and their survival threatened.

The principle of survival of the fittest says that the specialization of the different species occurs by evolving physiological processes that can adapt to special circumstances of the environment (snake, heat sensors; bat, sound sensors), so, if there is the order in the universe there seems to be, then it would be incongruous that man would evolve such a complex social environment and not simultaneously evolve the means for coping with it. Man is susceptible to more kinds of illness than any other species, and worse, despite progress in conquering the physical dangers, the number of ways man's well being and survival can be threatened has increased far out of proportion to the number of hazards faced by all species throughout all history.

But, it seems, man *is* surviving, and this suggests that *homo sapiens* has evolved mechanisms to cope with his new environment. Table 6 lists the newly evolved mechanisms man has evolved for resisting the inroads of his stresses. Since his stress is conceptual in nature, so too are his survival tools. Since human responses to human stress are primarily conceptual and these are implemented by the mind's thought processes, so too is the way human beings resist and relieve stress conceptual in nature. The most effective coping involves understanding and awareness, products of complex syntheses of experience, culture, learning, and thought.

It becomes reasonable for us, then, to conclude that the feelings we have as we experience stress are created by the mechanisms of our intellect and that human emotions are much more a matter of intelligent considerations than of a reflex primitive nature. The next chapter describes the way the mind, intellect, and imagery operate both to manufacture stress and deal with it to prevent and relieve its effects.

Chapter 9
The dis-ease process

In the eye of the beholder ... Stress is manufactured in the mind ... When "thought patterns" create stress ... Covert operations ... The mental steps to dis-ease. Previewing Figure 1 ... Expectations and perceptions ... Curiosity. Key to the intellect

In the eye of the beholder

Because stress is such an amalgam of social circumstances, the vagaries of human nature, and mind, body, and feeling reactions, stress is very difficult to conceptualize. Stress does not translate well into easy formulas that clearly explain its causes and cures. It seems to include an extraordinary number of unrelated kinds of circumstances, problems, obstacles, miseries, unhappiness, and perplexities that somehow pop up at different times and in different settings.

The alarming scope of problems and ills attributed to the stress of life (as in Tables 1, 2 and 3) poses a disturbing number of questions about the nature of stress and the way it damages mind and body. This chapter presents a new concept about the way the mind and its thinking (cognitive) mechanisms function when they produce stress and then either cope with it or succumb to its distress and the more serious stress ills.

By far the most tantalizing enigma of stress is how all the ordinary circumstances and events of life can wreak such physical havoc on our bodies and our brains. There must be some highly developed inner process that orchestrates the way happenings outside the self can discomfort the emotions and undermine body functions. Experiencing stress, no matter how vague or ill-defined the signs and symptoms are or how consciously aware we are of them, means, nonetheless, that we have not only interpreted our circumstances as unfavorable to our well being but that thought has been transformed into something that abuses the physical operation of mind or body.

The idea that thought-patterns cause stress is a strange and difficult concept to handle in terms of health and illness. It asks us to believe that intangible events moving along erratically through space and time not only can upset the physical functioning of the body and cause physical ills, but can, as well, change the chemistry of the brain and cause mental and emotional ills. Stress is not a particular person or group of people or any one thing that causes difficulties, stress is really *patterns* of the way people, places, hopes, and reality that involve you all come together and are perceived as threatening to personal well being. Most people think of stress as some difficult situation in life that has to be coped with. And rightly so, that is exactly what stress is. But most people also think of the difficult situation and the stress problem as being "out there," and that is not so.

Everything we know about what goes on "out there" is the end product of a complex series of our own mental activities geared to manufacture a product called perception. Perception is the process of attaching meanings to whatever the senses detect and of making sense out of the sprawling, ever-changing patterns of people-us interactions that we see or hear or feel. Our senses detect the "raw" information of our worlds — sights, sounds, touches or smells — and the brain routes this information to special areas where it is compared and associated with information already stored in memory. The result of this data processing is then sent along to still other brain areas that evaluate the interpreted information, judge it, and make decisions about what meaning to give to which kinds of new information. The end product is our perception of what is going on "out there." Trying to sort out the reasons for troubling problems such as why Johnny is so unhappy at school really exercises our persistence for searching and observing and taxes our reasoning powers before we can form a perception (our conclusions) in some satisfactory way.

This string of mental operations is relatively straightforward when our senses are detecting information about the physical environment. But where human behavior is concerned, our abilities for perception (assessing accurately) have very little reliable information to work with. In the realm of life's activities what the mind perceives (i.e., has available to interpret), of course, is how other people are behaving, what we think they may be thinking, how they say what they say, or the way we interpret messages from shops, schools or any organization run by people. Given the common social custom of concealing feelings, masking shortcomings, and feigning success and happiness, we can perceive little more than what other people let us perceive about them. We really don't "know" people, so we do a lot of guessing about what they do and say and what they are thinking about. And we probably guess wrong half the time. Having to guess about important parts of our activities in life creates uncertainty, and uncertainty is stress. Digging out the causes of Johnny's unhappiness turns up just enough conflicting stories and opinions to make absolute decisions impossible and keeps us uncertain and stressed.

This may be the reason the notion that stress is "out there" became popular. Instead of feeling personally at fault, people would rather believe that stress lurks out there in situations filled with people, the ideas of people, or the rules everyone faces in the course of daily life that seem to cause so much confusion. Most professionals offhandedly assume that stress does "come from" events "out there," and since they know that stressful situations cause emotional reactions, they prefer the more professional sounding term "psychosocial" as a cover term to describe both the situations "out there" and the way we behave (react) in those situations. But in a tacit admission that stress is, in fact, manufactured in the mind, a few researchers recently have used the phrase "stress triggers" to indicate that what is "out there" is only an occasion that can trigger stress reactions and is not the stress itself.

Stress is, of course, not so much as what is out there as it is what we make of what is out there, that is, how we perceive our circumstances in life. And the stress trigger can be any event, any occurrence or situation that is different from what we expected or hoped for. In the long run, all stress, abrupt or gradual, profound or mild, fleeting or prolonged, is, perhaps not so surprisingly, dashed hopes and dreams.

Stress is manufactured in the mind

So, if stress is not "out there," where is it?

In the mind, of course. Stress comes out of the hopes and dreams we have for a reasonably satisfying life, and it comes from those hopes and dreams because we have been taught to have great hopes and lovely dreams. Hopes and dreams are, perhaps, the vital forces that supply the drive and energy for life, but when they are frustrated, their driving force can just as easily cause despair and illness. Life, we find, is not all the stuff of hopes and dreams, but is an endless series of challenges to the pursuit of our hopes and dreams. As we, as a society, have become more and more socialized, more and more social forces have come to shape our behavior. More and more *society* (and we too) demands more and better performing, more successes and more achieving and implies that any failures must be weaknesses of person. We feel compelled to be successful in marriage, in our job, in sports, in the home cooking and cleaning, in school activities, and even in our hobbies. The demands for performing and success never end, and they are not merely demands for some kind of success but for the very highest standards of performing and success.

There are today, it is clear, many different kinds of encounters with life that cause stress (see Chapter 5). What is stress for one person, however, may not be stress for someone else. Not everyone feels stressed because they weren't elected president of some group or because their daughter got married or because they got a bad grade in school. Some people are so worried about the possibility of earthquakes in California, for example, they move back to the Midwest or East, while the people there become so stressed by electrical storms and heavy snows and gray skies, they move to California. On the other hand, some kinds of stress affect everyone. Everyone feels stressed by unemployment, being jilted by a lover, or by failing a course in school. Yet, although the occasions for stress are the same and everyone feels the stress, not everyone feels stress in the same way.

When "thought patterns" create stress

The ways of stress are bewildering indeed, especially now we are realizing that the discomforts and ravages of stress are born in the shadow world of thought and ideas and impressions.

By now it should be clear that stress is fabricated out of the things we encounter in life that we decide interfere with living a satisfying, or at least a tolerable, life. The implications of this fact are extraordinary for understanding the phenomena we call health and illness. We are, of course, obliged to accept the idea that both the feelings of anguish we may have about difficult life events and the deep distresses of mind and body can arise solely from the way we perceive the things that happen to us in life. A twelve year old aborigine girl ritually isolated for a month emerges with the joy and satisfaction of having become a woman; a twelve year old American girl isolated for a month emerges with a behavior problem. An overachiever can threaten suicide over a grade of C while an underachiever can be deliriously happy with it.

Stress is in the eye of the beholder. Well, not all of it, but it is really the important operations of the mind that determine what the eye will see and it is what the eye *thinks* it "sees" that causes stress. "I don't think my boss likes me" is *not* a casual observation, it is the attempt to be casual and tentative about a deep seated nagging worry that has been brewing for some time. Worry about whether the boss does or doesn't like me is a stress that not only diminishes my potential and enjoyment, but is a stress that can erode my gut and create an ulcer.

The way thoughts and impressions manufacture the stress one feels occurs in the sophisticated systems of the mind-brain that carry out the thinking we do. These systems are sometimes referred to as information processing systems because they "process" the information (or data) the mind uses in thinking (i.e., they sort out incoming information, organize it, judge it, etc.)

Manufacturing stress is not, however, due to any defect in the functioning of our information processing systems. Since all of our thoughts, ideas, and impressions are constructed by exactly the same processes whether we create stress or well-beingness, the first mystery about stress we have to solve is to discover why the mind makes certain things stressful at one time but can make those exact same things not stressful at other times. The answer lies in a little elementary logic: if both the thoughts and feelings of well being and the thoughts and feelings of stress are developed by the same information processing systems, then we can conclude that our thought processing systems are not at fault. If our thinking apparatus is functioning O.K., then chances are we do not create stress intentionally.

What, then, is at fault? What can happen during thinking that can make some things stressful at one time and not at other times? If our intelligence systems function fairly well most of the time and create stress only some of the time, then the only reason they can spew out a poor thought product is when they don't have the right information to produce a good thought product (i.e., to create effective thoughts and feelings of well being). If, for example, you are writing a book about cat behavior and don't include information about the behavior of Siamese cats, then the book will suffer in quality (well being) and will have to undergo treatment (putting in information) if it is to have a satisfactory future.

Covert operations

The impress of stress is so prevalent in modern life and is becoming so frighteningly magnified with every social and commercial change that *the chances of every single person incubating a stress disease are approaching 100 percent.*

And we know, too, that the mind-brain energy consumed in coping with the constant stresses of today weakens the immune systems of the body, reducing their disease defense capacities and lowering the resistance of the body to other ills. The importance of recognizing stress ills lies in recognizing that there is a treacherous and exceptionally prolonged incubation period between onset and the appearance of measureable effects of distress, a period when the signs and symptoms of stress can be disguised by tricks of the mind, or compensated for, or even absent, but a time period in which the stress of life nonetheless can undermine the energy of body and psyche. The fact that the active part of the stress dis-ease process takes place so covertly is a strong plea to examine the events of the process itself.

The difficulty is, of course, that covert is covert, and clues are scarce about how stress scenarios are written in the unknown recesses of the mind. And although Freud and Jung never said it was easy to sort out pieces of the unconscious mind puzzle, they never said it was difficult, either.

It is widely believed that emotional and psychosomatic disorders are emotional reactions to generally subconscious (unconscious) conflicts between the individual's desire to have a more satisfying way of life and a belief that something is blocking the way to fulfill that desire. The question remains: how can the unconscious be so clever as to pick up on bits of this and that to create some major conflict between dreams and obstacles to dreams? How does an unconscious mind interpret a complex social life and conclude that an important part of it is leading to troubles or misery? What is the internal wisdom that can judge success or failure?

More amazingly still, the unconscious intellect performs a still more complicated task. It creates defenses to protect the ego. Professionals generally agree that episodes of anxiety and unhappiness are dealt with by still other products of "unconscious" mental activity. Psychologists call these defense mechanisms because it is believed they operate to distort or deny the source of the anxiety. The most common defense mechanisms are repression (unconsciously preventing painful memories from reaching consciousness), rationalization (finding socially acceptable reasons for one's behavior to mask the real reasons), sublimation (redirecting unacceptable behavior impulses into acceptable channels, usually unconsciously), and regression (retreating behind more childish levels of behavior).

Note carefully — each of the defenses to protect the psyche devised by the unconscious requires a *sophisticated intellect.* Each ego-protecting defense the unconscious creates requires quite a masterful use of intelligence. When and how, for example, does the unconscious decide that a certain frustration needs a defense? What are the processes involved in planning and selecting a de-

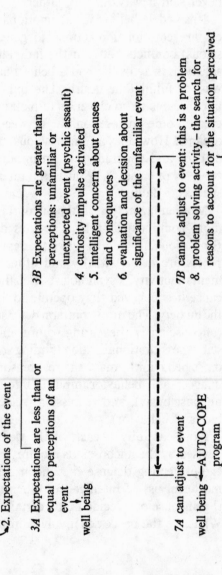

Figure 1
Flow chart of processes leading to states of well being
or states of stress and stress reactions

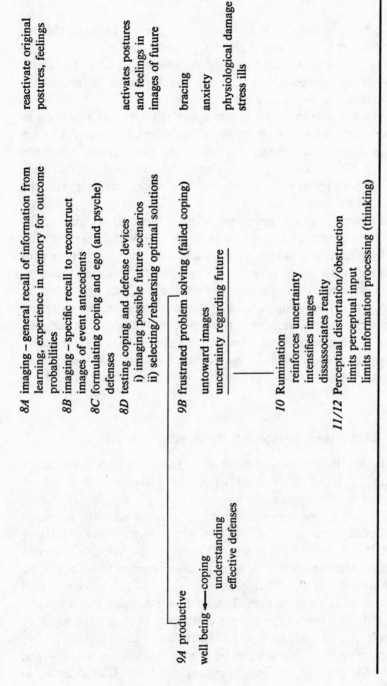

8A imaging – general recall of information from learning, experience in memory for outcome probabilities   reactivate original postures, feelings

8B imaging – specific recall to reconstruct images of event antecedents

8C formulating coping and ego (and psyche) defenses

8D testing coping and defense devices   activates postures and feelings in images of future
    i) imaging possible future scenarios
    ii) selecting/rehearsing optimal solutions

9A productive
well being → coping
    understanding
    effective defenses

9B frustrated problem solving (failed coping)

untoward images
uncertainty regarding future   bracing
    anxiety

10 Rumination
reinforces uncertainty
intensifies images
dissassociates reality

11/12 Perceptual distortion/obstruction   physiological damage stress ills
limits perceptual input
limits information processing (thinking)

fense; what is the nature of the communication between the unconscious that says, 'this is the defense, now carry it out,' and the consciousness that must somehow consent to perform the behavior the unconscious dictates? And finally, how does all this unconscious activity do its damage to the body?

I think the role of the unconscious mind in our reactions to experiences in life can be viewed much more positively. As I see the evidence, the defense systems of the unconscious mind are developed to *protect* the psyche and ego from assaults, and they are defenses based on the best problem solving possible with the information available.

As a matter of fact there is abundant evidence that points to the reasoning power of the unconscious as a powerful intellect that works efficiently and productively and only rarely produces conflicts and neuroses. Where, for example, where *really* do Freudian slips come from? Aren't they, in fact, the result of highly logical subconscious thinking that takes some impressions about something or someone, associates these perceptions with past impressions or judgments and then creates some marvelously clever comment on some event of the moment with the only "slip" being that it slipped through a conscious monitoring and got said out loud?

The mental steps to dis-ease. Previewing Figure 1

The mental events that determine whether a person succumbs to the distress of stress or works out ways to cope with stress are diagrammed in Figure 1.

The mind processes all the information it receives in life to synthesize — paradoxically — two very different ways of relating the self to its environment and to the rest of the universe. One end product of experience is the forming of expectations about how life should be while the other product is the way the working mind interprets life's experiences. The latter are our perceptions about events in life. Both expectations and perceptions are the result of complicated processes in which the mind organizes its available information in some systematic way according to what it has learned in the past, and just to make things complicated, expectations and perceptions constantly influence each other. Perceptions depend to a large degree on what we *expect* our circumstances to be, and conversely, our expectations are shaped by the different ways we interpret our circumstances at different times.

When our perceptions of what is happening as we interact socially with people and people-things are reasonably similar to what we expected the interactions to be, life moves on placidly. Psychologically we feel pretty good about things. But when we perceive things happening that are different from what we expected, we become concerned. Our expectations or our perceptions may not be accurate or realistic, but we assume them to be reasonably correct since, after all, our minds have created both. Then, as the mind becomes aware (often unconsciously) of some disturbing difference between expectations and perceptions, the mind reacts in a very special way. Just as nature abhors a vacuum, so does the human mind abhor disharmony in living and moves always to restore harmony. (Mom always used to be here when we got home from school. Now we never know when she'll be here. I'll ask Dad and if he doesn't know, I'll have to start following her to find out what she's doing.)

The mind, in fact, is impelled to restore harmony by a remarkable faculty — its curiosity. Curiosity is an underrated, understudied instinct possessed by all forms of life. Whenever anything unfamiliar in the environment is sensed by any life form, curiosity is reflexly activated (literally compelled) to explore the unfamiliar to determine whether the environment is still safe or not. This mental reflex serves a generally unrecognized function, that of gathering knowledge about the unknown in the environment so that the unfamiliar can be identified and become "familiar."

In human beings curiosity is expressed as inquisitiveness: who, why, what, where, when? The questions reveal our instinctive compulsion to search for answers, and the compulsion in turn means that there is something new and unfamiliar and perplexing in the environment. (Children sometimes seem to be eternally curious, but they are merely exercising one of the most innate of human impulses.) Until the time when curiosity can be satisfied there is uncertainty, and uncertainty is stress and a problem to be solved (i.e., what is this unfamiliar thing?).

When, for example, we are having special guests for dinner and I plan a superb meal all to be cooked in the oven and I find the electricity has gone off, there is a jolting disparity between my expectations and the real situation I perceive. As time marches on and I wait, expectantly, for the power to come on again, my tensions mount as dinner time grows near and the promise of power goes unfulfilled. I sense approaching disaster, embarrassment, and disappointment. I wrestle with the problem, reacting to the images of disaster in my mind, not knowing how to cope with this little problem that suddenly looms so large. I explore possible solutions, tense and near tears with exasperation when no solution seems good enough to end the fears and worries. Then when a possible solution pops up from out of the depths of my unconscious resources, I can feel myself relaxing. Finally, in a confessing phone call, our friends suggest that we can exchange dinners — they will come for my elegant dinner tomorrow or the next day and tonight they will take us to a good restaurant.

Stress has come and gone — almost. It may be a mini-stress but its impact wrenched body and soul for a few hours and I will probably always remember the distress of the moment. My body will remember, too, and brace itself at the memory.

The effects stress have on people are in direct proportion to the degree of difficulty in solving the stress problem, and this in turn depends upon the intensity and effect of the images about the circumstances on the mind and body. The mini-stress of housebreaking a new puppy can be almost nonexistent for the person familiar with the technique; it can be horrendously exasperating stress for the person who has no idea how to do it. The stress of losing a job in the middle of a severe depression can tax one's emotional and coping resources almost to the breaking point. The tensions that come from unresolved problems is the stress that harms.

As the mind works to deal with the stress problems of life, it conjures up images — re-creating scenes of the worrisome events and making images of a grim future that tend to swing back and forth to dream-images of the way it hopes the future can be. These are the images of problem solving. On the one hand are the images of the past, images that re-create experiences for the mind to explore for possible causes in different places and at different times, images that are scanned by the inner mind for any clue from the past that might shed light on why what is happening now is so different from what was expected or hoped for. On the other hand, there are, as well, images of the future, a guessing game when the mind creates images of scenes where the stress is resolved and scans to find which solution best fits the facts as they are known. It is the images, we will discover, that can both cause and cure dis-ease.

If the mind cannot find a solution to its stress, there comes a time when the mind runs out of cope. With no more ability to cope well enough to get by, the mind is swallowed by dis-ease and distress. Uncertainties swell to anxiety and the mind's images become negative and gloomy and intense because they feed on the uncertainties and the uncertainties feed on the images. The self has failed and the failure is still another unexpected difference from what the self expected. Faced with another unfamiliar circumstance, the curiosity impulse is aroused again. Now it relentlessly pursues why this mind-being has failed, and it pulls the mind operations into a tight circle of insistent rumination and morbid preoccupation so intense that the perceptions become disorted and impaired.

Expectations and perceptions

Strictly speaking, nothing that causes us "stress" is inherently, in itself, stressful. It is only when we *interpret* things or events that they become endowed with the qualities of stress. Take the junior executive who feels the stress of his job. The people he works with, the job responsibilities, the work situation itself — none of these is stressful in itself. It is only when he relates his hopes, his self-analyses, and his reactions to the people and the work that his circumstances become stressful.

The mental activity that most greatly influences what one perceives from the environment is *expectations*. Expectations, too, are the sum of thoughts about ourselves and other people and people-situations, a sort of integrated sum of experience, hopes, desires, and reason. I am always amazed by how we balance hopes with reality, and how often we seem to adjust to disappointments and dashed hopes or bad luck. Then I remember how much most people feel they must "put up a good front" and live up to a social ethic that says intelligent, understanding, mature adults should always be able to cope, and any sign that they can't cope is taken as a defect in intelligence or maturity. And I remember further that grown men *do* cry and no matter what a person's behavior seems on the outside, there can be a bruised psyche on the inside. We feel great hurt and sorrow when life fails our hopes and expectations.

Expectations are products of learning and experience; perceptions are how we interpret our circumstances, while the circumstances of life are events to be observed and interpreted for what they mean to us. When I invite guests for dinner, I expect they will come unless I hear otherwise. If, an hour after time for dinner, they have not arrived, this is a circumstance I observe. A fact. But I am a typical human being, so immediately I begin to wonder why they haven't come — why my expectations haven't been fulfilled. I speculate on possible reasons why they are late — an accident, some emergency, a flat tire, a traffic jam. As each possible reason comes to mind, I use my best common sense to guess the reason. There has been no phone call, so their reason for being late must be either terribly important or not important at all. That is, if there were an accident, I would *expect them to call.* That rules out all the in-between reasons. When another hour passes and my guests fail to arrive, I become more preoccupied with wonder why they haven't come. I am very concerned for their safety, concerned about what to do about dinner, and I'm annoyed, upset, and tense with waiting and not knowing. There has been enough time for them to phone me, so my guesses come down to two: either there has been a terrible emergency or they forgot the date. By this time my feelings are deeply involved. I am in part fearful for their safety and in part angry and hurt because they haven't called or they forgot. When I favor one answer, I have one kind of feeling, and when I favor the other, my feelings change. My mind is generating my feelings.

This, briefly, is the modus operandi of the mind creating stress. The guests not coming is simply a fact. It has no meaning until it is given meaning by the person who observes the fact. In law, for example, the facts of a case, known as the evidence, are interpreted within the special context of a set of laws. The same is true in science. Scientific facts have little meaning until they are interpreted rigidly and systematically as they relate to facts about the same or related phenomena. The facts of the circumstances we encounter in life can be interpreted as precisely as legal or scientific facts. They can be, but usually are not, almost always because related facts needed to give any isolated observation some meaning are either missing or unknown. In the case of my missing guests, the missing data were the facts about whether there was an emergency, whether the telephone lines were down, whether they are chronically forgetful people, where they were at the moment of dinner time, whether they were sick, etc., etc.

Why we perceive things the way we do, or how, is such a fundamental part of human life, it is difficult to realize the complexity of mental activity that goes into the simple act of perception. To perceive means to attach meaning and a degree of significance to the *totality* of what the senses detect. It is complicated because what the senses detect from the environment depends almost entirely on what the senses are paying attention to. And what the senses (the eyes and ears mainly) pay attention to depends a good bit on one's "perceptual set" — that is, what one customarily looks for in the environment, that in turn depends upon experience, training, culture, and a host of beliefs, emotions and attitudes. To perceive is actually to apply quite selectively the sum of one's experience to the information streaming in through the senses to the interpretive parts of the brain.

I have defined stress as: "An unfavorable perception of the social environment and its dynamics that threatens social and psychological well being."

The key is perception — that is, how a person sees his social situation and his role in social relationships and in society in general. The term *social* includes everything pertaining to the behavior of human beings, singly, in groups, or even when they are represented in business or government. When it comes right down to it, nearly all of modern life is made up of interactions with people or with the products of people's activities. And the amount of stress we suffer comes from the way we perceive these interactions and how well we can adjust to them.

A difficult family situation, for example, where one spouse's parents live with the family and seem to be the source of a hundred daily problems, from conflicts about rearing children to a lack of privacy, is a situation that is stressful for everyone involved. But it is particularly stressful because each person sees the situation from his own perceptual set, from his own perspective, colored by his own particular experiences, his own beliefs, his habits, and his attitudes about his own situation, all of which makes communication and the gathering of information very difficult. The resulting interaction of so many different perceptions and expectations makes communication even more difficult and intensifies the potential for stress.

The extraordinary number of influences that can intersect and create stress are summarized in Table 7 (Appendix 1). Each factor covers a multitude of variations that makes each stress so intensely personal.

Curiosity. Key to the intellect

Curiosity is one of those qualities of the human personality that is so ordinary and so instinctive that very little is known about it. It may be, however, the mental mechanism that energizes the entire stress dis-ease sequence. Ethologists have shown curiosity to be an instinct of most unusual qualities. Unlike any other innate behavior, curiosity has no objective to accomplish outside of itself such as hunger, territoriality, nesting, stalking, or bird songs do. It is the only inherited or learned behavior that occurs without any purpose to achieve, fulfill, or complete anything other than its own act. It occurs only to gather information, without any other known motivation, and oddly, it can be instantly turned off when any other feeling or emotion is aroused.

The result of being curious is learning, but it is the *process* of learning that fulfills or rewards the curiosity instinct, not what is learned. This is clear because when people or animals learn something, that learned something need not be used immediately. Instead, the information, now "known," is filed away until it is needed. Only then can it be determined that anything at all was learned.

I suspect our innate impulse to be curious whenever we detect anything new and unexpected is much more than simply the compulsion to explore what is unfamiliar in the environment. In some form or other, all life seems also to possess what may be a related quality — an innate drive to restore order whenever order is disturbed. When a bird's nest is violated by a predator but not wholly destroyed, the bird usually restores the order of the nest with frenzied activity. When we trip and spill lightly to the ground, we instinctively brush away the dirt and smooth our clothes back into their proper order. And when reality clashes with what we feel are quite reasonable or modest expectations, we lash out with our curiosity probes to find out why and restore order in our lives.

I suspect also that our sense of order and innate desire to avoid chaos and to maintain order is the reason we tend to take the same seat in any meeting that has more than one session (as a class). Typically, if you are bold enough to change seats at intermission, the previous occupant shows mild upset at least. The status quo is important in keeping life orderly.

If I seem to be dwelling on curiosity over much, it is for a good reason. Curiosity plays a multiple role in human well beingness. It is essential for learning and crucial to the development of all awarenesses, including self-awareness. And failing to satisfy curiosity may well be the root of all stress.

When curiosity is not satisfied, the effect is stress. A common, innocuous experience of frustrated curiosity is when a friend tells you a tantalizing riddle and then won't tell you the answer. The immediate reaction is a search for the answer along with another Why? — why did he tell me the riddle if he won't tell me the answer? The questions why and what is it are the outward signs of the curiosity drive. The girl, whose awful stress is having been raped, asks why me? why did he do that to me?

When curiosity is satisfied, stress begins to be relieved. The momentary touch of the stress of not knowing the answer to the riddle, for example, vanishes as soon as the answer is explained. (And, remember the big sigh that sort of explodes when he does tell you the answer? That's the relaxation of the body's tension, the bracing to be found silly or dumb.) For the girl whose stress is rape, psychologists now recognize the need to answer the questions. They have developed ways to relieve the deep effects of stress by creating "hot lines," special kinds of group discussions and special psychotherapies.

The curiosity drive plays a dual role. It is the devil's whiphand of stress and the healer's helper in distress.

Chapter 10
Simon says cope

The cauldron that brews stress . . . The stress of problem solving . . . Inner bicker (good worry, bad worry, and problem solving worry) . . . Images—the making and the unmaking of distress . . . The images of distress . . . The consequences of frustrated problem solving . . . Time and space in disease

The cauldron that brews stress

In the next phases of the dis-ease process a series of mental operations "execute a program" pretty much the way a computer does. By comparing an expectation with a perception of some event (see Figure 1), internal perception detects a threat to the psyche and this is the command to the brain's computer to identify the (social) hazard and cope with it. The first thing the brain's computer does is shift its curiosity probes to work for the thought processes. Curiosity now must search for and gather information for identifying the nature of the threat to the psyche and for evaluating just how much of a hazard the threat might be. In this role, curiosity makes a survey of items contributing to the un-desired event, much like a poll taker, feeds this information into the processes that compare the situation to events already in the memory banks and makes a decision about what significance the unexpected, undesired event has for future well being.

When the mind detects some event that might be a hazard to the psyche, the mind goes on alert, often only subconsciously. At first, not enough information is available to decide whether there really is a potential hazard, so now that attention has been alerted, the first mental step is to start identifying the possible threat by cataloguing the information that the curiosity probes send in. Initially this phase is one of "thoughtfully" processing the information. That is, the mind surveys the information, extracts a sort of general notion about what it means, looks over the normal consequences of situations of this kind, then makes decisions about whether some familiar coping device (such as, I'll just ignore that) will work or not.

If, for example, I detect evidence that the factory where I work is changing its work schedules in some rather unusual way, I (my curiosity probes) look for signs that might confirm or deny my impression. The mind is interested but not alarmed or worried. It is simply gathering facts.

The questions the intellect poses generally are *intelligent* concerns about social behavior and relationships — and the subsequent sensations, the feelings and emotions follow the intellectual activity and are *expressions of the intellect concerned about the unsatisfactory way social relationships are perceived and appreciated and projected into the future* (i.e., stress is an unfavorable perception of the future). It is extremely important to recognize how very much all of this intellectual activity occurs within the unconscious domain of the mind. Stop a moment to tune your awareness to the fact that concerns and worries emerge *into* consciousness and that conscious activity has relatively little to do with shaping your perceptions.

After curiosity's *search* program explores the consequences of the troublesome situation, a *decide* program makes one of two different kinds of decisions: one decision says, "oh, I can live with that; I can adjust to that little setback," or it decides the problem isn't worth worrying about or should be ignored or it decides the answer is already in the memory files. It automatically then just goes on to its old reliable list of ways to cope with things and selects the best one. Whichever solution is selected, the mental concern immediately eases and the self is restored to a state of well being.

It is the second kind of decision that leads to stress. This is the decision that says, "I don't understand what is going on," or "I just can't deal with that," or "I just don't know what to do." This is the kind of inner upset that, as the saying goes, really rattles your cage. When the *decide* program assesses the potential hazard as a real threat to the well being of the psyche, it recognizes that stress does, indeed, exist. By reason of a very special linkage between a unique set of thought-behavior patterns and a unique set of human behaviors at special times and special places, the mind perceives a problem that bodes ill for the future.

The stress of problem solving

Solving problems within the dimensions of behavior and social relationships is very different from solving problems in math or physics. Solving personal stress problems involves a good bit of information colored by feelings and attitudes as well as by erratic assumptions that may or may not change as more information is gathered. Solving people-problems can be a surprisingly long process.

Personal problems involve a host of unknown qualities and influences that can take different forms even within the same problem depending upon our mood at the time. In the case of a dispute with the neighbor, for example, about the dogs barking all through the night. Suppose the neighbor insists that the dogs are simply doing their watchdog duty and it's none of your business anyway. Now you have a problem and it really does threaten your future well being. Your mind projects the agony of a hundred more sleepless nights with your emotions becoming ragged and your body faltering because of lack of sleep. Your active mind envisions more ways the neighbor might show his thoughtlessness, from sweeping trash onto your yard to violence, if you pursue your request for quiet. The longer the problem goes unresolved, the more it feeds upon itself and is magnified. Stress is living with an unresolved problem.

There are, also, occasional complications. The first is that personal problems are difficult to define, especially about who is doing what and why. Then, as if stress problems weren't already confusing and difficult enough, there are often problems with the solutions we develop or would like. Usually the solution you like best is impossible (Honey I got a great job today — no more unemployment checks!); often no one answer is best (the court's custody decision gives you no flexibility); or too often we cope with problems impulsively and more hastily than the stress warrants because *we are expected to cope.*

When the mind begins to suspect that it may not be able to develop reasonable, workable, satisfactory solutions (coping; ego defenses), it begins to see its problems as threats to its emotional and social well being. Then, when the usual techniques for handling problems fail and the problems continue, unresolved, our problem solving efforts are frustrated. It is at this point the destructive stress process begins.

Almost always, however, the failure to find answers to one's problems is *not* the failure of the intellect. Virtually every human being has the intellectual capacity to solve almost any problem. The only reason it might not is because the intellect lacks the right kind of information needed to solve the problem.

It is only when problem solving gets into difficulty that the emotions are aroused. When problem solving becomes difficult, we can feel apprehension and anxiety, insecurity and uncertainty, frustration, irritation, or hostility or failure or loss of self-esteem. Emotions *follow* the intellectual work with stress problems, they do not precede them.

Inner bicker (good worry, bad worry, and problem solving worry)

And what is the usual reaction of one's psyche when its inner perceptions detect a possible threat to its well being? Worry. Worry is the natural first reaction to any kind of problem. When we say, "I'm worried about writing that report," it really means we are searching our memory banks for the best kinds of answers to the problem of writing a report.

For most of life's ordinary problems the mind usually comes up with fairly satisfactory solutions to its problems, the operating techniques we call coping devices or defense mechanisms. Most of us most of the time can think our way through problems. We can rationalize, follow customs, substitute another goal, or find some way to protect our egos against disappointment or frustration. This is *productive* worry, the kind of worry that produces answers to our problems that are good enough either to let us survive well or at least get by in life. It is only when we *can't* find answers to our problems that worry can be destructive.

The question WHY? is the curiosity impulse of the intellect and the mental prod that needles the mind to worry. "Why did he do that to me?" "Why did I do that?" "Why did I say that?" "Why did that have to happen to me?" "What (why) did I do wrong?" and a thousand other whys are the curiosity probes that the mind thrusts out to try to understand its human condition.

If worry is really asking the question, why? and is goaded by curiosity to find answers, then *worry is actually problem solving activity*. If we can identify worry this way, then we ought to be able at least to figure out how we could worry better, or use worrying more effectively, or know when to worry and when not to worry.

Normal worry, for example, means we are paying attention to the problem at hand, considering how it started and the best ways for handling it. A little more than average worry means we're having trouble solving a problem and are concerned. Excessive worry means that we have failed in our problem solving. And this is when anxiety and fear for our personal welfare override our intelligent direction of behavior and we are launched on the road to neurotic or physical ills.

It is the familiar concept of worry that best describes the way we wrestle with the stress problems of life and it has, as well, fascinating implications about the stress dis-ease process. It encompasses all of the subjective, private emotions of social stress reactions and it implies, too, the dominant role of cognitive activity. Worry covers both conscious and unconscious worry and can be made up of combinations of all kinds of feelings of concern, insecurity, uncertainty, inadequacy, conflict, frustration, apprehension, and related feelings and emotions. All of these expressions of subjective reactions to difficulties in life are rooted in an *intellectual concern* about one's social life such as adequacy of social performance, the meeting of social criteria for behavior and achieving and success, or ensuring a sense of social well being and social survival. *The subjective sensations are all expressions of a disturbed intellect,* i.e., an intellect disturbed about the way one's social relationships are appreciated and interpreted.

Worry does not always nor even usually evoke emotional reactions. People worry about paying bills, about the energy crisis, about the education of children, about what color to paint the walls or about what to serve guests, without much emotion at all. It is only when effective worry begins to fail that emotional reactions occur. The primary process is intelligent problem solving; emotions are secondary.

Let's examine worry and the dis-ease process as stress develops in a specific situation. Take one of the newer stresses, the stress of sexual harassment of working women. The scene is the workplace, an environment where the woman has come to believe she can prove her abilities and be successful. An important supervisor approaches her with sexual advances and she responds with varieties of coping devices she has learned before. The encounters are spaced over days and weeks and keep her in a state of uncertainty and tension. The woman expected a business relationship but she very quickly realizes she is being cornered into a sexual relationship.

Our lady is concerned. She doesn't first panic, emote wildly, break out into a sweat or hyperventilate — those are all symptoms of exhausted coping resources. This lady is still in the initial phases of the stress process, that of defining her problem and searching for a good answer. The lady first observes, looks for clues about what the future might bring, sorts out all her information that could help to solve the problem, and then tries out different ways of coping, first in mental images she projects into the future and then in the real life situation. The man, however, persists and eventually her coping fails.

As time goes on the problem becomes more and more disturbing. The lady worries more and more. Her psychological well being is threatened and her future is in jeopardy. Concern becomes worry and worry begins to flood the mind with images and fears for the future. She is now fully aware how serious the problem is. Two different conflicts, in fact, intrude into her awareness, neither crystal clear but obvious danger signals nonetheless. There is the enormous conflict about personal values, whether to submit and use the skirmish for personal gain or report the incident and chance being ignored. And there is the conflict about the job itself, whether to stick with it and hope the problem can go away or to give it up now and start over. This is a perfect example of what I emphasize so often about the stress dis-ease process — if I have a problem, it *is* reasonable (intelligent) to worry and become mentally and physically alerted as a way of concentrating on solving the problem.

Images — the making and the unmaking of distress

I am beginning to suspect that mental images hold all the keys to health and illness as well as the keys to achieving, fulfillment, and well being of the human spirit.

Images are a way of abstracting units of related recollections that are important to us in some way. They *represent* complex things and events in ways that can be best appreciated and fit into one's personalized memory banks, such as the ways of seeing, hearing, feeling, conceptualizing, etc. Musicians, for example, often have feeling-images about music that integrate all the things that can make it sound the way it should sound, the mood that can create a particular sound, or a sense of the movements needed to produce the sound. No single feeling or idea works; it is the sensation of the *whole,* integrated feeling-image that makes for understanding and for good performance.

In problem solving, images are summoned up in the mind as units of information about different aspects of the problem. If I am working a jigsaw puzzle, for example, I form a mental image that gives me information about the shape or size or potential place of a piece. Remember, it does not have to be a visual image. It can be some vague feeling about dimensions or shape, perhaps some idea about how the shape might feel. Or, if I want to balance my check book, I rehearse quickly, almost subliminally, in imagination the successive operations of adding, subtracting, multiplying, etc. Again, a visual image is not necessary. We need only a "memory state" in which quasi-awareness *scans* groups of associated elements that form a picture or symbol or idea needed for the task at hand such as problem solving. The mental picture or strings of ideas is a *mental image.*

Quite possibly, imagery may be the most critical influence affecting the well being of human beings. Mental images are, in a large sense, the mind's tools for displaying and scanning whole patterns of related material — real or imagined — a uniquely efficient way of extracting important information. (Note again: images are not necessarily or, even often, visual.) When some event from the past is recalled and reconstructed as a mental image, the event can be scanned, how it started can be scanned, each small item or detain can be scanned, the associated beliefs, attitudes, and feelings can be examined and *re-experienced*. We use images from the past to gather clues for problem solving, or to enjoy memories or to learn from past experience.

Equally as important and perhaps most important to human welfare is the ability of human beings to construct images about the future. When anything in the future is considered, images are constructed out of what is known about the future, what is desired for a future event, and often the feelings that may be experienced in the future can be projected and experienced now and planned for.

Mental images allow human beings to learn from experience without having to repeat experiences until learning occurs. That is, they allow us to make mistakes in the mind only. Images can be good entertainment, as when we daydream or dream or fantasize, but they can also punish us for our mistakes as when we repeatedly review mistakes and play the mental "what if" game.

Whether images are from the past or are images projected into the future, the mind intentionally manipulates different parts of any image. With an image reconstructed from the past you may want to explore a "what if" situation (what if I hadn't said that; what if he hadn't been there), while with an image of the future you can rehearse your behavior and reactions as a way of helping you decide the best and most useful way to behave in the future.

During problem solving (worrying) we all use mental images in many ways. First, we attempt to reconstruct the situation, and we call up as many memories as possible about the circumstances that are related to the problem. Since *we* are involved, our thoughts and emotions and bodies are also part of the memories. We essentially re-enact the problem — over and over — in all its variations and for all the different times and places that might have contributed to the problem. *And for every memory our mental images reconstruct the physical postures of our physical reactions.*

But by far the most fundamental and significant feature of mental images is their stubborn bond with the physiology of the body. The best examples of the role of imagery in stress and its effects on the body come from Jacobson's work on anxiety and muscle tension. In working with varieties of supervisors who took part in decision-making conferences, for example, he was able to show that the muscle tensions they showed (and he recorded) were exact duplicates of the tensions they felt during the conferences although, of course, much less intense. The forehead muscles were contracted in an attention mode, the neck and shoulder muscles also showed an attention posture — even the muscles around the ears were tense as if trying to listen intently. But these were the *muscle tensions caused by the memory* of the conferences — events represented by images of the conferences. Jacobson called them tension-images.

To get an idea of the power of imagery, analyze what happens when you imagine sucking on that sour lemon (see page 62). The salivary juices flow, and sometimes one has the sensation of changed gastric motility. These are exactly the same physical effects that physically sucking a sour lemon produces. But now the effect is produced by imagination only. What the lemon-image example means is that, first, a conscious thought can direct the mind to create a specific image. The mind doesn't simply go "presto!" and conjure up the image . . . not at all. The conscious mind tells something else in the mind to re-create a very specific sensation and perform a specific act. Some mental operation not known to conscious awareness searches the memory and associates the instruction with the memory of a sensation need to produce an image. Once the image is formed, another mental operation (intention) says, "O.K., stimulate the nerves to the salivary glands." For, you see, we can also imagine sucking a sour lemon in the abstract, and whether or not the image stimulates salivation depends entirely on what the state of our attention, motivations, and decisions is at the moment of imagery.

The effects of imagination on the body are everywhere. Aside from the inferences we can make about the role of unconscious mental activity in imagination, there are two extremely interesting and fundamental principles we can deduce. The first is that the more specific the image, the more specific the effect. That is, the image becomes more capable of exciting *exactly* those physical mechanisms of the body to produce the physical reactions to the image. (This may explain why imagery therapy works and it also suggests we could improve imagery therapy.) And the second principle we can deduce about imagination is that *mental images can cause a very real expenditure of physical energy* (see Jacobson; also Table 8).

I am beginning to believe that the effect of mental images on the body's physiology may be the critical mechanism producing both stress and reactions to stress. Certainly we are now learning that imagery can *reverse* not only the effects of stress (as in self-suggestion, etc.), but actually assist healing the physical disorders stress causes. Along with system susceptibilities such as a "weak" cardiovascular system or with initial psychic traumas (reacting to a spanking by holding the breath and later developing asthma) — the role of mental images may explain why stress reactions can be transformed into so many different kinds of distress.

The images of distress

Dredging up the past in imagery in search of clues to resolve a stress problem is not the only way in which imagery plays its important role in the stress dis-ease process. Imagery is also absolutely essential in problem solving. In the very special domain of human interactions, a great deal of the solving of personal problems is mental trial-and-error. That is, the information we have to work with may or may not be reliable. After all, it comes from the uncertainties of interpreting human behavior and so we never know exactly what facts we can use in trying to solve our stress problems. We have to try out different possible solutions in the mind. We say to ourselves such things as, well, if he really meant that, then I can tell him how I feel, or we try another solution when we decide he really didn't mean what he said. That is, we formulate possible solutions to our stress problems in our minds and project them forward in time in our imagination. We continue the dialogue with ourselves, saying such things as, "tomorrow I'll confront him with the way I feel," or "next week in that conference I will argue my case," or "they say I have grieved enough so tomorrow I'll join the gang for lunch."

The images are all action-images. They project the self into a situation directly related to the situation that created the stress. And because they are action-images, *the body reacts exactly as imagined.* The muscles tense and the inner, vital systems shift to tension states. The stress tensions are re-created and created in images.

As problem solving fails, the perception of the social problem intensifies. Images become more and more disconcerting and ominous, and the situation comes to be perceived as a threat to social and psychological well being because the future is uncertain. Since no intelligent or emotional defense has been forthcoming, it seems likely that the threat to social well being becomes generalized to the whole being and so includes the physical body as well. Only at this late stage in the stress process does a threat to physical well being emerge and can then appropriately stimulate the arousal response as a physical defense mechanism.

As coping with the stress (the problem solving) becomes more difficult, the mental images tend to focus more and more on the circumstances of the stress and with the stress*ee* in the image; the stress postures are mimicked and body tensions add. Then, as problem solving becomes still more difficult and uncertainty increases, mental images of fearful expectations hover subliminally and the body carries an expectancy posture. That is, the body braces itself both to be hyper-alert to fresh psychic assaults and to adopt a resisting mode that will signal the mind to hesitate and think first before acting. *Bracing is a response to a thought-product* and much different from the reflex arousal response.

The consequences of frustrated problem solving

The failure or apparent inability of the mind to cope with stress represents a mind that has exhausted its resources. It literally has no place to go — it has explored every possible answer to the problem with all the information it can muster and none works or is practical. The impasse, however, doesn't stop the mind. It is, as I have described, driven by its innate drive to know and to understand.

This curiosity drive, goaded by uncertainty and by unfavorable images, is now totally thwarted yet it refuses to quit and simply starts asking the same questions over again — and over and over. The mind ruminates, i.e., it chews the same cud over and over again. It mentally reviews every bit of information it has and projects the same old answers into the future — again and again. The problem can't be solved (actually the mind *thinks* it can't be solved) yet the mind cannot rest until it finds some answers. It starts a circular activity — recirculating the information, attitudes, and conclusions it already has until the weight of so much recycled, negative-going information disables the problem solving process and the mind no longer searches for new information and no longer tries to solve its problems.

Instead, because the same old unsatisfactory or frightening images are constantly being recirculated, the constant attention to negative images reinforces all the emotions of stress and anxiety. Rumination has still another very destructive effect: it maintains *attention on the distress* rather than on problem solving. With the attention turned to the feelings of distress, the perceptual field becomes narrowed. Less and less attention is paid to what is actually going on and more and more attention is paid to the disasters of the images. In this state everything one experiences is interpreted in a way that fits with or reinforces some undesirable or inappropriate solution. The mind becomes preoccupied with the sensations of uncertainty and unrest and doom. Things are no longer as they are but as they fit one or another disastrous outcome. This state of the mind is typified by the observation, "Oh, she hears only what she want to hear and she sees only what she wants to see."

At the same time, and presumably for the same reason, the perception of important internal signals about physiological activities becomes obstructed. Sometimes known as "cortical inhibition," the appreciation faculties of the cortex fail to detect the tensions developing in the body and so they continue to build.

Without the brain's higher regulation, the primitive muscle tissue simply adapts to higher and higher levels of muscle tension. Further, with the mind ruminating on its difficulties, it sees them as continuing threats to well being and so it continues to send messages down to the lower muscle regulating centers to stay alert to the danger (to stay tense, ready to take action).

By this time anxiety and disturbing images have so activated the body the body rushes messages to the brain that it is overtensed. The mind feels the sensations but can do nothing to relax the tensions because it is still sending message to the body that the body must stay alert so that the self can protect itself. The anxiety, the feelings of anxiety, and the body tensions all combine to shift the mind's attention to the disturbed feelings rather than keeping the attention on problem solving. In this way the "cortical inhibition" reinforces rumination and diverts the mind from its problem solving activity. The total effect then accelerates dis-ease into disease.

Time and space in dis-ease

Failures of emotional or physical health caused by the stress of life take time to develop. Stress is not a continuous pressure from the outside — the circumstances of life are always changing. People adapt and adjust to situations. The person under job stress doesn't have the stress *all* the time. Many days or weeks can go well even when the job stress hangs overhead like a storm cloud. Nor are the stress circumstances always in the same place. One part of the stress may be a co-worker in the next office, another part may be the boss in a distant office, and still another part might be the pile of memos on the desk. The unique characteristic of stress is that the occasions for stress are discontinuous in time and space. It is the mind that has to piece together all the evidence from things happening at different times and in different places.

The mini-mood swings that are a part of ordinary human behavior reveal how our moods reflect the way our minds work with our stress events that are separated in space and time. Unable to project a satisfying future, the mind worries about the way life can or might be in the future. The mood brightens at every glimpse of hope that something may dispel the dismay, and the mood sinks into despair when the outlook is bleak. It is at those times of intense concern for the future that mind and body tense, fearful of the outcome and bracing for the worst. The longer stress problems stay unresolved, the more the tensions build, imperceptibly but inexorably until the tensions exceed the limits of the body's ability to control them.

The destructiveness of stress depends entirely upon how much stress the coping mechanisms can handle. When the circumstances are the commonly occurring stresses of life, such as job or family stress, or even the daily mini-stresses, the harm of stress occurs when there is simply too much of it — stress for too long or too many different stresses coming too close together. One may be muddling through job stress, but when family problems, financial problems and health problems are added, the total stress can exceed the resources and energy needed to cope.

And while the more dramatic circumstances of less common kinds of stress, such as unexpected loss or failure, would seem to be very different from the ordinary stress of life, the destructiveness of sudden, severe stress (grieving the death of a loved one; enforced separation from family; unexpected failure) runs a rather similar course. Although the impact occurs acutely, the meaning of events (social relationships and situations) prior to the disaster has been built up gradually, usually over many years, and any rupture of such a meaningful relationship takes a long time to adjust to and repair.

While potentially cataclysmic alterations of lifestyle are immediate rather than potential as are the psychic threats of ordinary stress, the emotional reactions are, nonetheless, also based on intellectual appraisals of the meaning of the loss to the self. The man who suddenly and unexpectedly loses his wife of thirty years must cope not only with profound grief, but with a radically changed lifestyle as well.

Recovery from the distress of stress always requires nearly as much (or sometimes more) weaving together of the changed perceptions, repair of images, building defenses of the psyche and lowering of tensions in as many different spaces and in as many different times as were involved to mend one's wholeness and harmony.

Chapter 11

The healing power of information and the subliminal mind

The role of the intellect in health and healing . . . The information that heals . . . How information relieves stress . . . The importance of body awareness . . . The information miracle — instant healing . . . The subliminal theatre of ease and dis-ease . . . The mystery of the covert healing wisdom . . . The dis-ease immune system, a creation of the psyche

The role of the intellect in health and healing

For me, the most exciting frontiers unfolding in our changing notions about health and illness are the tantalizing clues about the role of the intellect in achieving states of well being. The intellect has not been considered important either as a cause or a cure of emotional or physical distress. Nonetheless, the compelling characteristic of stress is that it *is* created by the mind through its intellectual activities that are not distorted or skewed or abnormal in any way. Stress is created out of perfectly normal intellectual activity.

What, really, is the intellect? What does it do?

Everyone, but *everyone,* possesses the mental means to be intelligent. The chief work of the intellect is to put our observations and impressions about things in life into orderly arrangements so that the relationships among things, events, or elements can be recognized as credible. Intelligence, the faculty of thought and reason, is the capacity to acquire and apply knowledge (information).

Although everyone would seem to possess the capacity for intelligence, obviously not all people are intelligent. I'm always shocked by the experts who assume that people are "dumb" or "slow" or not very bright simply because they don't think the way the experts tell us they are *supposed* to think. Au contraire, ma chérie! Most people who seem to be not so intelligent can almost invariably be found to be *informationally deprived* in some way. Some people are not only *not* given information in life, they are never shown even reasonably adequate ways to organize the information they do have. Other people are deprived of both academic and practical knowledge. The most common example is the information deprivation of many minorities who are rarely given information about the realities of the majority world they have to live in.

Stress is an awareness about a relationship with a person, people, or people-things (like the economy) that isn't what you expected or would like it to be and you become concerned about how things will go in the future.* One special characteristic of the stress of life is that it builds up from experiences in different places and spaces and at different times.

Since the circumstances of stress can be in many different places and at many different times, there must be some mechanism of the intelligence that can pull all the impressions together. Dad's work stress, for example, can include his interactions with a boss, co-workers, helpers, volunteer or associated sports groups, and the occasions of stress can be in the factory, in an office, in a conference room, in the cafeteria or the bowling alley. There is a theme of stress the mind carries with it, always alert for a clue here or there to flesh out the story. It is a theme that flows through all the spaces and times of the individual's experience. One of the most elegant but least recognized abilities of mind is its ability to construct and reconstruct sets of related social events, circumstances, dynamics and relationships to create reasonable pattern-images of *many events occurring through social time and social space* (and another role for imagery). Threats to future well being, real or imagined, are appreciated in consciousness only through intellectual mechanisms capable of processing *discontinuous* events and meanings in the social environments.

Since detecting a problem in the social environment can be

*For other ways of defining stress, see Appendix 2.

achieved only via the intelligent mind, it can be assumed that any reaction to discovering a problem will also occur in the intelligent domain (information processing) of the mind. The interpretation of a threat to social well being gives rise to *intellectual* concerns, i.e., concerns about one's social performance, about one's own special, psychological well being and survival. Subjective sensations (feelings, emotions) *follow* intellectual concern and are expressions of an intellect concerned about the way social relationships are perceived, appreciated, interpreted, and projected into the future.

There is, further, abundant evidence that stress develops only because the intellectual processes lack the information needed to understand what stress really is and how it affects mind and body. Even in the worst of stress intellectual functions operate normally enough with the information available to them. As I pointed out earlier, if I have a problem (stress), it *is* reasonable (intelligent) to worry and it *is* reasonable to become mentally and physically alerted as a way of paying attention and to keep concentrating on trying to solve the problem. Problems cannot, however, be solved if the information needed to solve them is not available.

If we human beings do possess such talented intellects that can detect hidden stress problems and then worry about them intelligently, why do so many of us suffer stress? The next section will help to answer that question.

The information that heals

Agatha Christie always had Hercule Poirot saying he would have to use his "little gray cells" to get the key to a mystery. The little gray cells are, of course, what make the mind and brain work, and finding relief from stress absolutely needs the help of the little gray cells.

Hercule Poirot, as Sherlock Holmes before him, was a Master of Logical Thought. It was, of course, their profession. But most people, unschooled and ungeniused in the art and science of problem solving, are left to their natural devices. And what most people do not know is that nearly everyone has a natural, high-level intellect just waiting for release from the bondage imposed by cultures and myths and fears. For most of us this intellect labors in the obscure, little known recesses of the "unconscious" mind.

A popular device in decision making illustrates this nicely. That is, taking a pause in the sorting out of the pros and cons to "sleep on it." So often when we put decision making on the back burner or when we really do sleep on it, a course of action surfaces and decisions become easier. Somehow we seem to come up with what we feel are the right decisions. We can only deduce that some "intelligent" process got our information all straightened out and put into logical order so that the conclusions made good sense. Many scientific studies report logical, productive thought during the deepest stages of sleep, but because we, ourselves, cannot observe or have a sensation of this mental activity, we say it occurs in the unconscious mind. The logic of the symbolic dream, too, is contrived without conscious awareness or help and can be astoundingly erudite.

The process of putting one's observations and thoughts into some systematically organized arrangement is carried out much more efficiently by unconscious mental processes than it is during conscious awareness. How many times have you suddenly said — out of the blue — "Oh, *now* I get it!" meaning that all of a sudden, maybe hours later, you understood something you didn't understand before. That little old unconscious mind was sorting out information all the time, organizing it in a proper order to be convincing, and then when it was done, it sent a signal to conscious awareness that it had the answer.

The most remarkable example of the ability of the mind to develop complex and highly successful stress reduction stategies is the kind Freud cited so many times. I, too, often use a similar example because it so perfectly illustrates both ingenious intellect and the fact that this intellect can flourish without any hint to conscious awareness. Freud began his most famous studies with analyses of what are called the paralytic hysterias. Elsewhere I have described a remarkable case of hysterical blindness I encountered in college. In this episode, two weeks before final exams, the most popular girl in our class, who was also a straight A student and beauty queen to boot, was hospitalized because she had suddenly become blind. The diagnosis was "hysterical" blindness.*

As the episode was later reconstructed, she had developed an unconscious conflict. Unconsciously she feared that because of her many activities, she might not get her usual A's and her failure would be exposed by the coming exams. Her unconscious intellect had seized upon an ideal answer — if she couldn't see the exam no one could criticize her for ducking it. In her case, Freud's unconscious defense was the incredible, complete, and specific *mental* block of nerve conduction in the visual cortex (where visual impulses from the eye are integrated into images). Through the years psychiatry has interpreted such unconscious defenses as inappropriate and pathological.† That just goes to show how removed from reality psychiatry can sometimes be. I contend this girl's unconscious intellect performed brilliantly. Her plight caused so much sympathy her professors scheduled new exams for her long after her recovery (which came right after finals) and, unencumbered by school activities, she studied and made all A's!

How information relieves distress

The vehicle that enables communication between the external world and the interior mind-brain-body world of the individual is information (knowledge). How we behave, what we think, and how we think all depend upon the information we have about us and about them and about how to use that information. When our information is inadequate or misleading or deceptive, there are conflicts between the external world of people and people-events and the interior concept-forming, decision-making functions of the mind. Stress is, basically, the consequence of a lack of information about both the mental and physical self.

No problem, arithmetic or life problem, can be solved if the information necessary for the solution is not available. Worse, the kinds of problems we face as we live our lives have little relation-

*The hysteria of the paralytic hysterias is not the hysteria of uncontrollable laughter or crying, but means "conversion" symptoms, that is, the transformation of a psychological conflict into physical symptoms. Patients usually maintain a *calm* mental attitude and with or without signs of mental aberrations.

†It is important to remember that most psychoanalytic explanations are based on comparisons of suspect behavior to behavior *expected* by society, and society's standards and expectations have undergone radical changes since these theories were formulated.

ship to the streamlined exactness of problems in arithmetic. To solve problems in the arena of human relationships we need a surprising variety of information that can throw light on the many interacting parts of the stress scenario.

One kind of information we need is information about the social reality, i.e., about how and what and why people think and behave the way they do in real life. And because human behavior is most often a facade that complies with the social consensus and hides private thoughts and motives and feelings, the best anyone can do is to store up a lot of good general information from experience about human behavior and about the dynamics of human social interactions.

Because stress arises out of the way we interpret our circumstances and interactions with people, and the vagaries of human behavior are such that it is easier to *mis*interpret than interpret behavior accurately. Thus another kind of information we need in solving stress problems is more accurate information about human behavior than most of us have in order to interpret people's behavior accurately. I've often thought we should teach people how to achieve a Reality Quotient that could keep them aware of the Practical Reality and how to cope with it while striving for the Ideal Reality (an R.Q. would be much more useful than an I.Q.).

Another major kind of information deficiency we live with is the lack of knowledge about what influences our own behavior and what makes *us* tick, how we, personally, think, develop attitudes and beliefs, and how and why we develop feelings, and how all these inner activities affect our external behavior and our performances and our achievements.

There are two other areas of our own personal domain where we lack enormous amounts of the kind of information we need to live with a minimum of stress. One is knowing how the *mind* works. We say such things as, "I should have been able to figure that out" or "I just can't decide." There hasn't been a great deal of knowledge accumulated about the actual everyday workings of the mind. (If you read about research on memory, for instance, try to figure out whether it has any possible relationship to you. Chances are it won't.) I often wish that University Extension Schools would give courses on, say, the psychology of everyday living, or how your mind really works (instead of lectures on experiments on rats), or on different ways people can think, and, most important, how to solve everyday stress problems.

Lastly, most people need information about how to apply all of the many kinds of information they need to solve their stress problems! Remember the all-A student in senior high who always made marvelous grades but never could seem to be able to be successful in a job? Or, have you ever gotten a kit to assemble and found a critical instruction much too obscure to follow? While most people believe they have enough information to do something, they often falter somewhere along the line because they can't figure out how to use the information they do have. The how-to-apply information is usually hidden in the how-to information, and the trick is to pay really strict attention to every tiny bit of information there is.

The importance of body awareness information

The other, and extremely important, kind of information human beings need to ensure well being is information about how the body works — that is, information about the physiology of the body, how the mind relates to the body, and the ways the body can be harmed and also healed.

Most people know very little about how our biology changes under stress and the signs we could watch for. And we have had no teaching at all (until very recently) about how to develop awarenesses of the body's different states. Most muscle tensions of stress, for example, are not felt at all. We become aware of the tensions only when we can relax enough that our attention is no longer focused on our stress or on how or if we are performing well enough to achieve our goals. Worse, we have not only *not* been taught to be aware of body sensations and the information these sensations give us, we have actually been taught *not* to pay attention to our feelings. In a reporter's story in the news the other day, he wrote about the funeral of a slain police officer. He wrote that a police officer weeping at the funeral "failed to hide his grief." The old stiff upper lip behavior may please the sergeant major, but it can be a formidable obstruction to becoming aware of the physical being. Our society has spawned many behavior codes that not merely repress feelings but deprive the self of the information it should have about its body — and mind — state. Many cultural injunctions inhibit becoming aware of the states of inner health or inner tensions (chest out, chin up), and so the body adapts to tensions, and as more stress is encountered, tensions keep on adding. For additional discussions about the importance of learning awareness of body states to detect stress levels and ways to deal with body distress, please see Chapter 4 and Chapter 12.

The information miracle — instant healing

Among the *mental* medical marvels are the cases of instant healing. I don't mean miracles as at Lourdes because I have some difficulty accepting instant reconstruction of torn tissues or fractured bodies. There are, however, thousands of miracle cures of psychical hurts with intense physical involvement that go unreported. Take the paralyzing anxiety of waiting for the diagnosis of your ailment you are sure is a serious cancer. Your soul and gut and muscles and heart have been tied up in knots perhaps for weeks. Then, "Perfectly benign," the doctor tells you. You flush with suppressed relief, the skin freezes momentarily in a clammy hold, then tingles with relief. Your head feels stuffed with data, decisions, images, fears, and then the stuffiness melts and drains and you feel a surge of excitement, then joy, and finally the sigh comes and the crisis has passed. The weeks of anxiety, knots in the stomach, catches in the breath, pounding heart, sweats of fear, the strain of sadness — they are all gone. In an instant. The instant healing of information.

The unique emotional "release" phenomenon that occurs sometimes in psychotherapy is another dramatic illustration of the instant healing of a psychic injury. As explained more fully in Chapter 12, there are times in therapy, and especially with Autogenic Training (an imagery-relaxation technique), when the patient's body begins to shake with uncontrollable spasms. Usually in five or so minutes after the attack passes the person experiences a marvelous euphoria. Tensions are gone, anxiety has disappeared, the body feels relaxed, ready to race or play. On a less intense emotional scale, people who bottle up their feelings while they cope with some emotional trauma and later break down in sobs usually experience a similar kind of relief.

In such cases it is theorized that the anxiety of uncertainty about the future sends messages from the interpretive cortex to the muscle control centers of the lower brain to keep the muscles uptight and tense in case the worst may happen (and messages *from* the muscles back to the brain are recognized by the higher brain and interpreted as sensations of tension, and these sensations then intensify the feelings of anxiety).* Because of various biological factors, these "keep-tense" messages from the cortex pile up at the lower brain-muscle junction, and when the anxiety is *mentally* relieved, the muscles begin to relax, and as they relax and stop sending their tension messages up to the brain, there is a reflex release of all the piled up (unused) "keep-tense" messages *from* the cortex. The flood of the released tension messages is so great and so helter-skelter, all the muscles respond in as coordinated a way as possible under the circumstances. The result is a kind of rhythmic, rapid, tensing-relaxing alternation we call shaking.

I tend to suspect there is more to the story. It seems likely that as the subliminal intellect begins to understand the causes for the stress, it also recognizes that the alertness and bracing are no longer necessary and are now, in fact, irrational reactions. This mental event may be the signal either to get rid of the "keep-tense" messages (they can't back up, so they have to flow on down to the muscles) or to send messages to the tension releasing mechanisms that in turn activate the flood of tension impulses that causes the shaking. Whichever way it works, it is an incredible instance of instant healing.

This somewhat involved mechanism for discharging tensions may also be the same mechanism that causes the good feelings and near euphoria so often experienced by runners and joggers.†

There is still another role of information that can cause almost

---

*See also pages 66 and 118.
†In each instance of instant "feel good" there is the likelihood that the muscle activity generates changes in the brain's endomorphin levels (the "brain's opiates," although I prefer the label the "brain's euphoriates").

instant healing. It may be, in fact, the most important role despite how silly it sounds — that we need the information that we need information. As I repeat at every opportunity, we all grow up believing we should be able to cope with most of life's problems, and most people hurl themselves impetuously into coping only to suffer frustrations because their coping doesn't work.

Take the family faced with having to take a set of parents into the home and be their main support as well. The stress is everywhere, in the coming added expenses, the physical energy needed to care for two more when the family is already working all day, the need to soft-pedal discussions of values that have changed, wondering how to handle visiting friends, and a thousand more thorny problems. Then a neighbor says, "Have you tried the Seniors Aid Society? They have all kinds of ideas about how to handle these kinds of problems. They know where to get help for free and might even be able to locate some cooperative housing for your parents." Instant relief. There *are* answers. Sure, we'd heard something about the help before, but when it's your problem, somehow the memory channels get clogged up with the worries, and we forget. Getting a "handle" on a problem gives noticeable instant relief.

For one thing, the problem becomes a step away from being so personal. Becoming aware that you need information before you can even start to work out your problems takes away a lot more blame for your situation than you think it might. It means you aren't so dumb after all and you can stop blaming yourself for not coping perfectly. Becoming aware you need information also stirs up hopes that with the right kind of information you *can* solve your problem. Now you begin to understand that the information you need really is out there somewhere and you can probably get it. The relief is also a relief from guilt feelings. We've all grown up with the idea we should be able to solve our problems pretty much by ourselves, and so now we suddenly realize that our helplessness is not something to feel guilty about. When we have information about anything we have been fearful about or concerned about, half the uncertainty disappears, and with it go the feelings of uneasiness and anxiety.

The subliminal theatre of ease and dis-ease

Some people and some professionals have a bit of trouble accepting the idea that a working intellect operates in the part of the mind unknown to conscious awareness. Among the experts there is still no consensus about what consciousness is or what unconsciousness is or what goes on in each. I have conducted more research and analyses on the unconscious than most of my mind-brain research colleagues, and I am convinced that there is an intellect in the parts of the mind for which we have little or no conscious awareness. Yet because there must be communication between the conscious and unconscious aspects of mind, I often use the phrase "subliminal intellect" as a sort of compromise term to describe the unconscious intellect and its potential to operate also in quasi-conscious awareness.* Whatever the state of awareness of our working intellect may be, this covert intellect accomplishes truly incredible feats of mind.

The most remarkable ability of the subliminal intellect is its capacity to put all the information it receives into a precise, orderly arrangement that appears to approximate the natural order of the universe. Getting data (information) in the right order is the process that allows logic to be applied so that deductions and conclusions can be made about the meaning of the information. Let me give you two examples here of how this subliminal operation of the intellect works; one example is of a mechanical event, and the other how new discoveries are made about the nature of the universe.

One of the marvelous things about the new personal computers is that as long as you assign numbers to the lines you use in writing a program, you can enter lines at any time, helter-skelter, then press the LIST key, and magically, every line is now listed in

---

*"Subliminal," as in subliminal perception, simply means that which is perceived (sound, image) exists below the threshold for conscious recognition. In subliminal perception, the proof of the phenomenon lies in demonstrating a direct response to a subliminally perceived instruction (such as a sample population actually buying more Snicky Snacks after being exposed to subliminal messages to buy Snicky Snacks) without any conscious awareness of either the message or the reaction. I mean to imply a similar situation with respect to the subliminal intellect — that is, that this intellect evaluates information and makes judgments and decisions and directs behavioral activity, all without conscious awareness that these mental events have occurred.

numerically consecutive order on the screen. The computer sorts the numbers according to a precise ordering program. There appears to be, perhaps not so strangely, a similar super sorting mechanism within the human mind-brain (not so strange since the human mind invented the numbering systems). We know that all science and especially the science of prediction rests upon man's ability to put things in order.

There is, moreover, a great deal of evidence for the existence of an ordering mechanism that operates subliminally within the unconscious mind. This subliminal intellect can often put scattered bits of information into a meaningful order that we cannot do during conscious awareness states. A well known subconscious information ordering episode concerns an organic chemist from the last century who dreamed the molecular structure of the benzene ring and was later able to prove it was correct.

The scientist no doubt had his head stuffed with information about the chemical properties and reactions of benzene, but in the waking state simply could not put the facts together in a way that met all known characteristics of benzene. But away from the distractions of myth and controversy and other mental pressure, the subliminal intellect could accomplish its ordering task much more easily. One can only guess that when the mind is supplied with adequate and relevant information, it can and does put it all into the order that best approximates the natural order of things in the universe and the intentions of the mind director, conscious or not.

I suspect any hesitancy in accepting the unconscious (subliminal) intellect as profound and quite possibly superior to the intellect of our conscious states may be the tenacious belief that human beings are designed in the image of a watchful goodness that could never allow its greatest gift, its intellect, to be hidden from conscious awareness. Instead, it is acceptable to endow the unconscious with great mental hazards that, as notions in psychiatry suggest, can injure or destroy its own being when it creates mental illness and unrealistic ways to cope with life. The fallacy of the belief is that the unconscious intellect *intentionally* creates misery. As I analyze the stress dis-ease process, there is no personal guilt or error. Misery comes only from circumstances that one feels are treating one unfairly, and from the lack of information about what led to the feeling and information about how to deal with the circumstances to relieve the miseries.

The subliminal intellect can, however, be prevented from carrying out its ordering task (understanding its circumstances). Strong beliefs, such as superstitions, can obstruct the subliminal intellect. Men who live with the macho image block their inner intelligence, as do the elderly who believe the myths about sex and the elderly. Or, the subliminal intellect can be blocked by allegiance to the consensual consciousness (I'm middle class, I should go to college), and it can be easily brainwashed in the presence of ignorance (why shouldn't I buy the Brooklyn Bridge?). All these beliefs are sustained by building psychic defenses and mental walls around the beliefs to form a cocoon and protect the mind-psyche structure of the belief from being pierced and prevent hurtful thought-arrows from gaining access to the psyche. When the psyche is cocooned in this way, the subliminal intellect operates in a way that inserts all new information through only one slot, so to speak, such that all new information can be associated only with the stuff of the psychic cocoon. If the armor is accidentally pierced by reason or is crushed by excessive stress, the subliminal intellect can be liberated to perform its usual chores. More usually, when some concept or some insight penetrates the armor and the armored one begins to feel the armor tear and can no longer maintain the defense, the subliminal intellect begins to restructure its informational reservoirs into systems that more nearly resemble the person-order of the universe.

The mystery of the covert healing wisdom

The healing wisdom of the subliminal intellect has been documented endlessly. Consider the well-known "waiting list" study. People who applied to an outpatient psychiatric clinic were separated into two groups, one receiving immediate crisis intervention treatment and the other group simply put on a waiting list — and they waited — untreated. After six weeks, improvement of the emotional distress was the same for both groups.

We all know, of course, that if we can live through the acute first hurt or pain or fear, our problems automatically become less traumatic and often seem to resolve themselves. It may be a bit of a shock to learn, however, that *no* treatment for emotional problems may be just as good as quality psychiatric treatment. Most people who get no help at all often report that somehow they got their "head together" and were able to figure things out.

Another well-known study illustrates this point and also how the innate intelligence can often be a better healer than standard treatments. This study involved delinquent boys, ages six to ten. One group received eight (8!) years of psychological counseling and psychotherapy while a parallel group received no treatment at all. It was found, after the eight years, that there were more delinquent episodes in the group receiving counseling and psychotherapy than in the boys who had no treatment or help at all.

This is only one of many studies in which no treatment has bested psychotherapy, yet nowhere in psychology circles has the obvious conclusion been voiced that "classical" psychotherapy may actually *prevent* the normalizing, healing process and may, instead, sustain diminished well being. As people have become more informed about their psyches and feelings and emotions, fewer and fewer cases of emotional pathology have been recorded. And with the emphasis shifting to concerns about fulfillment and self-realization, there is less and less classical psychotherapy and more and more psychological counseling.

What it all amounts to is that more information is being given to the unconscious (subliminal) intellect. As the holistic health concept has spread, enormous quantities of information have become available about how to achieve an emotional balance, how to make your feelings work for you, how to interact with groups, how to become aware of destructive emotions and images and replace them with positive, productive thoughts, images, and emotions. And new information has also become accessible about the body, how to become aware of tensions and relieve them, how to energize the physical body, balance it, exercise it, nourish it, and care for it. The subliminal intellect organizes all the information for you in a way that best meets your needs.

The more information people have about themselves, the better they can maintain states of well being. It has been noted, for example, that there has been a sudden decrease in all kinds of cardiovascular disease, especially hypertension. The improvement is variously attributed to better nutrition, awareness, more exercise and less smoking, but these influences are actually the result of more information about health and illness. When you hear that exercise makes you feel better and you try exercising, the most important motive for continuing to exercise is the feedback of feeling better you get from your body.

The broad new interests in jogging, better nutrition, yoga exercises, and the more exotic kinds of physical fitness techniques, such as Rolfing, Tai Chi or aerobic exercises, are all ways people are expressing new insights into the meaning of real health. These new ways of working with the body do strengthen the body's resistance to the various kinds of assaults, but there is an even more interesting side to the body exercises. Have you ever noticed that each one of them uses the mind to make the exercises effective? Yoga and Tai Chi are perfect examples of how the mind is used to discipline the body and then how this is used to discipline the mind. The result of this mutual teaching between mind and body is the maintenance of a state of well being and better resistance to disease and illness.

In every case it is the mind that directs the body. Even in jogging, one of the main attractions is the altered state of consciousness that happens when people come to identify with the total state of the body as it runs. And most people forget the mental discipline that precedes jogging. The mind must first accept the logic of jogging and develop some belief, however tentative, in its potential to improve the body condition. The the mind directs the body, prepares it for jogging, concentrates on the body movements, and grows in appreciation of the mind-body harmony it can produce.

But how does the mind come by this marvelous power to make the body perform, often in a way that is alien to one's personal preferences or one's own deep body feelings that physical exercise may be too punishing for a tired old body? What makes the prim fiftyish lady, who normally disdains sports clothes and early rising, suddenly buy jogging clothes, set the alarm for 6 A.M., and start off plodding down the street in a behavior she would otherwise find embarrassing? Psychologists cite motives such as the desire to be with the "in" groups, the desire to stay young, the hope of recapturing the feelings of youth, pride in the physical figure, hopes for a longer life, and other personal reasons. But whatever these influences might be, it is the mind that makes the judgment about the best way to achieve the desire and it is the mind that keeps the self motivated to continue.

Someone who illustrates this inner healing ability marvelously well tracked me down across the country to tell me about his miracle cure. Briefly, this man had endured excruciatingly painful cluster headaches almost incessantly for seven years. Being well off, he was able to go to every headache clinic in the country, every expert, every hospital. But there was no relief. He tried biofeedback with several clinicians and with psychologists in different clinics and was terribly disappointed by the lack of relief. Then in a bookstore he saw one of my books on biofeedback, bought it, read it diligently, and decided to give biofeedback another try. With still another doctor, he experienced still another "introductory" session of biofeedback. His headache disappeared. And never came back. The longer the headaches stayed away, the more he vowed to tell me the story.

Could this really have happened? How does it work?

My notion is that the conscious mind is often the victim of myths about health and the self (as in the effects of negative life scripts or dismal wish-fulfilling prophesies). At the same time, the mind is deprived of reliable information about mind-body operations and the requirements for well being. When the right information can get through the protective armor of consciousness right down to the subliminal intellect of the unconscious, this intellect starts putting the information into order and presto chango, the answer pops up. Very often the answer never really gets into consciousness, but it does the next best thing — it removes the conflict causing the pain or anguish.

After all, the headache man was beset by a dozen stresses. He knew he would have a headache every day, he felt he had to cope and get through the days. He knew the distress was putting him further and further behind in his work, and he knew the next headache remedy he would try probably would not work. That's a very heavy stress script to live with.

The man with the ceaseless headaches actually had every bit enough information he needed about his headaches and how to relieve them but he just couldn't seem to put it together right. Then he read the book and went to the doctor to start treatment all over. And suddenly his inner computer or psyche or subliminal intellect (probably all three) made sense out of the whole picture, and there was understanding and no more headaches. The inner intellect put all the information about his headaches and how they caused pain and how the body's physiology changed when the headaches were relieved into an order in such a way that it "learned" how to stay in a balanced mode. He kept saying that he couldn't explain what had happened, that there was simply some mind-body state he could feel but not describe.

It all sounds very mystical, but I'm convinced it isn't. Unlike a religious belief, there are no assumptions to be made. All we have to accept is that intangibles such as understanding and awareness had in some way learned to resist the things that had once caused his headaches. The best answer I can come up with is that the understanding-awareness acted to maintain the wholeness and harmony of the psyche and the whole being. And once the wholeness and harmony were restored, the being was less susceptible to assaults, whether chemical, physical, or psychical.

The process, indeed, seems very much like the process that leads to the mystical experience I described in *Supermind* — one *knows* but one cannot explain the overall way of knowing. And like the mystical experience, these awarenesses of the psyche are ineffable. How can you, for example, explain the feeling of the joy of the team winning, or why you cry at weddings? These are not one-dimensional feelings and awarenesses and recognitions, they belong to the whole being, to the psyche that is the Self. And when the psyche understands the assault and how to deal with it, there is healing.

Too often the game of life is played as one is expected to play it, accepting stress and dis-ease and compensating for psychic blows without realizing that it is not merely the ordinary stress of

life but an actual disease caused by unsatisfactory life events sow-
ing the invisible seeds of psychic infections. And while stress
silently wounds and bruises and even kills, to stem its dis-ease and
disease one needs to learn, mainly, three easy-to-learn kinds of
awarenesses:

- an awareness that usually, if not always, unsettling thoughts
  and feelings are signs of being under stress;
- an awareness that any interference with the harmony and
  wholeness of life is stress;
- an awareness that most body tensions are signs of being under
  stress.

The dis-ease immune system, a creation of the psyche

No doubt because we are only now reaching the frontiers of
learning about the mind-body interface, the words we use to describe intangible, abstract mind states and feelings tend to be more
confusing and ambiguous than truly informative. The word "consciousness," for example, is abused as much by the mind-brain
scientists as by anyone, and scientists routinely fail to specify
whether they are discussing conscious awareness or unconscious
mental activity (as in unconscious conflicts). I have described a
number of examples of the operations of the unconscious (subliminal) intellect, and to be consistent, we really should talk about
unconscious awarenesses as well as conscious awareness.

When, for example, we feel a deep commitment to someone or
have a strong rapport or feel empathetic, we really have two kinds
of awarenesses — a conscious awareness of the *fact* of a particular
state of mind and thought and feeling, and second, we have an
all over awareness, an all-pervading sensation through the entire
being that is almost impossible to describe. I suspect the latter
reflects a subliminally constructed consciousness about the total,
whole state of one's being. I suspect, too, that awarenesses that
seem to involve the entire being in a way that cannot be described
in words are complex awarenesses of the whole being, known to
the unconscious mind and poorly communicated to the conscious
mind because *conscious* awareness can focus on only a limited

number of events at any one time. Consciousness has some "ink-
ling" of the inner knowledge or feeling the unconscious mind is
aware of, but consciousness (as conscious awareness) cannot artic-
ulate the sensations except in vague analogies. Whole being awarenesses perhaps should be called psychic awarenesses (belonging to
the psyche) since it is the psyche that holds the whole network of
mind and body and feeling sensations together.

Elsewhere I present some new concepts about the human psyche. In essence, the research and analyses support Jung's description of the psyche as the innate, inner organizing center and
guiding force of the self and of the growth of Self during life, the
ground substance of self-realization. The new study of the psyche
also supports the dictionary definition of the psyche as, "the mind
functioning as the center of thought, feelings, and behavior, and
consciously or unconsciously adjusting and relating the body to its
social and physical environment" (*American Heritage Dictionary*,
1976).

As the concept of the psyche is expanded and updated in the
light of the new psychologies and changing psychosocial influences of the late twentieth century, it becomes clear *that the psyche
determines states of human well-beingness.* Because the psyche is
the bridge, the link joining mind and body and spirit, and because
it is the unifying principle that establishes mind-body harmony in
beingness, behavior, and feeling, it responds to all insults to mind
and body and spirit.

Mind, body, and spirit never react separately; whatever assaults
one diminishes the wholeness and health and well-being of their
core-link, the psyche, and when the psyche is affected, mind, body,
and spirit all respond. A physical ailment may be not only physically painful, its implications for secondary effects on job security
or economic well-being create both anxiety and depression of the
spirit as well. Stress assaults to the mind's beliefs and opinions or
to its values or hopes and dreams such as rejection, ridicule, being
ignored or forgotten, lead to deeply troubled emotions, usually
with equally troubled functions of the physical body. Similarly, an
insult to your moral integrity can make you both physically sick
and emotionally disturbed, while a disappointment or failure to
reach goals nearly always upsets the body and saps the spirit.

Physical, emotional, mental, or spiritual hurts, they are all psychic blows and they are all stress.

It is clear that stress affects first and most deeply the psyche. Because stress involves human relationships and causes uncertainty about life's future social relationships and concern about psychological well being, it strikes at the most vital of the foundations of human life — the center where mind and spirit work for fulfillment and self-realization. Stress jeopardizes the integrity and wholeness and harmony of the psyche.

Now, to complete our circle of thought from the notion of psychic awareness to the notion that stress is first and foremost psychic toxicity (assaults to the psyche; psychic bruises), still another very new concept emerges. Our evidence strongly suggests that the psyche contains and sustains an immune (defense) system that functions to prevent and relieve the effects of assaults to the psyche (stress). The immune system that defends against psychic assaults and psychic bruises looks to be a very specially evolved set of awarenesses and potential awarenesses.

It is well known that the body possesses an immune system that acts to defend the body against *physical* assaults. Tissue biochemicals, for example, tend to resist effects of injury and the body also possesses the capacity to manufacture antibodies that fight off invading infectious organisms. I suggest that the intangible nature of human beings also possesses its own immune system, a line of defense the psyche can develop to resist the effects of psychic assaults and psychic bruises (stress).

Awareness and consciousness and understanding are *not* the same notions regardless of how careless we have become in our language. Awareness and awarenesses are *mental sensations* — special, higher order, evolved sensations created by mind senses that recognize the products of higher mental activity such as beliefs, attitudes, thoughts, and feelings, the dozens of mental sensations that are usually just lumped together and called self-consciousness. Self-consciousness is not simply an awareness that one's own mental activities exist and an awareness that one's self is unique. Self-consciousness is a *collection* of awarenesses (the sensations accompanying understanding) of the self *as the whole participates in different qualities of the self.* They are like the gods in the Hindu pantheon where each whole deity is a manifestation of a different quality of the Supreme Being, and each special quality reveals the whole. *Psychic awarenesses belong only to the whole being,* and not to any one mind or body part (such as an awareness of fatigue or awareness of a problem or an awareness of being scared).

Awarenesses are the natural antidotes to stress. These extended senses of the psyche are the *mental sensations* of our beliefs and ideas and thought-sensations that encompass the whole being. The sense of your own name is one example. When people in the distance are talking and you can catch only a word here and there, you may suddenly be brought up short — did they say my name? You check. They did. You heard it, of course, with the subliminal mind, not the conscious mind.

The subliminal awareness of recognizing your own name in a very unlooked-for circumstance is very different from the primary sensing of a smell or touch. It is really an all-over feeling. You can feel the name recognition down to your toes. And note that your respiration halts for a second, you stand at attention if only for half a second, and some inner remote whisper says, "that's me!" But awarenesses are also awarenesses of exactly how something relates to you — to *all* of you. Awareness of your own very special identity is one of the self's most important protective, defense devices. It is not only essential to growth and maturity, but becoming aware of the wholeness and harmony of the self is profoundly therapeutic.

A striking, heartwarming example of the healing power of awareness is a simple self-suggestion. One cannot measure the enormous relief of so much psychic hurt in blacks as when the Rev. Jesse Jackson encourages them to repeat the phrase, *"I am somebody."* Thousands of people have come to *feel* being somebody, being someone special, having their own identity, being their own person, and feel the sensation *all over.* You can't pick "being somebody" apart to identify its causes the way you can, say, the feeling of Spring because of the sights and sounds and smells. Psychic awarenesses are created only when meanings for the whole being are understood by the whole. Awarenesses of the psyche's remarkable qualities that work for wholeness and harmony and for growth and individuation resist assaults to the psyche.

This, my friends, is what I believe to be the psyche's defense against psychic hurts: the special awarenesses of special qualities of *the whole being,* the awarenesses taught by the psychic senses, by the mind senses that belong to the psyche. These are *not* simply intellectual appraisals or isolated, specific feelings about special properties of the self; they are *sensations of the wholeness* of the self as the self participates in each quality of the self.

Chapter 12

Structured stress relief (Programs for acquiring stress immunity through mind-body-psyche awareness)

As the world turns . . . The need for personally tailored stress relief programs . . . Designing a stress management program . . . Program modules for tension relief and problem solving . . . Part I. The Quiet Time . . . 1. Easing mental tensions . . . 2. Easing body tensions . . . 3. Anxiety reduction . . . Part II. Mind Work Time . . . 4. Preparing the mind to discover and appreciate its inner intelligence . . . 5. Sharpening mental skills . . . 6. Information gathering . . . 7. Exercising support systems . . . 8. Problem solving . . . Part III. Action time . . . 9. Action exercises . . . 10. Transferring awarenesses and solutions to real life situations

As the world turns

The revolutions within the healing arts in recent years have led to some extraordinary changes in attitudes about health and healing. There has been, for example:

- a shift toward making the patient a partner in the healing process
- a new understanding of health that has seen widespread and dramatic changes in lifestyles
- a recognition of the importance of the *whole* person in dealing with health and illness (the holistic approach)
- a recognition that the mind is an important (and perhaps the most important) factor determining health and illness

Each of these new perspectives on health is concerned with two penetrating new insights into the nature of well beingness and healing. One recognizes the role of thought processes in the susceptibility to illness while the other recognizes the healing capacity of the human mind. It is becoming clear that self-helping exercises and stress-healing techniques are effective because they strengthen the faculties of mind. Rather than being the passive object of treatment that is given drugs and advice, the mind is beginning to take an active role in healing and in all health maintenance procedures.

Just as the body grows and flourishes with physical nourishment so the mind flourishes and is healed as it is nourished. Nourishment for the mind is information. And much the way the medicines we take cause healing because they help the body's immune (defense) systems or stimulate the body to produce healing chemicals, so does the mind use information to stimulate the psyche to develop new awarenesses about the self. It is these awarenesses that become the immune system of the mind and protect the psyche against assaults and the ravages of stress.

It is, of course, a strange notion to swallow — the idea that information and the mind may be the truest healing force of all. It is difficult to accept the fact that some intangible nonphysical thing such as information alone can heal the physical body, especially when we cannot track the way information heals the way we can trace chemical healers in the body. Even when we know how well information can heal, what taxes our ability to believe is that information heals only when we become sensitive to information about the true value and integrity of the self and psyche and body.

Each mind that faces stress, each hurt psyche is different. Each has a different fund of information, each has different information needs, and each handles information in a different way. To perform the healing magic for each of our forever unique situations of stress that condemns us to diminished well being, each stressee must seek out the special nourishment that its psyche needs.

We who are in search of healing for the psyche are like venturers on the moon. We are familiar with many of the bits and pieces we need to undo stress but we have not yet learned how to put them all together. The key seems to lie within the domain of each person's psyche, for it is the cerebral-psyche connection that performs the magical transformations from unwellness to well being with nothing more than words or symbols or the complex language of human behavior.

The need for personally tailored stress relief programs

Stress is 90 percent how the mind looks at difficulties in life and relieving stress is 100 percent the way the mind uses its resources to resist the effects of stress and learns how to deal with stress without distress.

If we review the stress dis-ease process (see Figure 1), the fundamental causes of stress are easily recognized as a distressing perception of one's circumstances and its implications for future well being. The stress itself is actually the effect of uncertainty, frustrated problem solving (unsuccessful coping), and negative images that evoke mind and body tensions. The entire process occurs within the thought and idea generating systems of the mind — and, so perplexingly, in the deep recesses of its subliminal operations.

We have seen, however, that the mind's thinking apparatus functions quite well even during the worst of stressful situations. Distress, dis-ease, and the marginal miseries arise from being *frustrated* in coping with our difficulties, an unsettling mind state caused by lack of the information necessary to solve problems (to cope). Coping depends upon finding the right information we need for our own very personal problems, working to access the subliminal intellect and sharpening mental skills.

Stress is, however, a very private phenomenon. Each individual has quite personally shaped expectations, each perceives life uniquely, and each solves psychological and social problems in special, personal ways. While the *stages* of the mental operations causing any particular kind of stress can be identified, the *contents* are always personal and individual.

Realizing the uniquely personal nature of stress leads naturally to the idea that self-help stress relief programs are *only* ways to combat stress. Since, however, stress is created because

the mind lacks information, guidance by physicians, psychotherapists, or counselors is absolutely essential, whether given personally, in groups, or via books, workshops or tapes. Professional treatment becomes essential (a) when a physical disorder
exists or is suspected (see Table 1), (b) when emotional distress
noticeably interferes with any of life's activities, and (c) when
any of the various self-help stress reduction exercises is not
thoroughly understood.

Because the origins of stress are submerged in a complex mixture of experiences, memories, and emotions, it is not usually
possible to tackle stress problems head-on. By the time the feelings
of stress are recognized, most of the mental events causing the
stress feelings have either occurred long ago or are well along in
the process. This means that overtaking the process must be a
two-pronged attack on both the mental and physical changes the
stress is causing. The peculiarity of most stress reduction techniques is that they actually do affect both mind and body, but each
technique emphasizes either mind *or* body.

One way to ensure a concerted attack on all the effects of stress
is to be careful to balance one's stress reduction program evenly
between both mind awareness and body awareness practices.

The initial steps of the stress management program outlined in
the following pages not only prepare the mind to deal with stress
but provide a significant respite from the stress tensions. This in
turn allows the natural resistances of mind and body to build up
again. The steps for stress relief are designed to deal very specifically with the two major effects of living with the stress of life,
that is, to relieve mind and body tensions that interfere with
coping (problem solving) and to provide a strategy for solving
problems.

Designing a stress management program

There are three kinds of stress management programs:

1) Those that provide relief from both the mental and physiological effects of *ongoing* stress
2) Those that reduce the existing subjective, muscular, and
   visceral tensions of *"official"* stress ills

3) Those that aid in *maintaining* a state of well being and in preventing stress from establishing a beachhead

The objectives of stress management programs should *not* be mainly to relax and relieve the tensions — the objective should be to resolve the difficulties causing the dis-ease. *Unguided* relaxation, unguided self-suggestion or imagery are *not* efficient ways to relieve distress, but when they are are structured to the needs of the stressee and integrated within a systematic program designed to eliminate the roots of stress, they can be invaluable aids.

A stress management program does *not* automatically resolve stress problems. All such programs can do is provide the most effective procedures for tension relief, problem solving, and coping. Just as stress requires the interaction of circumstances with human perception before it exists, so also does the control of stress require the interaction of two elements, the information contained in the various helping programs and the mind to receive the information — *your* mind. The intensely personal nature of stress means that *only the person enduring the stress can change the course of events to ease the psychic pain.*

Your task is: (1) to define both your feelings and the circumstances leading to the stress feelings (diagnosis), (2) to seek and find the information you need to resolve the stress problem and to design effective coping devices, and (3) to put what is learned from the program into practice in everyday life. Stress management programs provide ways to help you accomplish these tasks.

One important step in developing a personal, self-help stress control program is establishing a "diagnosis," that is, defining the source and the circumstances of the stress as accurately as possible. A complete diagnosis is usually not possible until practice with both mind and body tension reduction procedures yields new insights in the unconscious and are then relayed in some way to the conscious mind for its appreciation, either through mind-body sensations or actual thoughts and concepts. Nonetheless, a start on an accurate diagnosis is important because relief from stress is achieved only by understanding its causes and effects. The information in Tables 2, 3, 4, and 5 should be helpful in building an accurate diagnosis.

Program Modules for tension relief and problem solving

A complete stress management program should contain five phases:

1) Preparation of the mind to exercise its mental skills.
   Using varieties of techniques to assist in eliminating distractions, minimizing thoughts colored by feelings, and to give the mind instructions and guidelines for working more efficiently.
2) Preparing the body to detect its tensions.
   Developing awarenesses of body states by using various techniques (such as relaxation or imagery) to assist in eliminating body tensions and the tension messages from the body to the mind that prevent the mind from operating efficiently.
3) Information gathering.
   Exploring ways to gain access to the subliminal intellect, cultivating new awarenesses and psychical senses, and mobilizing relevant memory resources.
4) Problem solving.
   Defining stress problems precisely, integrating information (consciously or unconsciously), working to solve problems systematically, selecting effective coping options, and setting the stage for transferring decisions to action.
5) Transferring learning and problem solving to real life.
   Practicing awareness skills and instituting relief measures promptly when the onset of stress is detected.

In the following sections 10 stress management program modules are described.

To select the program modules to use, make your choices based on how you feel. For example, if you are emotionally upset, it will be very difficult to work with meditation exercises to quiet the mind and prepare it for problem solving work. Feeling this way, it would be best to start by relieving body tensions and developing new awarenesses of the body. On the other hand, if you are concerned about a specific problem and feel an urgency to solve that problem, then the best starting point is the module that helps to prepare the mind for retrieving hidden mental skills and for problem solving. If, however, a serious stress ill has been diagnosed, the first objective is to reduce body tensions so one would use the relaxation techniques that could accomplish this in the quickest way.

Ten mind and body exercise modules for designing a stress management program

Part I. The Quiet Time
    Module 1. Easing mental tensions
    Module 2. Easing body tensions
    Module 3. Anxiety reduction
Part II. Mind Work Time
    Module 4. Preparing the mind to discover and appreciate its inner intelligence
    Module 5. Sharpening mental skills
    Module 6. Information gathering
    Module 7. Exercising support systems
    Module 8. Problem solving
Part III. Action time
    Module 9. Action exercises
    Module 10. Transferring awarenesses and solutions to real life situations
Please note:

THIS IS A HOW-TO-HOW-TO, NOT A HOW-TO PROGRAM FOR STRESS MANAGEMENT

The suggestions in each exercise are designed to act only as *guidelines* to show the special relevance of each technique to the stress dis-ease process and its potential for reversing tensions. Most people interested in stress control already have a good acquaintance with a number of techniques such as tense-relax exercises, guided imagery, the journal process and so on, but most people who struggle to cope with stress or to keep it manageable, need to know *exactly* the purpose of each exercise and what it can do, and the best ways to achieve the objectives of each technique as well as knowing the procedure. In References I have listed a number of helpful books (many in paperback) grouped according to which stress relief technique they emphasize, such as relaxation, imagery, awareness, etc.

Although the following program modules form a comprehensive, unitary sequence, each module can be used alone or in combination with any other module and adapted to individual interests, objectives, and needs. Since they are meant to be principally guidelines, each module is described as briefly as possible, beginning with some background material, a brief statement of objectives, and then some examples of the strategies that might be used to achieve each objective. Occasionally I have included additional comments or notes where I felt they were warranted.

Part I. The Quiet Time

Module 1. Easing mental tensions
Objectives

1) To calm the mind and ease mental tensions
2) To suspend the natural impulse for mental activity
3) To silence disturbing thoughts, feelings, and images
4) To create an inner climate for mental discipline
5) To aid in recovering and using full mental capabilities
6) To prevent tension messages being sent from the mind-brain to the body

When the mind is concerned about a problem it detects in life, the concern tends to focus on uncertainties and feelings that the uncertainty generates. This prevents the mind from scanning both the outside environment and the inner memory for useful information. As the need to find answers increases, the mind twinges with an anxious urgency that sends messages to the body to brace itself against further assaults to the psyche. Before the mind can function effectively enough to solve its stress problems, its tensions need to be relieved by learning to calm the mind and minimize distraction to create a mind state favorable for the delicate job of receiving inner messages from the subliminal intellect.

Strategies*

1) Timed, regular breathing exercises (see Appendix 3)†
2) Uncomplicated meditation exercises

Things to remember

1) The mind does not function well without specific instructions, therefore, always spell out your instructions and goals with the inner voice. Repetitions, with intervals for allowing the mind to follow the instructions, are important. Remember, this is *not* a spiritual meditation. This is working toward a very specific goal of easing the tension of the mind.

2) Be mindful of your attention. It will be either "free-floating" with the rhythm of your respiration or focused on giving the mind instructions or on trying to assume a passive mode of being so that information emerging from memory or from other states of consciousness can be recognized.

*Strategy is one of those strange English words for which you can grasp the *content* of its meaning but for which you can never find a *specific* definition. I interpret strategy as a Master Plan, i.e., a course of action for achieving a goal built up from plans for reaching various levels or parts of the ultimate goal. In stress management programs the grand strategy is to relieve and prevent stress, and the strategy for each different procedure of the program is a way to achieve one of the goals necessary to achieve the ultimate goal. A stategy also implies uncertainty about the best procedure to use to reach the goal, so the mind must be alert to how the procedure is working as well as using it. Thus strategies are also ways of accumulating information (learning) how to best reach the goal. Jacobson's tense-relax exercises, for example, are techniques for *learning how to learn* true relaxation; many imagery exercises are ways (stategies) for "getting in touch with yourself," actually ways to learn how to learn about the inner, covert operations of the self and psyche. The learning is innate; stategies provide the innate learning abilities with the information to test stategies and determine what is best for personal well being.

†See Chapter 6, "The Breath of Life," in *Freedom from Stress* by Phil Nuernberger (Honesdale, Penn.: Himalayan International Institute Publishers, 1981).

Auxiliary or supplemental exercises (see Module 2)

1) Body awareness exercises
   When mind and body tensions are present, they add to each other. When the mind is concerned (mild tension), it sends bracing message to the body, and when the body is tense, it sends messages to the mind about how tense the body is, reminding it that body tension means anxiety and so the mind, in turn, reacts by feeling that tension and anxiety.

2) Contemplation
   Contemplation, which is the exhaustive mental examination of a single event or object in all its possible manifestations, requires considerable mental discipline. It is, however, a particularly appropriate mind activity during the problem solving phase of stress relief and recovery of the well-being process, and can follow the Quiet Time whenever the mind has become adequately disciplined.

Comments:

One of the wonders of the modern age is the way T.M. (Transcendental Meditation) created a sensation by telling the American people they needed a quiet time each day. As originally described, T.M. recommended twice daily periods of quiet sitting for fifteen minutes each in which the time was used to quiet the mind. There have been several interpretations about the way one could quiet the mind, notably trying not to think, although other devotees recommend focusing the mind on a particular object or thought. At the time of its peak popularity and with research funded by an incredible wealth from student fees, a number of research studies indicated many amazing kinds of improved health in T.M. practitioners. Other studies, in academic institutions, reported that people performing T.M. were actually in stages of light sleep. With obvious bias on both sides, one can only turn to reports of the T.M. meditators themselves, and these have been overwhelmingly positive.

It is, unfortunately, no longer possible to judge the benefits of T.M. objectively since many practitioners have turned to other (or supplemental) kinds of meditation or self-improvement techniques. Nonetheless, it seems clear that the intentional act of being completely quiet several times a day does have considerable benefit, particularly for the relief of mind and body tensions.

What exactly can a quiet time do for mental and physical health, and why should simply being quiet improve one's well being? And how does it do it?

There are a surprising number of reasons why regular quiet times make people feel better. First, the stress of life is almost constant pressure to perform. Even if stress is not actually present, the mind nonetheless remembers the past and probable future presence of stress and is always occupied and troubled to some degree by the need to deal with it.

The Quiet Time is a respite from the mental pressure of the constant demands of life, a respite that has very real effects on the physiology of the mind and body. Whenever the mind shifts its attention from the pressures it feels to freeing the mind from the usual crush of thoughts that vie for attention, it is actually removing the effect of stress thoughts on both the activity of the brain and on the functions of the body. In a way it's a bit like the effect of a tranquilizer in a person with troubling anxiety — the mind becomes calmed, and with that calmness the tension messages to the body decrease and the body then can begin to rest. Calming the mind has exactly the opposite effect from the tension build-up that stress causes. Just as tensions build imperceptibly as one lives with stress, so do tensions relax imperceptibly as the mind becomes calm.

The effect of a Quiet Time is not merely nullifying tension-producing thoughts. Aside from the question of whether "emptying the mind" automatically leads to a sleep state or to a true detachment and new knowledge (and this Zen ideal of freeing the mind from all distractions to tune into the universal — or even inner — consciousness is usually achieved only after long and serious practice), the acts involved in the practice of meditation have special effects in themselves long before such states are achieved. In fact, in yogic meditation each of the mind acts constitutes a special period of training. When one tries to empty the mind and ban distracting thoughts, the focus is first on the doing. That is, one has to *concentrate* on the intention. This means, automatically, a single focus, but for most people, no matter how hard they try to clear the mind, thoughts do intrude. While most meditative techniques recommend focusing on certain kinds of thoughts or mental pictures, other techniques make use of the intruding thoughts by aiming toward capturing them and focusing on them. The mind is rarely, if ever, without thought. The popular notion of no-mind is an unfortunate misinterpretation that such a state can be achieved without total devotion to serious, prolonged meditation practice. Without rigorous training and prolonged practice, the human mind is always flooded with thoughts, images, ideas, and sensations. Minimizing their presence is about as much as most mortals can do, but what most people *can* do is to put selected thoughts, images, ideas, and sensations to a useful purpose.

The Quiet Time allows the mind to be selective about what thoughts and feelings are important for further consideration. This is the preparation of the mind for contemplation. Sustaining the mind's focus on eliminating distracting thoughts — emptying the mind — is a mental act in itself. The result is a mind prepared to receive its thoughts away from the influences and distractions of the external world. It is a time to sort out thoughts and feelings. When the mind is turned inwardly, it moves into a different reality, the reality of the Self that is very different from the reality of the self busy with the world around it. What the mind discovers when it is by itself is what we call insight, for insights are simply understanding things we were too busy to understand before.

I have been using meditation and a Quiet Time almost interchangeably for several reasons. I feel strongly that the word meditation should be reserved to refer those special techniques of reflection or contemplation practiced for the purpose of spiritual enlightenment. Not all people have spiritual enlightenment as their first priority when they are searching for relief from stress, and other people sometimes have concerns about the religious implications of meditation. Although the traditional objectives of training in meditation may be only for the spiritually inclined, the *techniques* of meditation have valuable implications for dealing with distress.

Module 2. Easing body tensions.

Objectives

1) Easing physical tensions
2) Fixing an entry into rest and recovery
3) Removing tension messages from muscles to mind-brain
4) Preparing the mind to become aware of the natural body and body tension levels
5) Preparing the body to resist tensions
6) Becoming aware of the harmony of the physical and psychological energies

For the most part, the mind pays very little attention to body sensations. At the present time in the mind's education about the body, the mind recognizes danger signals from within when they come from disturbed body functions (infections, injuries, pain, fever). Note that the mind's appreciation of *potential* harm to the body is learned mainly through past experience with physical hazards. Muscle and visceral tensions are very new kinds of body disturbances, associated only with mental concerns, anxiety, or diminished well being. These tensions, moreover, develop slowly, in small increments of tension often over long periods of time, with the increments so gradual they escape perception.

Body tensions are the source of the *sensations* of concern, anxiety, and mental tension. It is generally believed that although body tensions fail to attract conscious attention (i.e., they are not felt), their tension signals nonetheless reach the more primitive interpretive areas of the brain where they are interpreted to mean that danger to the organism is present. *This* signal then tends to recruit sensations associated with anxiety that are appreciated in the liminal mind as feelings of tension, apprehension, or even anxiety. Then, because the mind is paying attention to its sensations of apprehension, it cannot focus adequate attention on doing something to solve its problems.

Strategies:

1) Breath regulation (yogic breathing exercises)
2) Jacobson's Progressive Relaxation (tense-relax exercises)
3) Autogenic Training (self-suggestion, imagery-relaxation exercises)
4) Yogic postures
5) Learning awareness of muscle tensions

Supplementary exercises to enhance body awareness

1) Physical activity programs, jazzercise, aerobics, jogging, swimming, dancing
2) Hot tub, Jacuzzi
3) Sensory isolation experiences
4) Bioenergetics
5) Structural integration, Rolfing

Comments:

The technique of Progressive Relaxation was developed many years ago by Dr. Edmund Jacobson, and many of the popular books he wrote on the subject are currently available in paperback. The technique is now more popularly known by the name of tense-relax exercises (See also Module 3).

The procedure is simple. First, a specific muscle or muscle group, such as muscles of the forearm, are tensed with as much effort as possible. Then the muscles are allowed to relax completely. The idea is to compare the sensations of tension with sensations of relaxation so that one can begin to detect lower and lower levels of muscle tension. It is really a way to gain awareness of muscle tension and how it feels to be truly relaxed (to become aware of the sensation of relaxation).

The exercises are systematic. Each muscle or muscle group is tensed and relaxed several times, waiting each time long enough to truly appreciate the sensation of relations. Then the same thing is done with another muscle group, and so on progressively around the body, ending with tense-relax exercises of the whole body.

Another popular technique used in relaxation training is Autogenic Training. This is a combination program of mental exercises that use self-suggestion and a form of meditation. Almost any kind of phrase can be used to suggest to one's self the feelings of relaxation, but scientific work has discovered two sensations critical to the relaxation process — the feelings of heaviness and warmth. So the phrases one says to one's self are something like "my hands feel heavy" and "my arms feel heavy." Phrases for every part of the body are used, and just as with the tense-relax exercises, the self-suggestion phrases are applied progressively around the body.

Next, you go around the body with phrases suggesting warmth, such as, "my hand is warm" and "my arm feels warm." Then the ideas are combined, and many variations of suggestions can be used. For example, you can say, "my hand feels warm and heavy," "my arm is relaxed, there is no tension" and so on. The phrases are said slowly for each part of the body, giving enough time between phrases for the desired sensation to be appreciated internally.

It is important in both the tense-relax exercises and in Autogenic Training to assume a passive attitude. If any effort is exerted, the effort leads to tension. With a passive attitude, one can just wait for the sensations of relaxation to occur. Once recognized, the state can be achieved when desired by returning to the passive state and feeling the sensations of relaxation.

Another helpful mind technique often used in relaxation exercises is imagery. Remember that mental images of problems make the body tense? Well, mental images can also be used to help the body relax. Try visualizing the most peaceful place or situation you know. It might be fishing on a lake far from civilization, or it might be a hot tub, or possibly sinking down in a feather bed. Visualize the scene completely, then re-live those tranquil sensations. This will often help to relieve tensions. Or, you can be specific about your mental images, and if your neck muscles, for example, are tense, you might visualize them and how the muscle cells might look when they are relaxed, or how the head feels when it is bent forward, relaxed. Any trick of imagination can be used to try to create or re-create feelings of relaxation.

There is a technique in psychotherapy that uses both mental imagery and relaxation procedures to treat emotional problems, particularly anxieties and mild phobias. This is called desensitization, meaning the procedure is used to desensitize or lessen the effect of those things causing the anxiety or fear.

The technique is easily adapted for stress reduction. Let's say you have developed considerable apprehension such as the "exam anxiety" that is so common among students. You know the material of the exam fairly well, at least you thought you did, but then the day before the exam you begin to get sick. You get sweaty, scared, your heart seems to flutter, maybe you have diarrhea — the typical acute anxiety syndrome.

In the desensitization procedure, the individual is first taught how to relax. Nowadays biofeedback is often used, or the relaxation exercises I described earlier. When some success in relaxing has been achieved, mental images about the exam situation are conjured up.

The images are arranged in sequences, from the least anxiety-producing images to the most anxiety arousing images. The first image, in the case of exam anxiety, might be walking into the building and through the halls to the exam room. The most fearful image might be the time of passing out of the exam papers, or an image of the professor.

The person first conjures up the least fearful image while trying to stay relaxed. When a mental image of the least anxiety-producing scene can be kept in the mind and the body can stay relaxed, the next most fearful image is used, and so on, until the individual learns how to stay relaxed while imagining the worst anxiety-producing scene. After this training, the learned relaxation is tried out during each sequence of the real situation, the person now being aware of the situations causing tension and consciously encouraging relaxation to occur.

Module 3. Anxiety reduction module

Objectives

To reduce subjective tensions, apprehensions and anxieties.

It was Edmund Jacobson whose research shed the most light on the relationship between anxiety and relaxation. As a medical physiologist he discovered that patients with symptoms of anxiety showed significant muscle tensions at rest, a finding that prompted him to theorize that anxiety and true relaxation are mutually exclusive states. He demonstrated what he called "tension-image patterns" (body tension patterns responding to images of tension-producing events) in individuals with anxiety. He also showed that mental images concerning the body *always* cause activation of physiological systems, and particularly activation of the muscle groups involved in the images.

Jacobson called the difference between felt and unfelt muscle tension "residual tension" and hypothesized that individuals could learn to become aware of the unfelt tensions by learning how to relax. He developed his famous tense-relax exercises (originally called Progressive Relaxation) from the observation that people could learn to detect smaller and smaller levels of muscle tension by comparing the familiar sensation of tension to states of relaxation. Because his research showed that muscle tension increased with the mere *image* of muscles working, Jacobson incorporated the use of imagery in his relaxation programs for treating anxiety and psychosomatic ills.

The images were used to recall one's tension during actual tension-producing situations (re-living tense situations) and then were used to learn to discriminate levels of muscle tension during actual therapy (as in desensitization). The ultimate objective is to learn to produce deep relaxation despite negative images first and then to obliterate the images. Jacobson's concepts of events during social stress reactions and their treatment is summarized briefly in Table 8.

Most clinical and research evidence supports Jacobson's notion that anxiety and relaxation are mutually exclusive states. One particularly important implication of Jacobson's work is that cognitive activities play a crucial role in both the cause and cure of anxiety and psychosomatic and stress ills. Mental images are an integral part of the mechanisms causing stress reactions, and conversely, awareness of tensions and the practice of relaxation leads to a return toward normal physiological activity.

The use of mental images in stress relief programs also provides a useful tool for identifying social situations causing tension states. Although the experimental evidence is mainly subjective, clinical evidence suggests that learning to become aware of internal functions by directing the attention to them specifically actually aids in resisting the effects of social stress. Moreover, it is reported that awareness of the way muscles react to stress and how they can be intentionally relaxed (through "passively" directed attention) also leads

Table 8
Summary of Jacobson's anxiety-relaxation concept

Major assumptions

1. Anxiety and relaxation states are mutually exclusive.
2. Comparing tension to relaxation (tense-relax exercises) develops awareness of sensations of relaxation.
3. Anxiety is not caused by a problem "out there," but results from the unproductive expenditure of energy in trying to solve the problem.
4. The imagery during problem solving evokes physiologic activity and expends energy.

Anxiety (tension) reducing procedure

1. Identify the situations producing tensions.
2. Identify the reactions to these situations. That is, identify the tension-image patterns of the body.
3. Use the images of both the tension producing situations and the tension-image reaction patterns during relaxation learning.
4. Gradually eliminate the images while maintaining relaxation.

to improvements in perception and more productive thought.

Strategies:

Jacobson's Progressive Relaxation (see References)
Any of the popular tense-relax exercise books and tapes

Things to remember:

That feelings come from *images*
To experiment with *positive* images

Part II. Mind Work Time

Module 4. Preparing the mind to discover and appreciate its inner intelligence

Objectives:

1) Removing emotional debris, i.e., setting aside negative images about the self
2) Learning to identify observations and judgments that are emotionally biased, and developing an ability to appreciate the world both objectively and subjectively
3) Developing awareness of the inner intellect and discovering clues for its access
4) Exploring the mind senses that belong to the psyche and foster awareness of the wholeness and harmony of the self
5) Developing an awareness of patterns of behavior and circumstances that influence life
6) Developing an awareness of the time and space behavior of human beings
7) Becoming sensitive to the inner being
8) Practicing mental discipline

Just as people have recently become aware of inner feelings, hidden motives and desires, so each human being can become aware of the vast resources of mental skills that have developed in little used compartments of the mind and are withering in the back archives of their memories. Many of these skills can be uncovered, retrieved and sharpened for use in everyday life. The chief technique is quiet reflection, directing the attention to the special objectives noted above.

Strategies:

1. Extended meditation; contemplation exercises directed solely to each objective (above), to each psychic sense, to each kind of awareness as well as to love, happiness, joy, peace, etc., as practice in feeling the inner appreciation and essence of these human resources
2. Self-suggestion
3. Focus on developing psychic senses
4. Guided imagery

Contemplation

The natural, normal mind is always active. This is, I suppose, why yogic and Zen meditation practices stress discipline, concentration, single focus, and contemplative exercises. They *use* the mind's tendencies for action but channel them to the specific purpose of striving for spiritual enlightenment. Still, most of us must live in the real world, and even in meditation we are concerned with self and understanding and our relationship to the rest of the universe. The Quiet Time shifts the sphere of mind activity to use the natural tendencies of mind to prepare it to deal with stress effectively.

Contemplation is another word more associated with the spiritual life than with what the word really means — a special way of thinking. Contemplation actually means to observe thoughtfully, to ponder carefully, and is often used synonymously with meditation. What makes contemplation different from ordinary thinking (and problem solving mind work) is the implication that the thoughts are to sustain a concentration on one particular idea or sensation, mentally dissecting each quality carefully and objectively until that quality (or event or feeling) stands out in its own reality for what it is without the embellishments of emotion or opinion.

If I try to solve a difficult situation with my father, for example, in my contemplation I will seek to look at his qualities through many different kinds of eyes. I will review his behavior for what it actually was and is, without my feelings judging them to be good or bad. I will look at our relationship as if we were strangers and I am observing from some neutral corner. I will examine my own feelings from the outside looking at, not looking from within.

I will try not to judge, compare, or react. I will, instead, ask questions. I will question myself constantly whether each observation is truly objective, truly valid, and without prejudicing assumptions. For in my contemplation I am gathering facts, information to use in the Mind Work Time to solve my stress problems.

Because so many people view contemplation with awe and as a mind exercise reserved for spiritual needs, there is often some hesitancy in embarking upon what seems to be a difficult task for the mind. But when the idea of contemplation can be seen as simply a continuation of the mind clearing process, it seems more palatable and less of a task.

With mind quieting as the first step, ridding and shutting out disquieting thoughts but always keeping the mind active, the next mental maneuver is to direct the mind's activities toward useful purposes. Since the purpose of these exercises is to deal with stress, and since the crucial turning point of the whole stress dis-ease process is problem solving and the pressure to problem solve successfully then the obvious directive to the mind is to prepare for problem solving.

One appealing technique was once used in an experimental study of meditation. This was sitting in the meditation posture and looking at a large blue vase. The idea was to concentrate on the qualities of the blue vase, trying to appreciate each quality fully in both mind and body. Early in the meditation training, people selected one special quality after the other and reflected on each, qualities such as shape or color or blueness. At later stages of the training, the students were able to appreciate the blue vase as a single harmonious whole, with all the qualities blended into a single impression until, for some, the vase finally became a blend of the entire universe.

This kind of meditative, contemplative process has many interesting implications for use in winning over stress (I recommend working with it). The Quiet Time practitioner can select some particular impression — an object, an event, a feeling, a spontaneous thought or some observation about life — and examine the impression in all conceivable ways such as its looks, meaning, structure, form, style, etc. Out of this process comes formed impressions from the unconscious and past experiences and desire. But when looked at dispassionately, away from the social and psychological demands to react or perform, a new reality emerges. The emotional overtones that accompany reactions and the pressures disappear.

The object or event or thought can now be seen for what it actually is, untainted by errors of perception, each with its own reality yet all of the same reality. The mental process moves on (minds can never be empty of thought, even in samadhi), now in a new state with a new perspective in which errors of impressions are removed. And in this new state, the extraordinary wisdom of the psyche or spirit or inner repository of understanding can emerge.

As I describe elsewhere, the psyche contains the capability to organize all knowledge and information in an orderly way that harmonizes with the natural order of the universe. Total access to the psychical unconscious would seem to be a mystical state. But it is not necessary to achieve total union with the universal consciousness where all is orderly and in harmony to appreciate either bits of its infinite wisdom or the depths of its potential. All that is required is intention, effort, and practice.

Module 5. Sharpening mental skills

This is a module for exercising the awarenesses and mental skills uncovered by practice of Module 2.

Objectives:

1. To prepare the mind for successful problem solving
2. To exercise the mental skills needed for solving psychosocial problems
3. To keep the mind focused on its skills
4. To focus on becoming aware of the complex activities of the mind, that is, on developing an awareness of such complex mental activities as objectivity, logic, relevance, the scope of mind, and even monitoring processing time
5. Creating instructions for the conscious mind to initiate various searches for the information needed for problem solving

Strategies and exercises:

1. Contemplation
2. Mental exercises such as practicing logical thinking until the mind develops a sensation and an awareness of the particular state of mind needed for such thought
3. Identifying mind sets
4. Lateral thinking
5. Programming dreams
6. Testing the strength of the mind quiet

Example of mind work production

Since it is almost impossible to capture the process by which insights open up entirely new ways of understanding life and human relationships, the following experience is used to illustrate how illuminating attention to mind work time can be.

Not long ago I was talking with a TV actor who made an observation that opened my eyes to an influence affecting human lives and well being in a way I had never imagined. He said, "One of the most difficult situations for an actor is to be out-of-synch with the other actors."* I was stunned with the novelty of the observation and couldn't wait to explore it in contemplation.

What a marvelous observation! The implications kept swirling in my head. First, it was an objective observation, not an impression. My friend was not blaming himself for a distressing situation but was simply observing a fact. As I mulled over his remark, I began to realize that all human beings might experience being out-of-synch in listening, in speaking, in feeling, and even in playing. After all, the entire body operates by way of its internal biological clocks, and the body does indeed contain many critical timing structures (such as the sinus node for the heart).

Perhaps the body being out-of-synch could account for the off days that professional artists and athletes seem to have. Or being out-of-synch might account for why we so often later say to a friend, "but I said that, you just didn't hear me." And most important of all, being out-of-synch might explain some of our difficulties in everyday life. It had never occurred to me that whole bits of behavior or feelings or communications could be out-of-synch. The observations were rich rewards for the contemplative mind work time.

Module 6. Information gathering

Objectives

1) To identify the sources of stress
2) To accumulate objective information
3) To energize the inner intellect
4) To test the strength of mind quiet and focus

It makes very little difference whether one's goals are to minimize stress, cope with life or strive for self-realization and fulfillment, the fundamental process is similar. Both coping and striving to achieve are behaviors that require the ability to adjust to the

*That is, "in synch" (pronounced "sink") being those times when people's feelings and thoughts and actions coincide closely enough in time and place to create an inner sensation of harmony with another person or persons. Not in synch refers to those times when the thoughts, directions of behavior, types of motivation, etc., of different people are not only not harmonious but often obviously out-of-step with each other.

ever-changing flow of life in a way that works toward one's well being. To be successful in either requires knowledge about the ways to achieve coping or fulfillment and that knowledge is exactly the same as that needed to relieve or prevent diminished well being and stress ills.

Solving problems, or finding answers to life's difficulties or working to fulfill one's potential all involve working with far less than ideal (or even helpful) conditions and information. In fact, psychosocial problems (created by social circumstances and involving psychological — feeling — reactions) are *always* characterized by spots of deficient information and often by misleading or false information (disinformation). The characteristically poor quality of information about human behavior stems mainly from the irreconcilable difference between the way society decrees we should behave and the way we try to cover up our shortcomings, our social behavior or personal differences or conflicts with social standards of behavior. Teenagers are striking examples of how difficult it is to get a good reading on the sources of their behavior that may contribute to your stress problem. And without adequate information you can only guess and approximate the information you need, which makes the chances of a satisfactory solution much smaller than you would like.

Gathering the information one needs to cope successfully with stress problems and pursue one's dreams for fulfillment or undo the tensions of stress is not at all an easy task. There is the difficulty of uncovering accurate information from behind the social masks everyone wears (people are generally *not* "open"), the difficulty in fitting together bits and pieces of information with so much missing data, the difficulty of tapping into the arcane secrets of the unconscious that manufactures conflicts, the difficulty in distinguishing reality from myth, and a hundred other obstacles to the search for information about the origin and effects of one's stress problems. Still, we are recognizing that the healing power of the unconscious mind and the subliminal intellect is so remarkable that finding the information these mechanisms of mind need is worth the effort to gather the information they need.

Strategies and exercises

1. Identify predisposing factors
    By using information from relevant, prepared information about predisposing factors, about kinds of stress circumstances and the kinds of signs and symptoms of reactions to stress (see Tables 3, 4, and 5).
2. Initiate nonpractice session techniques for extracting information from the unconscious intellect (in addition to spontaneous insights already achieved through practice with earlier modules).
    a) Talking with friends, counselors, or psychotherapists
    b) Using the journal process (record keeping)
    c) Programming daydreams, hypnogogic state, dreams

Remember:

1. Document signs and symptoms. Observe small changes in feelings, mental state, behavior, body sensations, and *write them down.*
2. Define precisely areas of deficient information.
3. Discriminate between (be aware that there is) objective information and subjective (emotionally colored) information.
4. Appreciate (recognize and remember) the spread of the problem with all its ramifications over time and space.
5. Be aware that information heals and that information is energy (see Chapter 11).

Comments: Data gathering — tracing the roots of stress

The chances of diagnosing one's special kinds of stress is a 50–50–50 proposition. The first 50–50 is because about half of the people believe they know what their stresses are but really don't and the other half is sure they don't. If, for example, you suspect your spouse is cheating on you, this certainly should seem to qualify as your stress. It seems so obvious.

But it isn't. The *real* stress is not knowing how to cope with the future. So it's a 50–50 chance that even if you think you are right, you probably aren't. The time that determines present stress is the future. By experience most people know that what they do today inevitably shapes their future, but when the conditions of stress crowd in, it is difficult to think in terms of the future. The stress of the moment is the worry about how things are going to go in the future, disturbing images of the outcomes of the stress problems of today. But the present concerns hold the attention like a giant magnet that attracts all the fears of catastrophes (Murphy's Law). It is the feelings of failure and low worth and being a loser and other self-condemning thoughts that repel all the good thoughts about reality, common sense, seeking help, positive outcomes, and knowing there is support and refuge.

The conscious mind swings back and forth between upset and feeling O.K. At times it can become choked with emotion, with quasi, primitive surges of anger, hurt and pain bombarding the mind while all the time the inner needle of curiosity pricks holes in the psyche's armor until it weeps with the sadness of self-pity. Then, as if some engineer flips a swtich, the mind can just as suddenly swing into a sublime moment as when some plausible solution sneaks its way into consciousness, and bliss reigns. But not for long. A new, bitter, dread uncertainty intrudes and swings the mental pendulum the other way.

The swings of the feelings, the focus on the immediate concerns of the stress, and the shushed anxieties about the future rise up like barriers against the mind finding a corner to retreat in and look at its problems in the cool light of neutrality. The quiet corner, nonetheless, *is* there. All it needs is dusting off and caring attention.

Tracing stress messages

It is vital to stress relief to collect the most accurate information possible about the sources of one's stress. Since stress can be created from so many diverse influences, it is especially enlightening to detail each influence as precisely as possible. This means inventorying and sorting out good information from the bad (from useless or stress-provoking or distracting information).

The following are notes to use in the search for your sources of stress.

1. Sources of information

a. *Messages from the body.* You can use any kind of exercises to detect body messages simply by paying specific attention to different body parts, much like performing yogic postures, each of which is designed to make very specific information available about different parts of the body. Or you can think of the source of body information as something like the meridians that convey information to and from organs and various acupuncture points.

Or use imagery as a way of focusing attention on the body. It is important to learn how to discriminate subtle differences in body messages (as, for example, the differences between boredom and fatigue in running) and to distinguish between real and imaginary messages (such as feeling the pulse is running fast or you have a temperature and when you check, they are normal).

b. *Messages from the emotions.* Because our lives more and more take place in an environment of thoughts and ideas, our "emotions" are less primitive and have become more subtle feelings that reflect our attitudes and beliefs about the world we live in and about the lives we lead. Understanding our feelings and emotions is also confusing because psychology has tended to pay more attention to emotional *ills* than to ordinary feelings. The average person, enduring the inevitable stresses of life, thus has little confirmation of the meaning of altered inner feelings.

Such changes, nonetheless, may be the most important clues to the onset of stress ills. As society has become so informed and sophisticated, so too has the range of inner experience been expanded. "Educated" feelings, born of experience, education, considered thought and value judgments are expressions of productive mental and psychical growth and they, too, as well as our heritage of less mature feelings and "emotions," can suffer negative change and can signal psychic hurt.

Since a great deal of our emergent, "educated" feelings are mired in the nebulous communications between conscious and unconscious awarenesses and have not yet been well defined, they are difficult to capture and hold up for inspection. Nonetheless, these higher forms of inner feelings are so important to understand in dealing with stress, it is extremely important to search the memory for clues to the origins of one's feelings, attitudes, beliefs and concepts. Exercises particularly appropriate for this task are structured meditation and contemplation, record keeping, self-suggestion and programming dreams.

c. *Messages from the way we behave.* This is much like the Freudian slip except on the behaviorial level. Have you ever done something or behaved in some way that either immediately or later you can't image whatever "made" you do that? Examining your behavior in such instances almost always reveals important information about inner feelings. Even when you aren't surprised by your behavior, it is a good idea to examine it from time to time for clues about the state of your psyche.

d. *Messages from propaganda.* Life today is a hotbed of propaganda about human behavior, health and illness. The media bombard you with persuasions to one behavior or another, taunt you for the tiniest fault (your teeth are stained?), shame you for not exercising like a pro athlete then advise you to relax to avoid stress. Morality, politics, religion, and even various lifestyles are not without their messages appealing for your psychic vote. It takes a great deal of introspection to sort out the real you from the product the media is trying to make of you.

e. *Messages from reality.* These are the most hurtful messages and the messages most easily disguised by the mind's receiving set. One common complaint, for example, is the boy/girl who wants to know if the relationship is over when the girl/boy refuses a date, won't answer a letter or come to the phone. The reality says it's all over, but the first-line (and primitive) psychic defenses fight back. Desires are slow to grow up and match the mind's education, yet learning to be objective and able to evaluate reality is the mark of maturity and balance and inner harmony. Distinguishing the reality from hopes and dreams nearly always needs a disciplined attention.

f. *Gestalt messages.* Some of the most important messages in life emerge only when events or situations have begun to form patterns. It is a characteristic of being under stress that being preoccupied with images of potential psychic hurt obscures one's ability to piece together the meaning of scenarios happening around one. It is an important exercise to use the mind's senses to detect whether or not patterns or themes are developing around the stress problem.

g. *Scripts,* of course, are the admonitions, warnings or life scenarios that ring in our heads for a lifetime because they came from some respected or feared authority and they leap to mind, especially in stress circumstances no matter how irrelevant or unfair they may be. Freedom from scripts comes only with practice in recognizing how inappropriate they may be in determining our behavior. Recognizing life scripts comes, in turn, from gathering data about one's behavioral performances and considering that data by "analyzing" it (paying serious attention to it such as writing down thoughts about the stress problem, using the thoughts as the subject of contemplation).

2. Asking questions to check validity of your information

When it is part of the complex interacting milieu of human behavior, information about individual behavior and the meaning of social relationships is nearly always skewed by varieties of social conventions (such as softening remarks by using euphemisms). The reality of social interactions is further obscured by the need of human beings to have reliable codes of behavior. Now that living has become so people-dependent and social values change so quickly, our authorities for social behavior (and beliefs) have become both expanded and diluted and confusing. These factors complicate our own introspections enormously. One relief from this dilemma is to ask questions about the validity and reliability of our own observations in order to determine whether they are really accurate assessments of the circumstances we think are causing us our stress.

3. Record keeping — observing yourself

Nothing, perhaps, is more revealing about the state of the inner self than when someone else describes your behavior. Nowadays we call the process of returning information about some performance back to the performer, "feedback," and it is a fact of behavior that behavior is always altered, or shaped, by the kind of information fed back to it. For the most part, commenting on peoples' behavior is not well accepted social behavior, and so most of us have very little data to work with about how our behavior is seen by other people and how that affects our relationships.

There are, however, some pretty good substitutes but they do take a fair amount of effort. For example, whenever you write a diary and read it later, you are feeding back information about yourself. The act of the writing itself feeds back information because most people try to define their thoughts fairly precisely before writing them down. This way of paying attention to one's behavior can produce some extraordinary insights about one's self and one's stress problems. Let me explain:

Even though it may be simply a short checklist about moods or thoughts instead of a full diary, when people keep regular records about their feelings, behavior and activities, whatever stress they may have can often be relieved long before the reasons for the relief come into conscious awareness.

What appears to occur is the subliminal recognition of patterns of influences creating the stress, and this stimulates the subliminal intellect to create appropriate ways to deal with those influences. (The process is similar to the psychiatric notion of how the unconscious develops conflicts and then develops inappropriate defenses to protect the ego, but — Thank Goodness — this time we have a highly positive action of the unconscious intellect.) The subliminal intellect has an obvious advantage over conscious awareness in dealing with stress. While conscious awareness must be busy dealing with the immediate, practical problems of life, the subliminal intellect is free to cope with understanding and dealing with the stress that spreads over all of life's spaces and time.

The subliminal mind can range through time and space, gathering neglected or hidden clues, detecting inconsistencies in behavior patterns, and then put it all together to form behavior that relieves stress. The subliminal intellect might, for example, conclude that a certain group of people is always associated in some way with your feelings of stress and so it directs your behavior to avoid those people without any conscious awareness at all about why you have changed your behavior. Later, you may realize you are avoiding them, wonder why, and suddenly discover they really were the cause of your stress. The subliminal intellect just got there first.

Excursions into record keeping should be personally developed records. I do not see much use for the "standard" psychology rating systems that ask you to record how much and when you felt depressed or had anxiety because that means *you've already got it* and that's a sign that needs a therapist's attention. Most people who live with stress have concerns and worries and apprehension, but relatively little overt anxiety. The chief idea of stress relief and stress prevention programs, such as this one, is to deal with the psychic distress and diminished well being *before* stress become so serious it disables mind or body.

The problem for most of us who linger in states *between* health and illness is to try to identify our stresses as exactly as we can so that we can deal with them effectively. The person who is 15 pounds overweight and is not sure why, for example, is in a very different state of psyche from the person who is 150 pounds overweight. One has a problem while the other has a **PROBLEM.** And while both can be equally stressful, each each needs a highly personal kind of attention.

Record keeping can accomplish an extraordinary detecting of inner, buried feelings and influences that fuel stress reactions. The key to making records useful and fun is to make them interesting. That is, *rate* different shades and degrees of feelings, emotions, and body states or feelings, each on a scale of 1 to 10.

Distinguish feelings and emotions by the degree of physical (body) involvement accompanying the state, with feelings having minimal physical involvement and emotions having the most involvement of the body.

Example #1. *Feelings* (such as self-pity, happy, ambivalent, expectant, worried, discouraged, etc., etc.) (See also appendix 4)

	Sun.	Mon.	Tues.	Wed.	Thurs.	Fri.	Sat.
discouraged	9	9	8	2	2	5	3

(where 0 = not at all discouraged and 10 = totally discouraged)

	Sun.	Mon.	Tues.	Wed.	Thurs.	Fri.	Sat.
mentally excited	5	4	6	9	9	7	3

(where 0 = not interested in anything and 10 = interested in everything or very interested in day's activities)

Example #2 *Emotions*

	Sun.	Mon.	Tues.	Wed.	Thurs.	Fri.	Sat.
irritated	1	2	9	8	5	2	2

(where 0 = not irritated and 10 = very irritated)

	Sun.	Mon.	Tues.	Wed.	Thurs.	Fri.	Sat.
happy	4	4	1	0	5	9	8

(where 0 = not very and 10 = very, very)

Example #3 *Body (physical) state*

	Sun.	Mon.	Tues.	Wed.	Thurs.	Fri.	Sat.
muscles	4	4	3	3	8	7	8

(where 0 = totally relaxed and 10 = totally uptight)

	Sun.	Mon.	Tues.	Wed.	Thurs.	Fri.	Sat.
inside (viscera)	4	4	2	1	5	6	5

(where 0 = feel great inside and 10 = gut feeling uptight)

	Sun.	Mon.	Tues.	Wed.	Thurs.	Fri.	Sat.
head	6	7	8	9	2	2	4

(where 0 = dopey and 10 = head is really operating)

special notes (see also Appendix 2)
  1. make your own list of descriptive adjectives (add them as you think of them) of what moods and feelings are most important to you to know or change.
  2. score yourself at any suitable interval, such as daily, morning, afternoon, evening, and night, or even hourly if it makes you feel good.
  3. when you want to follow mood or feeling or body state changes DO NOT place much emphasis on any one day's

score, but note trends over a significant number of days; also compare trends for a variety of descriptions of your feeling and body states.

4. isolate highest scoring words (good or bad) and use them as subjects for meditation and contemplation.

4. Other techniques for extracting insights from within

One common difficulty in dealing with the stress of life is that we tend to be as faddish in coping with stress as we are in the rest of life. That is, we adopt traditional ways of coping even when those traditional ways were devised only yesterday by the local psychologist. More often than not we cope without even thinking about how we are really handling a stress problem. One of the reasons is because some authority says that one or another coping device "works" ("tell him how you feel"), and when it doesn't work (he fired me!), rather than trying to figure out why, we just go back to the drawing board for another coping technique. The consequence is that the causes of the stress become more and more submerged beneath irrelevant garbage and become more and more difficult to bring into critical consciousness. And this is why I emphasize the process of self-inspection for the information we need to solve stress problems.

Here is another technique: Listen to your own voice. For example, tape some monologue and some conversations you have with a friend, as well as with someone you don't know every well. Later, listen attentively while you play the tape a number of times. But be sure to take notes *each time*. The tapes will be a goldmine of feedback, but tackle this exercise with as much objectivity as you can muster. In other words, don't fault yourself, just observe. Withhold judgments until you can see whole patterns.

5. Organizing your information

a) *Write down* all the information (data) you gather. It's a chore at first but quickly gets easy to do.

b) Discriminate the importance of each kind of information using scales of 1 to 10 (e.g., he's jealous given a score of 7 means "I think so but I'm not really sure").

c) List the additional information you think you need in order to make some conclusion about the sources of your stress and how to cope with it and what you can do about getting it.

d) List all the influences you think may be affecting your stress situation and find some way to make each item especially meaningful, such as assigning values to each factor, analyzing how to get all the information you need about it and ideas about how to handle it.

e) Feel liberated enough to call a therapist.

f) Absolutely, from any professional, request a list of things you can do for yourself.

g) Tell a friend.

6. Probing outside help

For example, make a few phone calls to find a physician who has family medicine training or who is particularly understanding. Call the local medical association and the local association of clinical psychologists and ask for those work with physicians.

And don't "buy" the first therapist you see if it doesn't feel right. Most important are (1) that you feel comfortable talking with the professional and (2) that he or she doesn't seem to discount your complaints, vague though they may be.

7. Surveying the psychologists' stash

In workshops or University Extension courses or special interest group meetings, many therapeutic techniques can be explored for the information and help they can give. There can be, for example, discussions about the nature and psychology of human beings, about creating and using support systems; the journal process; modified, individual, reality-oriented psychotherapy; group therapy; counseling; rational emotive therapy; family therapy; behavioral therapies; marriage encounter; dream analysis; guided imagery; Gestalt therapy; psychosynthesis; transactional analysis; meditation; bioenergetics; assertiveness training; psychodrama; and a host of other new psychotechnologies.

8. Other anti-stress games to play

a) Develop a game plan — a book of strategies for playing the game of life.
b) Sketch out scripts and scenarios you'd like to do.
c) Write down lectures about you and for you.
d) Write out some monologues and dialogues featuring you and your wishes and predictions about you.
e) Tru1behavioral rehearsal, programming dreams, being alone for as long as you can stand it, saying only positive thing to yourself.
f) Manipulate your thinking process by trying lateral thinking, carefully selecting words to describe your feelings, contrasting subjective and objective observations in your head, experimenting with being ultra-logical, trying brainstorming (blue-sky thoughts or stream of consciousness without logic).
g) Manipulate images. Try out positive vs. negative images, self-images, idealized and distorted images, success and failure images.

Module 7. Exercising support systems

Objectives

1) To learn to access useful services
2) To enlist psychological support and encouragement
3) To select informal counseling
4) To reinforce successes
5) To have help in maintaining objectivity

There is no more lonely a task than dealing with stress. Aside from the concern or unhappiness, worry or sadness, anxiety or frustration, there is always the added pressure that people are expected to cope, whatever. Most people do try to cope or to solve their personal problems in life by themselves, a cultural trait that simply makes the problem solving process much more difficult than it should be. First, it cuts off a great deal of potentially useful information that other people's knowledge and insights can give, and secondly, it weakens the spirit of the psyche by depriving it of support and encouragement. The "I can do it myself" idea is not very appropriate since stress comes from interactions among people.

It is becoming recognized that in the present complex, fast moving society of today, support systems are a necessity. They not only provide psychological support to ease psychic pain, they encourage and provide new information because different people are exposed to different situations and so they gather other kinds of useful information about human behavior, about different options for dealing with stress problems and different ways to gather useful information.

Strategies:

(Note — evaluate each possibility for its own particular kind of support and don't expect anything more than what each is capable of providing. Moreover, keep each support and support group compartmentalized and separate.)

1) Groups organized to serve special psychological support functions (groups dealing with incest, loss of a child, single parenting, etc.)
2) Social group activities; community service
3) Adult education courses
4) Group physical activities such as sports, walking, bird watching (even the birds can be supporting)
5) Self-improvement workshops

Module 8. Problem solving

Objectives

1) To state the stress problem precisely
2) To organize all relevant information in logical order
3) To make exact evaluations of the information gathered, making sure that all nonrelevant information is discarded

4) To ensure that the conclusions you make about the meaning of the information you are using are objective and logical

5) To develop effective problem solutions that have adequate and appropriate options for handling the problem

By the time this exercise module is approached, actually solving the problem should be a fairly straightforward process (and probably already accomplished, at least tentatively). Data (information) has been gathered, separated from emotionally colored observations, and contributions from the subliminal intellect have been appreciated and made part of the problem-solving skills. All that remains is to complete the mechanics of the problem solving so that solutions to your stress problems are as valid and reliable as they can be. The following strategies also function as a checklist to confirm solutions.

Strategies:

1) Working backwards from the desired goals
2) Using analogies
3) Keep starting over if necessary without being self-recriminating
4) Testing solutions by projecting their full images into varieties of possible future situations
5) Checking all possible outcomes against the existing reality
6) Parsing all problems into goals, information, logic testing, and error checking

Comments:
The focus on problem solving introduces a new concept into stress management. After all, the distress of living with stress is caused exclusively by frustrated problem solving. And while relaxation and imagery can often lead to a more healthful lifestyle and do relieve stress and so help the mind and body feel better, such techniques do not directly help to solve the problems causing stress. Since the inciting and continuing pressure of the stress

phenomenon is the need to solve one's problems, understanding how to solve problems is of paramount importance in stress relief programs.

Problem solving entails only two appraoches. One uses some known procedure to finding the answer while the other approach is finding a new way to find the answer. It isn't much of a choice. Problem solving really rests on following known guidelines or known stategies.

The most important elements for successful problem solving are: (1) establishing goals, (2) recruiting the information, (3) eliminating constraints such as unproductive associations (girls are no good at math), working backwards, etc., (4) eliminating all redundancy, (5) getting into the right attitude, (6) asking enough questions, (7) detecting patterns in the information, (8) organizing the information (observations) in logical order, (9) discriminating general from specific conclusions or inferences, (10) giving accurate values to all information used, (11) identifying interfering influences (emotions, culture, language), (12) giving one's self permission to doubt information and conclusions, (13) ensuring understanding of all different concepts needed to solve the problems at hand, (14) using objective evaluations, (15) withholding judgments until the problem is solved objectively and logically, and (16) being as completely logical as possible.

Note especially how many psychological factors are integral to the problem solving process.

Below is a checklist you can use to determine how well you followed the problem-solving (coping) procedure:

Have I defined the problem objectively?

Have I explored all my options?

Have I written down the problem, the options, and the advantages and disadvantages of different possible solutions — *on paper?*

How would I rate my mental state?

How would I rate my physical feeling state?

Part III. Action Time

Module 9. Action exercises

Objectives

1) Preparing the self and psyche and body to transfer the learned skills and problem solutions to real life situations
2) To try out individual parts of a stress relief action program and gain experience in them before or along with carrying out the solutions arrived at in the problem solving process

One of the reasons effective problem solving is so difficult to accomplish is because we human beings have developed a remarkable talent for fantasy. We fantasize nice solutions in our heads and then behave in a way that tends to blind us to the fact that the solution isn't working very well in real life.

Most human beings haven't developed the skills needed to cope with real life problems with real life people or people-things (else we wouldn't have such a flood of new counselors and therapists). No one seems to have the final answer. Every day we hear about completely new skills suddenly being recognized in some young genius just named editor of a big city newspaper or Presidential advisor or we hear the startling news that a woman has just been named a bishop in the Church. The news confirms that new kinds of skills are being rewarded and we are now facing the fact that we must learn new skills to deal with this changing world. The fact of modern life is that it demands newer and newer life skills every day, and our social and psychological survival and well being depend upon learning these new skills as soon and as easily as we can.

Worse, many of the skills we need to solve today's problems have long been associated with undesirable social behavior, such as the modern social behavior of women toward men (assertive?). Another skill long buried in social mores has been (for the middle class) keeping up a front in hard times. Changing economics, along with increasing understanding of the nature of human beings, has given permission to people suffering economic reversals to admit it, discuss it, and openly seek assistance.

Strategies

1) Confrontation exercises
   "Psyching" one's self up, carrying through with memorizing memory clues, seeking strokes, being "up front," facing everything honestly . . .
2) Practicing communication exercises (see popular books on how to be a good conversationalist)
3) Behavioral rehearsal. Developing a script and rehearsing it before facing the situation
4) Practicing management of time and space
5) Designing a truth table, that is, simply listing one's options for effective solution of a stress problem in order of their best to least potential and making a time estimate for the option either to be productive or to fail
   The results then serve as a guide for use with Module 10 to know when to move on to a different strategy.

Hints:
Some imaginative approaches to solving stress problems have been developed over the years. One strategy is like that used by my major professor when I presented him with an extensive analysis of my research data. He instructed me to start again and analyze the data in three very different ways. I was stunned because I believed I had used the *only* way there was to analyze data. But he was right, and the struggle with different ways of looking at my data produced some startling and very useful new insights. It is simply a matter of working to get a different perspective instead of simply accepting the usual perspective.

Then there is the Dale Carnegie way — taking the very worst that could happen to you and accepting that fate. Almost inevitably you know the worst will never happen and your mind becomes free to work on solving your problem.

Some people visualize a number of alternative solutions to their problems and try them out solely in imagination. I believe that full behaviorial rehearsal works better since visualization tends to get warped by images of hopes and dreams.

And finally, just to make sure you are coping totally, you could check it with the desensitization procedure (page 204).

Module 10. Transferring awarenesses of problem solutions to real life situations

Objectives

1) To detect any onset of body tensions promptly and to initiate mind and body relaxation immediately
2) Promptly silencing disturbing thoughts and feelings so that action on dealing with the stress problem can be carried out effectively and efficiently
3) Putting decisions made from the problem solving into effect promptly
4) Using truth tables (observing cutoff points for different action options to ensure not following unproductive avenues)
5) Using the newly emerging psychic skills to detect evidence of potential problems before they actually develop

This module really means to begin a new way of life. It becomes a way of being aware and protecting the psyche without effort and without worry. Too many people practice relaxation and meditation without thinking about using the awarenesses they may develop in their everyday lives.

True, lasting relief from the stress of life can be achieved only by working through each step (module) from preparing mind and body to work to solve one's stress problem systematically and practicing the entire anti-stress package until it becomes second nature.

Remember: Fantasy is always more fun than reality, but reality without stress can be magical. To undo stress, take it one day at a time. Stress is society's addiction.

Appendices
References
Index

Appendix 1

Table 7

Principal factors in the stress equation

Extrinsic factors

1. Social pressures
   (expectations of others)
     family expectations
     standards of society
     supervisors
     career influences
     economic influences
     competition pressures
2. Complicating factors
     unclear expectations
     poor communications by
        others
     lack of support
     too much responsibility
     inadequate time for
        performance
     unpleasant behavior of others

Intrinsic factors

1. Expectations
     personal pressure to perform
     personal dissatisfactions
     unrealistic expectations
2. Perceptions
     misperceptions
     misinterpretations
3. Complicating factors
     personality glitches
     poor communications

Interaction factors
communications
hidden agendas
philosophic differences
mismatched behavioral customs
pressures from economy
social prejudices

Appendix 2. Definitions of the Stress of Life

Because the stress of life *is* life, there are a thousand ways we can express what stress means to us.

From Tables 4 and 5 we can deduce, for example, some of the features common to *all* stress. We can see that stress arises out of human relationships, that it involves uncertainty about one's future social life (how others may act toward me, feel about me, what they may think of me, etc.), and that all stress involves concerns about one's own psychological well being. We can also deduce that stress is the way a person perceives or interprets his relationships to people and to the things that people do that influence one's life. Stress is felt only when an individual senses something in his social activities that may jeopardize achieving or keeping his health and happiness.

As I have struggled to define stress at different times, the following descriptions come to mind. Each emphasizes a different quality of stress, and I repeat them here because they convey the enormously wide scope of the stress problem.

- stress is the circumstances affecting people in the course of a lifetime that require adjustments of attitudes, feelings, and behavior to achieve states of well being.

- the stress of life is the jostling back and forth of human beings seeking self-realization and fulfillment in the human surroundings they seek them in.

- stress is the emotional distress and mental or physical ills when people don't, won't or can't cope.

- the stress of life is the encounters we have in life that make living more difficult than we think it should be — encounters with people, people-things or people-surrogates (like the IRS), encounters that challenge our abilities and our hopes and dreams.

• whenever a person senses, intuits, or becomes even subconsciously aware that there is a problem in any meaningful phase of social activities and relationships that signals future difficulties, that person perceives stress and reacts to it.

If we need to be "scientific" about definitions, then all of these impressions can be reduced to the definition I propose: The stress of life is any perception of the social environment and its dynamics believed to be a threat to psychological and social well being.

Appendix 3. Breathing exercises

Although it is my intention to concentrate this discussion on why it is so important for each individual to construct a personally designed stress control program and to provide the reasons why which exercises are useful for which stage of the stress process and your own special needs, I suspect it may be helpful for some readers to have an "entry level" introduction to stress control.

There are, in fact, rather few *kinds* of stress control aids. There are (1) relaxation exercises, (2) meditation and/or contemplation, (3) imagery or guided imagery, (4) problem solving techniques and practice, and (5) psychotherapy or counseling.

The goal of stress control, briefly, is to eliminate distractions that interfere with the innate intelligence that operates to ensure the wholeness and harmony of the individual.

It all starts with learning to become aware of the state of one's inner health and of any imbalances that may interfere with achieving and fulfilling and productive coping with life. The most universal awareness learning exercises are the breathing exercises long associated with yoga.

Breathing exercises

Although there are occasional variations on the theme, most breathing exercises used preparatory to meditation and contemplation (mind work) are almost identical. The following simple procedure was taken from the book *Meditations* developed by Swami Satyananda Saraswati, edited by Swami Nishchalananda Saraswati and published by the Bihar School of Yoga, Mongyr, India.*

Breathing exercises in the practice of yoga are never considered to be solely the physical practice of breath control. They are, instead, considered to be a means of manipulation of the subtle psychic energy body (life energy). The method is known as

*Reprinted by permission of Bihar School of Yoga.

pranayama (prana meaning the vital energy in the body, bio-energy, and yama meaning a rule of self-restraint designed to remove emotional distractions in preparation for higher yoga practices). "Pranayama serves as the basis for many types of meditation. It is used within the practices themselves; it prepares the aspirant's body and mind for the safe and successful practice of meditation; and it serves as a system for introverting the mind prior to sitting for meditation. It is of utmost importance" (from *Meditations*).

"Basic breath control in inhalation (pooraka), inner retention (antar kumbhaka), exhalation (rechaka), and outer retention (bahiranga) is the most important prerequisite for the practice of pranayama sadhana (sadhana = spiritual practice that aims at eventually experiencing self-realization or divine knowledge). Progressively practice each of the following stages of *nadi shodhana* until they can be done without any strain or shortness of breath being felt. If any difficulty is encountered during your practice, stop until you can gain the advice of a competent yoga teacher."

"Nadi shodhana, if practiced properly and without strain, is the greatest of pranayamas for purifying the body and stilling the mind. Some people, however, are not suited to its practice and so the aspirant should be sensitive to changes taking place in his body and mind as a result of the sadhana."

Stage one

Sit in any meditative asana (posture).

Close your eyes and become aware of your whole body. Observe that it is perfectly still, light and relaxed.

Now shift your attention to the natural breathing process taking place within your body.

Become aware of every inhalation and exhalation that you take.

Gradually slow down your breathing until you can count slowly to five with every inhalation and exhalation (the entire cycle).

You must also count the number of rounds (cycles of inhalation and exhalation) you take.

Count fifty complete breaths. Then open your eyes and relax.

Practice daily for one week; then proceed to stage two.

Stage two

Sit as in stage one.

Bring your right hand to your face and place your index and middle fingers on your eyebrow center in nasagra mudra (thumb and ring fingers placed on each side of nostrils, ready to close nostrils).

Be sure your head and torso are perfectly straight and relaxed.

Inhale through both nostrils.

Close your right nostril with your thumb and exhale slowly through your left nostril while counting to five.

Keep your right nostril closed and inhale through your left nostril while counting to five.

Now open your right nostril, close the left one with your ring finger and exhale through the right nostril while counting. Then exhale through the left.

Inhale through the left and exhale through right.

Continue in this way for 25 complete cycles of two breaths each — i.e., out left, in left, out right, in right.

At the end of the last round, exhale through the left nostril, inhale through the left, exhale through both nostrils and then open your eyes and relax.

Add five rounds daily to your practice period until you are completely comfortable practicing fifty full rounds per day. Then proceed to the next stage.

Stage three

From stage two, slowly elongate the duration of inhalation to a count of ten over a period of one week, or longer if necessary.

Do not strain or try to force your breathing beyond its natural capacity.

Your capacity will increase naturally over time.

Practice fifty rounds daily until you have mastered this stage.

Stage four

Practice stage two as has been described, but with one addition.

After you inhale, with every breath retain the breath inside your lungs for a count of five.

Close your glottis while retaining to lock the air inside.

After a retention of five, open the nostril opposite to that through which you inhaled.

Inhale very slightly, and then exhale through the same nostril for a count of five.

Practice this stage fifty times daily until it is completely comfortable and then proceed to the next stage.

Stage five

Practice as in stage four, but add outer retention for a count of five after every exhalation.

After outer retention, always breathe out very slightly before inhaling.

Breathing out slightly after retention and breathing in slightly after inner retention are very important points to remember when practicing pranayama, as this is the only way to control the breath when practicing long periods of retention. When you have mastered this stage, go on to the next.

Stage six

Practice as in stage five, but gradually increase the count of inhalation, retention, exhalation, and retention by one count daily, until your reach a count of ten for each.

Do not strain.

Increase gradually until you can practice ten with full control.

Stage seven

Practice as before, but inhale for a count of five, retain for ten, exhale for ten and retain outside for five.

Stage eight

Increase your count to 5:20:10:10

Do not strain.

Increase very gradually over a period of days, weeks or months as required.

Stage nine

Gradually increase your duration of count as much as is comfortably possible without strain, maintaining the same ratio of 1:

4:2:2 for inhalation, retention, exhalation and retention. Thus, you can continue and practice 8:32:16:16 or 6:24:12:12 or 10:40:20:20, whichever is comfortable.

These constitute the major set of breathing exercises. There are other minor variations as well as more advanced exercises. I heartily recommend looking for the *Meditations* book because it contains a series of tape transcriptions of actual classes in a variety of yoga procedures, including "inner visualizations," "abstract visualizations" and other techniques that offer extraordinary detail. From personal experience, I can heartily recommend the publications on yoga and its philosophy of the Bihar School of Yoga. They are always satisfyingly detailed and complete.

Note in the breathing exercises about the remarkable attention to even the smallest detail and the concern for well being.

Appendix 4. Word Descriptors for Scoring Moods and Feelings

If you are pressed for descriptive adjectives to describe yourself in your journal or other record keeping about your possible stress, here are some I gleaned from a psychology dictionary:

alienated, ambivalent, antagonized, apathetic, anxious, apprehensive, angry, anchorless, abandoned, abused, accident prone, aged, bored, bitter, brainwashed, compulsive, dissatisfied, doubting, doomed, dumb, defensive, distrusting, deprived, depressed, despondent, depersonalized, distracted, discriminated against, disorganized, dominated, day dreamy, excluded, erratic, exploited, fixated, frustrated, forgetful, fearful, like a failure, guilty, greedy, gloomy, hostile, hysterical, hopeless, inadequate, incompetent, incomplete, inferior, insecure, immature, irritable, impulsive, inhibited, inefficient, irrational, illogical, isolated, jealous, limited, lethargic, lonely, losing self-esteem, melancholy, having a mental block, moody, having a midlife crisis, maladjusted, masochistic, neurotic, non compos mentis, not accepted, oppressed, pressured, procrastinating, perfectionistic, persecuted, permissive, preoccupied, passive, paranoid, rejected, repressed, rebellious, remorseful, scattered, schizoid, sexually upset, unproductive, self-pitying, sad, shy, unstable, unhappy, up-and-down, unmotivated, unreasonable, unsociable, underachieving, uncoordinated, without goals, worried, withdrawn, like a statistic, like a token, like a victim.

There, now. Any hurt psyche, any depressed, self-pitying stressee should have a neurotic's picnic with all those descriptors of psychic hurt.

But when you are really suffering stress, it is difficult to describe your feelings exactly. So, if you are seriously trying to solve your stress problems, these may be of some help in scoring daily moods.

References

It is a tradition to "document" writing about science by listing references to original articles in scientific or other authoritative, credible sources. The custom began in academic and professional circles partly as the courtesy of supplying a convenient list of references for interested researchers, partly to lend authority and credibility to the piece of writing and partly to ensure suitable acknowledgment of the efforts and thoughts of other researchers.

I have long felt that while the traditional kinds of references may satisfy specialists who enjoy researching details, not one in fifty readers of nontechnial material ("popular" books) has access to technical references and fewer still ever trouble to track down references. Moreover, listing pages of scientific references merely references embedded data (requiring study) and they rarely contain discussions or overviews of topics useful to nontechnical readers. Scientific articles simply aren't designed to integrate new ideas about phenomena; they principally supply data to document pieces of ideas.

On the other hand, there are many fine, readable books on the market today that discuss both broad and specific aspects of phenomena such as the psychology of human behavior, psychotherapy, stress, and wellness. These provide infinitely better opportunities for understanding such phenomena than do esoteric references, and they also give the reader important feelings and awarenesses about human behavior and human nature. Since the main thesis of *Between Health and Illness* represents my own analyses and syntheses about modern stress phenomena, except for my own scientific articles there is a paucity of relevant reference material. There is, however, considerable related material (background, existing concepts, techniques, etc.) in a number of interesting trade publications that I believe can be much more helpful to the average reader than can purely scientific, often sterile, references, and so below I am providing a partial list of these that have served me well. I trust my break with the referencing tradition will be useful.

Awarenesses

1. *Self-Perception: The Psychology of Personal Awareness,* Chris L. Kleinke. W. H. Freeman and Co., S.F., 1978.
2. *The Psychic Grid,* Beatrice Bruteau. Quest Books, 1979.
3. *Bioenergetics,* Alexander Lowen. Penguin Books, 1975.
4. *Language Awareness,* eds. Paul Eschholtz, Alfred Rosa, Virginia Clark. St. Martin's Press, 1978.
5. *Self-Change,* Michael J. Mahoney. W. W. Norton & Co., 1979.
6. *New Rules,* Daniel Yankelovich. Random House, 1981.
7. *Outgrowing Self-deception,* Gardner Murphy. Basic Books, 1975.
8. *Anatomy of an Illness,* Norman Cousins. Bantam Books, 1979.
9. *Awareness Through Movement,* Moshe Feldenkrais. Harper & Row, 1972.
10. *The Alexander Technique,* W. Barlow. Alfred A. Knopf, 1973.
11. *Sensory Awareness: The Rediscovery of Experiencing,* C. Brooks. The Viking Press, 1974.
12. *The Aerobics Way,* Kenneth Cooper. M. Evans Co., N.Y., 1977.
13. *T'ai Chi Ch'uan: An Ancient Chinese Way to Achieve Health and Tranquillity,* S. Delza. 1972.
14. *Body Time,* Gay Luce. Bantam Books, 1973.
15. *On Becoming a Person,* Carl Rogers. Houghton Mifflin, 1961.
16. *The Silent Pulse,* George Leonard. E. P. Dutton, 1978.
17. *Space, Time & Medicine,* Larry Dossey. Shambala Publications, 1982.
18. *The Human Connection,* Ashley Montagu. McGraw-Hill, 1979.
19. *The Nature of Human Aggression,* Ashley Montagu. Oxford University Press, 1976.
20. *Being and Caring,* Victor Daniels and Laurence J. Horowitz. San Francisco Book Company, 1976.
21. *Focusing,* Eugene Gendlin. Bantam Books, 1978.
22. *Free Yourself from Pain,* David E. Bressler. Simon & Schuster, 1979.

23. *New Mind, New Body,* Barbara B. Brown. Bantam Books, 1974.
24. *Supermind,* Barbara B. Brown. Harper & Row, 1980.

Imagery

1. *Creative Dreaming,* Patricia Garfield. Ballantine Books, 1974.
2. *The Inner World of Daydreaming,* Jerome Singer. Harper Colophon Books, 1975.
3. *Creative Visualization,* Shakti Gawain. Whatever Publishing, Mill Valley, California, 1978.
4. *The New Psychology of Dreaming,* Richard M. Jones. The Viking Press, 1970.
5. *Galton's Walk,* Herbert F. Crovitz. Harper & Row, 1970.
6. *Experiences in Visual Thinking,* R. H. McKim. Brooks/Cole Publishing Co., 1972.
7. *Mental Imagery,* A. Richardson. Springer Publishing, N.Y., 1969.
8. *Seeing with the Mind's Eye,* M. Samuels and N. Samuels. Random House, 1975.
9. *Go See the Movie in Your Head,* J. E. Shorr. Popular Library, N.Y., 1977.
10. *Imagery and Daydream Methods in Psychotherapy and Behavior Modification,* J. L. Singer. Academic Press, 1974.

Relaxation

1. *Release from Nervous Tension,* David Harold Fink. Simon & Schuster, 1953.
2. *You Must Relax,* Edmund Jacobson. McGraw-Hill Paperbacks, 1978.
3. *Tension Control for Businessmen,* Edmund Jacobson. McGraw-Hill Paperbacks, 1968.
4. *Relax,* eds. John White and James Fadiman. The Confucian Press, 1976.
5. *The Relaxation Response,* Herbert Benson. William Morrow and Company, 1975.
6. *Stress and the Art of Biofeedback,* Barbara Brown. Harper & Row and Bantam Books, 1977.
7. *The Stress of Life,* Hans Selye. McGraw-Hill Paperbacks, 1956.

8. *Stress Without Distress,* Hans Selye. J. B. Lippincott Co., 1974.
9. *Freedom from Stress,* Phil Nuernberger. Himalayan International Institute, Honesdale, Penn. 1981.
10. *Relieve Tension the Autogenic Way,* H. Lindeman. Peter H. Wyden, Inc., 1973.
11. *Autogenic Therapy,* vol. 1–6, W. Luthe. Grune & Stratton, 1969.
12. *You and A.T.: Autogenic Training,* K. Rosa. E.P. Dutton & Co., 1976.
13. *Progressive Relaxation,* Edmund Jacobson. University of Chicago Press, 1938.
14. *The Complete Book of Sleep,* Dianne Hales. Addison-Wesley Publishing Co., 1981.

Meditation

1. *TM: Discovering Inner Energy and Overcoming Stress,* Harold Bloomfield, et al. Delacorte Press, 1975.
2. *How to Meditate: A Guide to Self-Discovery,* Lawrence Le-Shan. Bantam Books, 1975.
3. *Meditation in Action,* Chogyam Trumpa. Shambala Publications, 1969.
4. *Cutting Through Spiritual Materialism,* Chogyam Trungpa. Shambala Publications, 1973.

Yoga

1. *Light on Yoga,* B. K. S. Iyengar. Geroge Allen & Unwin, London, 1966.
2. *Yoga, the Key to Life,* James McCartney. Rider & Company, London, 1969.
3. *The Awakening of Kundalini,* Gopi Krishna. E.P. Dutton & Co., 1975.
4. *Yoga for Physical Fitness,* R. L. Hittleman. Prentice-Hall, 1964.
5. *Introduction to Yoga,* R. L. Hittleman. Bantam Books, 1969.
6. *Yoga Sutras: The Textbook of Yoga Psychology,* R. Mishra. Doubleday, 1973.
7. *Fundamentals of Yoga,* R. L. Hittleman, Doubleday, 1974.

Problem solving

1. *Patterns of Problem Solving,* Moshe Rubinstein. Prentice-Hall, Inc., 1975.
2. *Problem-Solving Therapy,* Jay Haley. Harper Colophon Books, 1976.
3. *The Art of Creative Thinking,* Gerard I. Nierenberg. Cornerstone Library (Simon & Schuster), 1982.
4. *Styles of Thinking,* Allen F. Harrison and Robert M. Bramson. Anchor Press/Doubleday, 1982.
5. *Thinking Better,* David Lewis and James Greene. Rawson, Wade Publishers, N.Y., 1982.
6. *Human Information Processing,* Peter Lindsay and Donald Norman, Academic Press, 1972.
7. *Brain Games,* R. B. Fisher. Schocken Books, N.Y., 1982.

Miscellaneous popular books on human emotions, human problems and human solutions

1. *Shyness,* Philip G. Zimbardo. Jove/HBJ (Harcourt Brace Javanovich), 1977.
2. *The Psychology of Self-esteem,* Nathaniel Brandon. Bantam Books, 1969.
3. *How to Survive the Loss of a Love,* Melba Colgrove, Harold Bloomfield, and Peter McWilliams. Bantam Books, 1976.
4. *When Bad Things Happen to Good People,* Harold S. Kushner. Avon Books, 1981.
5. *The Intimate Enemy,* George Bach and Peter Wyden. Avon Books, 1968.
6. *Creative Aggression,* George Bach and Herb Goldberg. Avon Books, 1974.
7. *When I say NO, I feel guilty,* Manuel J. Smith. Bantam Books, 1975.
8. *Games People Play,* Eric Berne. Ballantine Books, 1964.
9. *Beyond Games and Scripts,* Eric Berne. Ballantine Books, 1976.
10. *Scripts People Live,* Claude M. Steiner. Bantam Books, 1974.
11. *I'm OK, You're OK,* Thomas A. Harris. Avon Books 1967.

12. *Type A Behavior and Your Heart,* Meyer Friedman and Ray Rosenman. Fawcett Publications, 1974.

13. *Depression and the Body,* Alexander Lowen. Pelican Books, 1972.

14. *Contact: The First Four Minutes,* Leonard Zumin. Ballantine Books, 1973.

15. *A Way of Being,* Carl Rogers. Houghton Mifflin, 1980.

16. *Peoplemaking,* Virginia Satir. Science and Behavior Books, Palo Alto, 1972.

17. *Letting Go,* Zev Wanderer and Tracy Cabot. Warner Books, 1979.

18. *Explorers of Humankind,* ed. Thomas Hanna. Harper & Row, 1979.

19. *Instant Relief: The Encyclopedia of Self-Help,* Tom Greening and Dick Hobson. Seaview Books, N.Y., 1979.

20. *Snapping,* Flo Conway and Jim Siegelman. J. B. Lippincott Company, 1978.

21. *How to Make Yourself Miserable,* D. Greenburg and M. Jacobs. Random House, 1966.

22. *Life Stress and Illness,* E. Gunderson and R. Rahe. Charles C. Thomas Publishers, 1974.

23. *On Becoming a Person,* Carl Rogers, Houghton Mifflin, 1961.

24. *Passages,* Gail Sheehy, E. P. Dutton & Co., 1976.

25. *Getting Well Again,* Carl Simonton, Stephanie Matthews-Simonton, and J. Creighton. J. P. Tarcher, Inc., 1978.

26. *The Way Your Body Works,* B. Stonehouse. Crown Publishers, 1974.

27. *The Johns Hopkins Atlas of Human Functional Anatomy.* Johns Hopkins University Press, 1977.

28. *Mind and Emotion,* George Mandler. John Wiley & Sons, 1975.

29. *Anger! The Misunderstood Emotion,* Carol Tavris. Simon & Schuster, 1982.

30. *The Natural History of the Mind,* Gordon Rattray Taylor. Penguin Book, 1979.

31. *Brain: The Last Frontier,* Richard M. Restak. Warner Books, 1979.

Index